TRAVELS
with
LOUIS

TRAVELS
with
LOUIS

Two Decades of Writing
for Gourmet

TERRY WEEKS

Travels with Louis is comprised of articles published in
Gourmet magazine between 1980 and 1993.
All articles appear as originally published.

Illustrations and cover design by Marjorie Weeks
Interior book design by Carolyn Eckert
ISBN 978-1-937650-59-9
Library of Congress Control Number 2015942170

SMALL
BATCH
BOOKS

493 SOUTH PLEASANT STREET
AMHERST, MASSACHUSETTS 01002
413.230.3943
SMALLBATCHBOOKS.COM

Remembering Kipper, who started the whole thing.
April 15, 1948–December 31, 2011
Missed every day.

Contents

SOUTHERN CLIMES

NEW ENGLAND

EXTRA TREATS

POSTSCRIPT

FOREWORD

"I was born into a family that considered food important."

ERRY WEEKS'S FATHER was a doctor in Manhattan who loved a good meal and who, from the time she was little, took her out with him to eat at the city's restaurants. "My mother said food was my father's first thought in the morning and his last at night." Her mother was Colombian, and brought her own sense of food to the household in which Weeks grew up; from an early age, Weeks and her brother traveled with their parents every year to Colombia by ship for extended visits with their mother's family.

In the 1940s, when Weeks was in her teens, there were many high-end French restaurants in New York where her father liked to eat. Among the best was Chambord. It was in a chancy neighborhood on Third Avenue in the 40s, under the El. One of her earliest food memories is of eating their Sole Véronique, with its luscious *velouté* and white grapes.

After two years at Barnard, she left college to marry Louis Weeks, a Columbia University Law student. As it happened, she had never boiled the proverbial egg. For her first attempt at cooking a meal, she was confronted by a still-frozen hunk of ground beef, burst into tears, and decided their only recourse was to hire a cook. "Louis said we weren't going to do that, and I'd just have to learn." She bought *The Joy of Cooking* (it was 1946, still fifteen years before Julia Child's *Mastering the Art of French Cooking*) and set about teaching herself how to cook. "I got pretty good at it because I liked to eat, and I knew if I didn't cook it well, no one else was going to. But I would never have become the cook I became if Louis hadn't taken such an interest in what he was eating."

The two took their first trip to Europe together (and Louis Weeks's first altogether) in 1960, leaving their three children with a nanny and two sets of nearby grandparents. Sailing on the *Liberté*, "We had every great French dish on the menu, for seven days."

Traveling wasn't only about eating, but some of the high points were. "I remember going with Louis to La Pyramide in Vienne, Burgundy. The chef there had been Fernand Point, one of the first three-star chefs. Point had died a few years earlier, but his wife still owned and ran the restaurant. We had a chicken with black truffles under the skin that was famous in the region— *poulet demi deuil*, chicken in half-mourning."

At home on Long Island, Weeks had a young Scotswoman named Martha Harper to help with the children. Martha ended up staying for twenty years. She cooked her way through *The Art of French Cooking*. "Martha wasn't a trained cook, but I saw her mashing potatoes for the children and knew she had it. She was one of those rare naturally talented cooks." For all those years, every evening when she brought the food to the dinner table Martha would say, "Bon appétit, whatever that means."

Weeks went back to Barnard in the mid-'70s to finish her BA. Unlike her first two years at Barnard, this time she never missed a class or turned in an assignment late. "Not even physics, a requirement at the time, and maybe the only thing that has ever truly terrified me." (See "Back to School . . . ," page 359.)

Weeks and her husband traveled enthusiastically with the family, Weeks keeping detailed travel diaries. In 1979, after a family Christmas in Nevis and St. Kitts, one of the children said one day, "You should write about food, Mom, it's the only thing you ever put in your travel diary." Inspired by this challenge, she wrote an account of their Christmas trip—in longhand on a yellow legal pad—had someone type it for her, and sent it off to *Gourmet*.

After Barnard, Weeks had gone to the New School to learn the mechanics of preparing a manuscript for publication. "In class there, I was the only one writing about food. It made me feel somewhat frivolous." About a month after she sent her article to *Gourmet*, the magazine called to say they would take it, and they would like to see anything else she wrote. The next piece she did for them was about three inns in New Hampshire, and they published that, too. (See "Three New Hampshire Inns," page 239.)

"Nevis and St. Kitts happened to be the only two Caribbean islands that had not been written about, and the unconventional occasion helped sell the article. It was an Anglican Christmas on a tropical island." The magazine sent her back to Nevis to collect more information, and the story was featured in the December 1981 issue.

And that is how a woman who came of age in the 1940s became a published writer in the 1980s. She did it without high expectations but also without trepidation, and suddenly, there it was.

The Weekses moved to Stonington, Connecticut, in 1982, into a large eighteenth-century house on Main Street, with a beautiful garden that was Louis Weeks's pride and joy. They did a lot of entertaining in that house, most weekends hosting dinner parties for guests from New York and friends from Stonington.

Weeks traveled and tasted the world for *Gourmet*'s audience of 800,000. Her articles were not only about food. She wrote about the history, geography, people, art, and industries that informed the food. Her *Gourmet* articles span nearly fifteen years, with the last one published in 1993. From 1982 to 1995, she and her husband spent winters in Old Town Key West, and she reviewed restaurants for Frank Taylor and David Ethridge's *Solares Hill* newspaper. For several years in the 1980s, she was also a food critic for Andy Birsh's *Restaurant Reporter* in New York, with the byline "TW" (Birsh never used writers' names, just initials). She would bring her husband, children, and friends along to restaurants she was reviewing, and the group would share food on one another's butter plates, while she spoke her notes into a handheld tape recorder. Weeks's husband often ordered the veal chop, on Birsh's advice that the most expensive item on the menu was a likely indicator of the quality of the kitchen. Invariably, he also ordered the crème brulée.

Louis Weeks died—not due to all this eating—in 2010, at age 92, and today Terry Weeks lives in Baltimore near one of her sons and his family.

When *Gourmet* closed up shop in November 2009, giving way to magazines with a more modern voice, and to the Food Network and an explosion of online cooking blogs and recipe sites, a large community of foodies mourned its sudden disappearance. Many readers had never thrown away a copy of *Gourmet*. Those who had, found they had nowhere to turn for archived issues.

The articles that follow, written by Terry Weeks and published in *Gourmet* between 1980 and 1993, are for all those readers with a passion for food and travel—be they cooks, diners, travelers, or bon vivants—who miss *Gourmet.*

—Kim Gallagher
September 2014

love,
Kim

BRITISH ISLES

GOURMET | MAY 1983

South Wales

A TOUR OF WALES provides some of the most spectacular scenery to be found anywhere in the world. From the gentle green pastures and shaded trout streams of the Brecon Beacons in the south to the wild highland scenery of Snowdonia in the north, the country is varied and beautiful, mysterious and compelling. For sheer sightseeing alone it is well worth the journey, and, if you are propelled by history, particularly the Norman and Tudor ages, you have found yourself a country that will keep you in castles for weeks on end.

In the 250 years that followed William the Conqueror's victory at Hastings castles were erected by the dozens in Wales itself and on the border separating Wales from England. The earliest-built fortresses were actually lived in by the Normans as they moved deeper and deeper into South Wales from England; their square stone towers protected them from the recalcitrant Welsh whose lands they had appropriated. The later castles, constructed under the direction of Edward I of England, were used primarily as fortifications to maintain his shaky dominance over the Welsh. As a result, two and a half centuries of military architecture in varying states of preservation can be chronicled in Wales today.

We drove west from London on our way to Wales knowing two things: one, that we would combine military lore and country dining with idle days of beautiful back road driving, and, two, that we would reserve North Wales for another trip. It was an early summer day as we crossed the Wye River at the border town of Chepstow—gateway to South Wales—and were greeted by Draig Coch, the red dragon of Wales that appears on many road signs. A sharp turn, and immediately Chepstow Castle loomed into view high on a bluff overlooking the river and the lush, green surrounding countryside. This Norman castle's unusual rectangular keep was built between 1067 and 1072; its gatehouse, baileys, and towers were added later, thus creating an unconventional succession of wards. Cattle graze placidly in the shadow of its walls, and a gigantic yew stands in the upper bailey providing a touch of life to the pervading feeling of time past.

From Chepstow we followed the Wye north for five miles to Tintern Abbey, the roofless ruins of a chapel, abbot's lodgings, kitchens, infirmary hall, and cloisters that have been immortalized by William Wordsworth in verse and by Joseph M. W. Turner on canvas. The site, on a quiet bend of the river, is magnificent. The abbey church, dating from the thirteenth century with a stunning rose window, is all that stands today.

Carrying on north and west, we passed the village of Crickhowell to arrive at GLIFFAES COUNTRY HOUSE, a gray stone edifice built by one Reverend West in 1881 for his family of a dozen offspring, now run as a small hotel by Pita and Nick Brabner. The rooms are large, simply furnished, and comfortable, and the food is wholesome and plentiful. Amenities include a tennis court, and trout or salmon fishing trips can be arranged on the Usk River. What makes this hotel unique, however, and qualifies it to be listed among the important *gardens* of Europe is its park that overlooks the Usk. Rhododendrons in shades of pink and purple border the long drive, and there are fine specimens of swamp cypress, Spanish chestnut, juniper, and plane trees. In this enchanting locale we headquartered for several days.

One excursion over narrow back roads, virtually lanes, where not even two small cars can pass each other, past neat fields and rolling hills transformed into a geometric patchwork by well clipped thorn hedges and Queen Anne's lace, led to White Castle, a twelfth-century structure so named because once upon a time it was plastered in white. Like Tintern Abbey, these ruins inhabit a tranquil and pastoral setting. The loudest sound that can be heard is the occasional bleating of a goat or the barking of a sheepdog. A small stone house nearby advertises fresh thyme, parsley, mint, lettuce, and gooseberries for sale.

From there it is fourteen miles to Llanthon Abbey, where William de Lacy founded a religious community. The ruins of the church are in a particularly lovely meadow, backed by steep craggy hills. In 1538 the priory was surrendered to Henry VIII. Times were turbulent, and the priory fell into disrepair until it was bought by the poet Walter Savage Landor in 1807. Landor, a man of many moods and of great temperament, had elaborate plans to restore it, but his dreams exceeded his pocketbook and the project was abandoned eight years later. A pub on the grounds with a moss-covered roof and hanging baskets of petunias offers hearty homemade soups, coarse dark country bread, and frothy lager from the tap to make simple but satisfying lunches that on sunny days can be taken outdoors.

Route B 4423 north to Hay-on-Wye is a winding road that reveals some of the most glorious scenery in Wales. Fields are framed by flowering hawthorns, and chestnut and apple trees intersperse patches of fragrant blue scilla. The road snakes up to fields covered with spiny yellow gorse where hundreds of sheep graze perched like mountain climbers. An adventurous spirit is required by this country; some of the roads are unmarked and many are very steep. The local folk are kind and most patient, though, in giving directions, and what a joy it is to hear their Celtic tongue! Hay-on-Wye, a pretty market town that is known as the secondhand book capital of the world with shop after shop of antiquarian booksellers, is a browser's paradise.

Ten miles from Crickhowell in Llandewi Skirrid, near Abergavenny—all these lilting names in more or less the same area!—is the WALNUT TREE INN, a whitewashed house set by the side of a country road, which is actually a restaurant, there being, despite the name, no overnight accommodations. Its cheerful bar at midday is usually filled with regulars as well as travelers who have come to enjoy Chef/Proprietor Franco Taruschio's culinary expertise. Lunch in the bar can be a simple or an elaborate affair with choices such as the chef's own home-cured *bresaola* (dried beef), *gravlaks* (marinated salmon), lasagne, *trenette con pesto* (pasta with basil sauce), and roast duck with figs and strawberries.

Dinner is served in a pleasing dining room: Pottery, copper pots, and antique maps of Wales decorate the walls; plum-colored napery covers the tables; and, because flowers are Ann Taruschio's special love, lilacs, lupine, and daisies grace every setting. A vast menu combines the best of English cookery and some carefully chosen specialties from the chef's native Ancona. Cold trout in orange marinade and *salmon en croûte* with a sublime tarragon sauce are typical dinner selections. Desserts would satisfy the most discriminating. Honey and brandy *gelato* showcases the Italian expertise of ice-cream-making with double-rich Welsh cream, and a torte with three liqueurs and a chestnut mousse are among the other tempting choices. In sum, one would be hard-pressed to find in Wales a better restaurant than the Walnut Tree, which could hold its own in the most illustrious of company anywhere.

Our drive south to Caerphilly, renowned for its crumbly cheese, which, alas, is not made there anymore, took us through industrial areas—a not uncommon sight in this country of mines. A castle was our destination, however. Caerphilly, the largest castle in Wales, is an important example of military fortifications in Great Britain. Started in 1268 by the Norman lord of Glamorgan, Gilbert de Clare, to secure his newly annexed territories, the structure, partially restored, with a moat, is a truly impressive example of the concentric double-ring style of architecture—the same design used in the Tower of London. Its buttressed walls are reminiscent of Aigues-Mortes, an almost entirely walled medieval town in southern France.

We drove due west along the southern coast of Wales—the land of Merlin the wizard and Dylan Thomas—to the ancient town of Laugharne, on the estuary of the Taf, where the poet spent sixteen years in a charming white Georgian boathouse with bright blue trim. A shed wherein he wrote looks out over the lonely tidal basin. This last home of his has been turned into a small museum housing pictures of Dylan and his family, manuscripts, and other memorabilia. In the churchyard of St. Martin's in Laugharne a simple white wooden cross marks his grave, and black letters record his untimely death on November 9, 1953, in New York City.

ROBESTON HOUSE in Robeston Wathen, near Narberth, is an ideal spot from which to explore the Pembrokeshire Coast of Wales. Run by the Barretts, the pink stucco hotel has only five double bedrooms and one single. In this intimate setting, careful attention is the order of the day, from the geranium and amaryllis abloom in the conservatory to the antiques in the parlor and the bar. There is a pool, and fishing trips can be planned. The dining room conveys a comfortable glow. A Welsh dresser displays Portmeirion pottery, and the tables, of all shapes and sizes, have the rich patina of well-cared-for antiques and are set with white damask cloths, natural straw mats, and flowers. The Aynsley china called Pembroke is a reproduction of an eighteenth-century pattern, and with gleaming cutlery and handsome Dartington goblets there is the promise that one will dine well. The Barretts and Chef Wendy Johns see to that. Dinner one night consisted of creamy potted shrimp with cheese as a starter, kidneys with brandy and orange, and for my companion an unusual dish of diced lamb with mint and cumin. As is the custom throughout Wales, fresh seasonal vegetables, in this case grown in the hotel's own garden, are placed on the table. Carrots, cauliflower, and turnips were our choices that evening, and last but not least there are always glorious potatoes, bubbling and aromatic with garlic and Gruyére. Desserts here are deservedly popular. Walnut and lemon meringue cake and Sherry trifle were among the winners. After-dinner coffee is served with rich yellow cream, so thick a spoon is needed, nuggets of rock sugar, and smooth Welsh fudge, which is an event in itself. Culinary pleasures aside, part of the enjoyment of dining at Robeston House is the opportunity of watching the long England gloaming turn beds of bright red poppies, lavender lupines, and resplendent yellow laburnums dusky, blue, then midnight black.

Pembroke Castle is among the attractions of the Pembrokeshire Coast, the only coastal national park in Britain, with a continuous footpath for walkers, endless sandy secluded beaches, and varied wildlife. The twelfth-century castle is probably best known as the birthplace of Henry Tudor, Henry VII, who later fullfilled the prophecy that a Welshman would one day rule England. The Norman castle, with its unusual circular keep and curtain wall, is surrounded on three sides by water. A shop there sells traditional Welsh crafts, much in evidence in South Wales, and a National Trust store displays intriguing woolens—shawls, sweaters, capes, and blankets—along with excellent honey and that unusual fudge, which turns out to be specific to the region.

Directly south of the castle, almost at the tip of the peninsula in Saint Govan's Head, is Saint Govan's chapel. The simple cliffside room dates from at least the eleventh century. Saint Govan, history has it, was an Irishman who founded a monastery in Wexford and went on a pilgrimage late in his life to Pembroke. When he was attacked by pirates there the cliff opened to take him in; when the danger passed, it released him. Saint Govan was so impressed with the miracle that he built a single cell on the spot where he was saved and spent the remainder of his days in solitary prayer and contemplation. The view from his retreat is singularly striking.

Two castles in this area, though not as widely known as some, should be noted. Manorbier, in the village of the same name on the southeast coast, overlooking the Bristol Channel, is a perfect microcosm of a medieval nobleman's seat—a moated Norman manor house rather than a military stronghold. The town itself, overgrown with pink valerian and white Russian vine, is a restful spot in which to muse for an hour or two. Carew, on the northwest coast, is a thirteenth-century castle whose character changed considerably in Tudor times when sumptuous state apartments were added by Sir Rhys ap Thomas, one of Henry VII's chief Welsh supporters and at that time the richest man in Wales. The celebration Thomas gave when made a Knight of the Garter apparently lasted six days. Other structural changes to the castle were made by subsequent owners; unfortunately, the building is now considered unsafe and is closed to visitors. Obviously the crows and seagulls have not been so informed.

Continuing due west along the coast, we explored the delightful neighboring seaside towns of Broad Haven and Little Haven perched on the cliffs high above Saint Bride's Bay. The houses, all with flourishing flowers, are minuscule, but the beaches are vast. This is a favorite resort area in the summer In Little Haven there is a charming pub, the SWAN INN, which is filled with mementos of World War II and old pewter tankards that hang from low rafters. The experience of a pub lunch in Wales is a must. Invariably, the menu is chalked on a slate, one orders at the bar, finds a spot to sit at one of the small tables, and, lager or Amontillado in hand, waits. "Your" table may well be shared with strangers (who do not usually remain strangers for long), and eventually a plate of prawns in aspic with *aioli* or sardines—your order—does arrive. It is friendly and fun.

Saint David's on the northern peninsula of Saint Bride's Bay is Britain's smallest cathedral city. This picturesque spot overlooking the open sea is the birthplace of Wales' patron saint, after whom it is named, and was long ago the site of countless religious pilgrimages. The cathedral is a rare gem. Though it was started in the twelfth century, extensive alterations to its exterior make it appear to be of a much later style. There is a choice sixteenth-century oak ceiling, and the guidebooks solemnly inform the visitor that the floor is on such a slant that a marble can be rolled from the high altar to the west door.

The flower arrangements in the cathedral are done with loving care, and note the kneeling cushions, all in differing needlepoint designs. Edmund Tudor, father of Henry VII, is buried in the cathedral. Nearby are the ruins of the Bishop's Palace, now but a spacious quadrangle. Built between 1280 and 1350 by Bishops Bek and Gower, the building was widely used as a place of assembly for the many pilgrims who traveled to Saint David's. During the Reformation the palace was left derelict.

The coast road north from Saint David's winds through Fishguard, a pretty seaside town that was chosen for the filming of Dylan Thomas' *Under Milk Wood* several years ago. Heading due east, again through some breathtaking countryside, we arrived at the tiny town of Brechfa, set in the Cothi Valley on the edge of the Brechfa forest, to end our journey at the pink-washed sixteenth-century TY MAWR (great house) country hotel, run by Jill and Cliff Ross. There are only five bedrooms, all comfortably appointed.

It was evening, and after changing for dinner we studied the menu over a drink on the terrace. Dinner in the persimmon-colored dining room started with smoked mackerel with gooseberry sauce and velvety cream of mushroom soup followed by roast guinea hen and an individual meat pie. For dessert we shared first-rate brown-bread ice cream with Melba sauce and *zuccotto*, a rich molded cream-filled chocolate cake. Jill Ross is the cook—and a fine one—who produces interesting fare with local ingredients in a seemingly effortless manner. It is easy to understand why Ty Mawr is frequently the setting for weddings and parties. We had not one complaint.

A day or two in this bucolic setting could only be a balm to the spirit. Walks are a big leisure activity, and fishing trips can be organized by the management.

For us South Wales echoes the Normans, the Tudors, the Romans. Castles stand as sentries to history. Legends and folklore abound. This is a land of poets and knights. The very language intrigues. North Wales, entirely different, awaited.

North Wales

*W*E WOULD BEGIN our journey to North Wales in Mid Wales, in the county of Dyfed. From the small town of Brechfa we simply headed northeast to Llanybydder, where we stopped at a woolen mill, so typical of the many throughout Wales. Visitors are welcome; and don't miss the interesting and irresistible selection of colorful blankets, jackets, and sweaters for sale on the premises. From there the route north to Tregaron becomes more and more spectacular, culminating in the fifteen-mile unmarked old Drover's Hill road, which winds, climbs, and then descends through the Tywi forest.

After such breathtaking scenery one is ready for the LLWYNDERW HOTEL in Llanwrtyd Wells (just outside Abergwesyn), which is owned and operated by Michael Yates. A Georgian stone mansion of the late eighteenth century, situated a thousand feet above sea level, the hotel looks down on a lush valley in the heart of Powys lake country. Surrounded by mountains, the setting is tranquil and beautiful and a haven for birds, of which there are more than eighty different species in the vicinity. A small garden lies adjacent to the hotel, and tubs of yellow pansies stand as graceful sentries at the front door.

As beautiful as everything is outside, inside all is comfortable.

The front parlor contains an eclectic mix of furnishings and bibelots; the library, well stocked with books of poetry, history, and novels on Wales, doubles as the spot for a preprandial drink, there being no bar. The bedrooms, accommodating only twenty guests, are well appointed, with such handsome pieces as a fine Pembroke table and a particularly pretty inlaid oak dresser. The heated towel racks in the bathrooms add an extra touch of comfort to one's stay.

Country tables and a huge fireplace decorate the dining room, which is pleasing if somewhat out of character with the delicate feeling of the rest of the house. There is one seating for dinner, at seven forty-five precisely, and the menu is posted beforehand so that an appropriate wine may be selected. A typical meal starts with tomatoes Provençal, sorrel soup or first-rate vichyssoise, and continues with roasted guinea fowl stuffed with rice, sultanas, and nuts accompanied by the freshest new potatoes, braised endive, and carrots. Lemon mousse and spongecake round out the repast with coffee served in the library or one of the lounges.

The same care is taken at breakfast with freshly squeezed orange juice, a choice of eggs, and superior marmalades and honeys. Picnics may be ordered the night before so that guests can go on their way in the morning with delectable take-out fare. Llwynderw Hotel is the perfect place to rest and be refreshed in remarkable surroundings.

We were headed north, of course, through more dazzling terrain, past towns called Beulah and Rhayader, past stone walls and vast stretches of dappled meadowland with sheep grazing everywhere, to Dolgellau, a small brooding town with the Cambrian Mountains in the distance. Our destination was Harlech Castle on the west coast of Wales, facing Tremadog Bay on one side and the mountains of Snowdonia on the other. The castle was begun in 1285, and eight hundred men worked for nearly five years before it was completed. The sea, now a half mile or so away, then came to the very base of the structure, enabling the castle to be supplied by ship. The gigantic gatehouse, Harlech's most unusual feature, represents a progression in the development of military architecture. Heretofore the keep had been the strongest point of defense in the medieval castle. The wind blows wildly around Harlech's turrets, which hold sad memories; the castle was valiantly but unsuccessfully defended for seven long years by the men of the House of Lancaster against the Yorkists. Those soldiers were the inspiration for the well-known march "Men of Harlech."

Portmeirion, a surprise of an Italianate town ten miles north up the coast from Harlech, is the creation of a Welsh architect, Sir Clough Williams-Ellis, who visited Portofino, Italy, and became so enamored of it that he decided in 1926 to re-create part of the village on this unlikely spot in Wales. His charming folly consists of a piazza, campanile, village houses, statuary, and even waterfalls. Williams-Ellis also built a sumptuous hotel, once the showplace of Wales, which was unfortunately destroyed by fire two years ago. Plans are currently under way to rebuild. Portmeirion china, designed by Williams-Ellis' daughter, can, of course, be purchased here.

Narrow-gauge railways seem to have taken over northern Wales. One such is The Ffestiniog near Portmeirion. The line starts at Porthmadog harbor and runs for 9 3/4 miles. Literally thousands of tourists ride on these trains every year. Views of Harlech Castle and Mount Snowdon add much to the enjoyment of the journey.

Snowdonia National Park in northwest Wales is dramatic, wild country closely resembling the Scottish highlands. The mountains are impressive enough to serve as practice peaks for climbers bound for the Himalayas, including Mount Everest. The scenery is in marked contrast to that of South Wales' gentle rolling hills.

A tour of North Wales would be incomplete without a visit to Caernarvon, an agreeable town with a busy main square that was once the ceremonial capital of the country. Its magnificently preserved castle, considered by some to be the grandest in North Wales, was started in 1285, with most of the basic building completed by 1287. Its outer walls, nine feet thick, enclose three acres and once incorporated the town walls. Thirteen towers and a drawbridge of huge proportions guard the castle's wards. Edward II, the first Prince of Wales, was born there in 1284. The title was introduced by his father, Edward I, in 1301 to placate the subjugated Welsh. The title evolved to be conferred on the eldest son of the ruling British monarch. The first ceremony of investiture was in 1343, when Edward III invested his son, the Black Prince, "in a Parliament holden at Westminster . . . with these Ensigns of Honour: a Chaplet of Gold made in the manner of a garland, a Gold Ring set on his finger, and a Verge Rod or Spectre of Silver." Edward VIII became Prince of Wales at Caernarvon in 1911, and on July 1, 1969, Prince Charles was invested here by his mother. After his investiture Prince Charles traveled for four days to the cities and through the smallest villages to meet his loyal subjects, greeted wherever he went with cheers and rejoicing:

Among our ancient mountains,
And from our lovely vales,
Oh! let the prayer re-echo,
"God Bless the Prince of Wales."

There is a pictorial and recorded history in the northeast tower of the castle that imparts the pomp and grandeur of such a ceremony in this extraordinary setting. Because Caernarvon Castle has lost its interior curtain and is open from one end to the other, it has a superb sweep and feeling of space.

To the north and east, right along the coast in the town of Llandudno, is BODYSGALLEN HALL HOTEL, a fine old stone house built around 1620 and added to in the eighteenth, nineteenth, and twentieth centuries. Lovingly restored, it has been turned into a deluxe country house hotel by an organization called Historic House Hotels Ltd. No detail has been overlooked. The drawing room is an inviting paneled room. There is a frieze around the ceiling and chintz and orange lilies and sweet William in vases everywhere. Mullioned windows in the thick stone walls add to the feeling of well preserved antiquity. Beyond these lie the gardens of the house where a particularly charming Dutch Knot garden flourishes with golden marjoram, thyme, rosemary, and purple flowering sage. Masses of pink Valerian abound. The comfortable bedrooms offer oversized beds, thick carpets, and gleaming antiques. A final touch is the china jar filled with delicious homemade cookies on the bedside table. There are twenty such bedrooms in the hotel, several of which boast views of Conway Castle just two or three miles away. Some outbuildings on the seven-acre estate are being converted into additional suites.

The dining room of Bodysgallen Hall has pale apricot walls and darker apricot curtains and as such is formal and luxurious. The space fairly sparkles with immaculate white napery, shining crystal, and glistening silver, and the food, under the able direction of Chef Peter Jackson, Scottish born and Gleneagles trained, is equal to the surroundings. Dinner selections include perfect smoked local salmon, potted crab, or salmon trout with sorrel sauce and filet mignon with walnuts and grapes, noisettes of Welsh lamb accompanied by tarragon sauce, pork and wild mushrooms, or "tweed kettle," the chef's name for excellent poached salmon with hollandaise. The vegetables, always fresh and whenever possible picked from the hotel's vast garden, appear transformed as fried zucchini, puréed carrots, crunchy steamed green beans, or delectable potato croquettes. Brown bread ice cream, made extra rich by incomparable cream, black currant and grapefruit *sorbets*, and local strawberries are apt to end a memorable meal, and, if there is still room, the hotel has on hand some of the best Stilton ever tasted. A buffet lunch is served too, and the chef prides himself on the picnics that are made for the guests who want to tour. Nicholas Crawley, Savoy-trained Etonian, is the resident director of the hotel, and the Welsh-speaking staff is unfailingly pleasant and accommodating. There is no finer hotel in Wales today, and in a stay of three or four nights one can cover many of the more interesting sights in North Wales.

The first and nearest of these is Conway Castle, which is incorporated into the town walls, overlooks the Conway River, and is somewhat similar in layout to Caernarvon. Conceived by Edward I's military architect James of Saint George, the castle is unique in that its inner ward was designed in 1283 to house state apartments for Edward and his queen Eleanor, including such domestic arrangements as the great hall, king's hall, and the presence chamber. Because the walls of these buildings and the interior curtain are still intact, Conway does not share Caernarvon's feeling of openness and airiness but is a splendid site in its own right. At Conway Castle in 1399 Richard II was betrayed by the Earl of Northumberland to Henry of Bolingbroke.

Situated on the east bank of the Conway Valley, a few miles southeast of Bodysgallen Hall, is Bodnant Garden, residence of

Lord and Lady Aberconway. For many years Lord Aberconway has been the president of the Royal Horticultural Society, and, though Bodnant became part of the National Trust in 1949, he and his head gardener, Mr. Charles Puddle, look after the grounds on its behalf. There is no doubt that Bodnant is the finest garden in Wales and one of the finest in Britain. In springtime, when the celebrated azaleas and rhododendrons are flourishing and the impressive collection of magnolias are at their peak, it is a place of unsurpassed beauty. The renowned laburnum archway has to be seen to be believed; an avenue of these trees has been trained to grow over frames to form a tunnel. When the laburnum are in bloom during late May and early June a walk under their fragrant yellow blossoms is a magical experience. Roses, hydrangeas, and borders of massed perennials bloom throughout the summer. Delightful hours can be spent strolling past waterfalls, pools of water lilies, old cedars and cypresses, and statuary.

On the subject of gardens, the National Garden Scheme is an organization in the United Kingdom that makes available to the public the viewing of otherwise private gardens. For a modest fee, from which the Visiting Nurse Association benefits, various gardens are open on specific days. Most hotels have notices of the openings in their areas.

It is a short drive west along the north coast to the graceful suspension bridge that spans the Menai Strait and connects the island of Anglesey to the mainland. The bridge, probably the first of its kind, was designed by Thomas Telford in 1826. On the east coast of Anglesey stands the fairy-tale castle of Beaumaris, the last of the Edwardian castles. Designed by James of Saint George and started in 1295, the castle was left incomplete because of the high cost of construction. Its very site tells why. The setting is indeed choice, though: The ruin is encircled by a wide moat where swans glide gracefully. A wooden bridge has replaced the drawbridge, and there are twelve towers that were built to protect the entrance to the Menai Strait. This idyllic setting belies the sophistication of the defenses of Beaumaris, for it is the ultimate concentric castle and, as such, is the culmination of medieval military architecture.

On Anglesey is the great house Plas Newydd (meaning New Place), home of the Marquess of Anglesey, built in the early 1500s by the Griffith family of Penrhyn. Over the centuries the mansion has had many alterations and additions. The present, or seventh, Marquess gave Plas Newydd to the National Trust in 1976 but still keeps apartments there. The house is admittedly grand, though not overwhelming, and is furnished to emphasize comfort and brightness. The dining room, with a stunning Rex Whistler mural with astonishing trompe l'oeil panels at either end of the room, is the high point of a visit to Plas Newydd. In 1937 the sixth Marquess of Anglesey commissioned Rex Whistler to paint what was to be the last and most extensive of his murals. The main painting, on a single piece of canvas, is fifty-eight feet long and is done in oils. The picture represents the view from the house over the Menai Strait, but instead of the actual Welsh landscape with its farmhouses and forests the artist created a pastiche of architecture from many periods. Some of the buildings are recognizable—Saint Martin's-in-the-Fields and Trajan's Column. Other details are well known, such as the family's two bulldogs and pug and the small cello that belonged to the present Marquess when he was a boy.

On view as well is Lady Anglesey's bedroom on the first floor of the octagonal southeast tower. Decorated in pale pinks and white, the room contains a Sheraton bed with muslin hangings and ribboned spread—one of the most inviting sights imaginable.

The sixth Marquess and his wife, Lady Marjorie Manners, supervised the 1930s renovation of this space, with its views across the Strait toward Caernarvon.

A drive around Anglesey reveals rocky landscapes, deserted beaches, and busy sailing harbors and in the interior a mixture of pleasant farmland and pockets of industrialization. One small town, undistinguished in any other way, boasts the longest name in the world—Llanfairpwllgwywgyllgogerychwyrwdrob-wllllantysyliogogogoch—meaning Saint Mary's (church) by the white aspen over the whirlpool and Saint Tysilio's (church) by the red cave. The name is proudly displayed on several buildings.

THE GOLDEN PHEASANT HOTEL, a family-run country inn in Glyn Ceiriog, near Llangollen, is an ideal place from which to explore northeastern Wales. Pony-trekking is a great sport here as is game shooting. Jenny Turner runs the establishment without frills but with all the essentials. The drawing rooms and bedrooms are simple, neat, and cozy. The bathrooms are more than adequate. The dining room, with cottage furniture, a dresser holding blue-and-white china, and prints of every variety of pheasant on the walls, serves hearty country fare: game pâté and steak-and-kidney pie or perfectly roasted leg of lamb with mint sauce, gravy, and roast potatoes done to a turn. Dessert might include a glorious apple pie from the sideboard or Stilton. On nights when the hunters have been successful pheasant, quail, duck, or grouse might be offered. The inn is open year round, with the fishing season extending from March through September, the shooting season from August to October, and riding as long as the weather permits (and quite frequently when it does not). Jenny Turner's father and sister are in charge of the stables and the orchestration of all hunting and riding parties.

There is much to see in this particular corner of Wales. A

property of the National Trust, the Erdigg House, one mile south of the small city of Wrexham, stands in a park of nearly two thousand acres. A visit through the family rooms and especially the servants' hall where pictures of the old staff are displayed affords a fascinating glimpse into the workings of an English country house.

Not more than ten miles from Erdigg House in Llangollen is a completely different type of abode, another Plas Newydd. This one is a charming small black-and-white timbered cottage that stands in a neat formal garden and is covered inside and out with elaborate oak carvings. It was the residence for almost fifty years of the legendary "Ladies of Llangollen," Lady Eleanor Butler and Miss Sarah Ponsonby. From land-owning Anglo-Irish families, the two women ran off in 1778 to live "a life of sweet and delicious retirement" together. In May of that year they landed at Milford Haven in Wales, traveled the countryside, and arrived in Llangollen, which they found "the beautifulest country in the world." There they rented and subsequently bought Plas Newydd. The ladies, objects of curiosity at first, were soon accepted into the community, and because Llangollen was on one of the main routes from London to Ireland it was not long before their reputation spread. They started receiving visitors of world renown—the Duke of Gloucester, the Duke of Wellington, William Wordsworth, Sir Walter Scott, Josiah Wedgwood, to name but a few. Lady Eleanor died in 1829 at the age of ninety and Miss Sarah two years later at the age of seventy-six. They are both buried in the Llangollen churchyard.

Chirk Castle, a still-lived-in small border castle two miles west of the town of Chirk, was built in 1294 by Edward I to safeguard the conquest of Wales. Parkland surrounds the structure, home of the Myddelton family, and at its entrance is a remarkable iron gate, executed between 1719 and 1721 by Robert and Thomas Davies of Bersham. The site of the castle on a hill overlooking the Ceiriog Valley is particularly pleasant.

The interior of the castle has been renovated innumerable times and contains a great variety of furnishings ranging in style and period from the sixteenth to the nineteenth century. There is a coffered ceiling in the saloon, the elegance of which is usually associated with Adam. Venetian glass-framed mirrors adorn the walls of the drawing room as do portraits of Myddelton family members. The formal gardens have many examples of topiary work and a well tended rose garden. Astonishing are the civilities of certain castles at times!

The BOAT INN in Erbistock, northeast of Chirk, is a perfect spot for lunch. A charming sixteenth-century stone cottage on the river Dee, the inn serves a simple but appealing cold buffet—smoked trout, meat pies, salads, and sweets—as well as a more elaborate lunch in the main restaurant, where salmon with béarnaise sauce might be available on any given day.

Powis Castle, near Welshpool, nearly on the Shropshire border, is an appropriate place to wind up a visit to Wales. The castle of pink stone is set on an impressive site among massive old elms, maples, and Spanish chestnuts. Banks of rhododendrons line the drive. Like Chirk, Powis is an Edwardian castle whose construction was started in the late thirteenth century by the Gruffyd family. The castle was purchased in 1587 by Sir Edward Herbert, a younger son of the Earl of Pembroke. His son William was created Baron Powis in 1629, and additions and changes were made to the castle by his descendants in both the seventeenth and eighteenth centuries. In 1801 the family title became extinct, but in 1804 the estate passed to Henrietta Antonia, sister to the last earl, who married Edward Clive, the son of Clive of India, founder of the empire of British India. So it was that his collections from years of military service in India came to be displayed at Powis. The name of Clive is no longer used, and the castle was vested to the National Trust in 1952, but Lord Clive's great-great-great-grandson lives at Powis today. The long gallery, the grand staircase, and the state bedroom, where the bed is cordoned off in a style reminiscent of Louis XIV's bedroom in Versailles, are well worth a visit. But it is the gardens of Powis that are truly spectacular. They are planted on terraces reached by steep staircases that overlook vast lawns a hundred feet below. In addition to beds of perennials and shrubs that ordinarily flourish in this part of the world, there are specimens generally found in far more temperate climes—New Zealand cabbage tree and Mediterranean sweet bay or laurel tree. Here everything seems to grow in abundance and good health, a garden to remember in a memorable tour. After having visited so many of the castles of Wales, uninhabited for centuries, with silence and solitude imbedded in the very stone, Powis is a happy contrast.

A land of many temperaments, Wales offers her visitors the best of all possible worlds: history, magnificent beauty, and quietude. The differences between North and South Wales are haunting. Her poetry, though, is everywhere.

GOURMET | MARCH 1993

A HIGHLANDS FLING
Three Scottish Inns

UMORS OF THREE extraordinary inns in Scotland's west-ern Highlands had been persistent. We kept hearing that accommodations were comfortable, the country peaceful and beautiful, and—best of all—that three wonderful women of the west were doing marvelous things in the kitchen. All of this hearsay we found to be gospel.

Our first stop was THE AIRDS HOTEL in Port Appin, on Loch Linnhe. We picked up our rental car at Prestwick and head-ed north on the route that winds past bonny Loch Lomond and Loch Fyne, known for a particularly succulent variety of break-fast kipper. Yellow gorse, or *planta-genista* (from which came the name Plantagenet), bluebells, and brilliant mustard plants turn the landscape into a carpet of color. Pink rhododendrons the size of dinner plates embellish the gardens of even the smallest houses. But, with all these signs of late spring, hills in the dis-tance still have their cover of snow.

Inveraray, a town with some interesting shops for Scottish goods and the family seat of the duke and duchess of Argyll, is worth a stop. Inveraray Castle, now in ruin, was headquarters of Clan Campbell; the turreted palace one visits today dates from the eighteenth century. The Great Hall and Armoury, state · rooms, tapestries, and period furniture are impressive. There is a pleasant spot for lunch and tea here as well as a shop with attractive gifts and keepsakes.

Airds, meaning "high place on promontory," is an old ferry inn from the early sixteenth century. The interior of the white-stucco hotel is elegant without being "done up" or pretentious. Guests enter through a glassed-in conservatory where begonias and geraniums bask in the sunshine and all chairs face the garden and the loch. The front hall and stairs are covered in a red carpet with a thistle print. Two parlors are cozily furnished in velvets, chintzes, and patterned rugs. Fires blaze and crackle all day long. Flowers are everywhere. Arranged by next-door neighbor Joan Wakefield, bowls of primroses, carnations, and pale spider chrysanthemums (often from her own garden) add immeasurably to the feel of the place. On the walls a stunning series of gold-framed prints depicts kilted Highland hunters with deer and game. Piles of books and magazines and a tall-case clock loudly ticking away the minutes set a lazy scene. Preprandial drinks and after-dinner coffee are served here.

The fourteen bedrooms are furnished in the same stylish manner. Comfortable as can be, with telephone and television, each one is different. Our room had a queen-sized bed with matching chintz spread and curtains printed with pink, blue, and green posies. Reading lights were bright, and, though the room was not large, there were two comfortable chairs and an antique dressing table. Closet space was more than adequate; and hangers—a seemingly unimportant item about which I can have very strong feelings—were state of the art. Bathrooms at Airds are nearly as large as the bedrooms: Tubs are commodious, towels are fluffy, towel racks are heated, and there is a supply of fragrant soap and bath foam—in other words, all the niceties.

Betty and Eric Allen have owned Airds since 1978, improving and refurbishing as they went along. Betty is one of Scotland's premier cooks, proud possessor of the prestigious Chef Laureate award of the British Academy of Gastronomes. Dinner at Airds is an event that guests look forward to all day. Menus and wine lists are left in bedrooms in the afternoon, and guests are asked to order both dinner and wine by seven-thirty. (Dinner is at eight.) Eric Allen has a truly impressive wine list—clearly the result of a serious avocation—with more than four hundred different choices, including dozens of Bordeaux and Burgundies as well as the house wines, which are specially bottled in France for the hotel.

Our first evening we sipped a glass of wine in one of the parlors and tasted canapés of smoked salmon on pastry rounds. Crisp white table linens and napkins tied with plaid ribbons give the low-ceilinged dining room an opulent air. Eric Allen always wears the kilt, and the expertly trained young women who work in the hotel wear long skirts in the Stewart of Appin tartan. The day's light fades slowly and late in northwestern Scotland's springtime, and the dinner hour is enhanced by this long, soft gloaming.

As starters we selected breast of wood pigeon salad—thinly sliced meat accompanied by perfectly dressed field and oak-leaf lettuces—and a mushroom and onion cream flan, which had an intensely woodsy taste and was served on flaky pastry. Cream of Stilton soup, smooth and well seasoned, followed. Main courses were roast saddle of hare with an onion *confit* and fillet of beef. The Allens often have game on the menu and take the greatest possible pains to have it the best; this is true, however, whether the main course is game, fish, or fowl. Vegetables are served family style, as is usually the case in England and Scotland: A small vegetable dish is put on each table, and guests help themselves. New potatoes, crisp snow peas, and lightly cooked cabbage with juniper were this evening's selection. A 1982 Nuits-Saint-Georges complemented our dinner nicely.

Sweets are cause for celebration here. Date pudding with butterscotch sauce is worth any resulting guilt, and Athole brose, made of malt liquor, oatmeal, and cream, is rich as can be. A selection of Scottish farmhouse cheeses is always offered; Lanark Blue (a sheep's milk cheese), Bonchester, and pungent smoked Orkney were distinctive and delicious.

One of the great joys of a stay at Airds is that there is little to do. Walking is a major pastime. One path, from Port Appin to North Shim, covers nearly two miles. Hills are steep, but the road is smooth and provides bucolic scenes of flocks of sheep with milk-white lambs, deer, and cows grazing serenely. Wild anemones, primroses, buttercups, fiddle-heads, and gorse that smells strangely of coconut oil are some of the flora. Another footpath, also beginning near the hotel, is identified by a wooden marker that reads CLACH THOULL, Celtic for "hole in the rock." Cleared by the Scottish Rights of Way Society, this is a gentle half-hour stroll, indeed past a boulder with a hole, to the dock at Port Appin, from which a small ferry goes occasionally to the island of Lis-more; a dockside restaurant serves meals and teas and coffee.

The town of Port Appin consists of the community Co-op–cum–post office, which sells groceries, newspapers, stamps, and toiletries; a few houses; and Cala Gallery Craft Shop. Handcrafted woolens and pottery are sold here, and the owners have quite a collection of nineteenth- and early-twentieth-century bottles. Bicycles are also available for rent. If you require activities that are slightly more organized, a handbook in each bedroom at Airds gives information on excursions to salmon farms and smokeries, local distilleries, and boat trips on neighboring lochs.

Our second dinner was every bit as good as the first. We feasted on *mousseline* of scallops with a Barsac cream sauce, the mollusks enhanced by the sweet wine, and *gravlaks* with a pungent mustard and dill sauce. Soup was cream of swede (turnip) and leek, smooth and flavorful. Poached fillet of trout was so pink that it resembled what we call salmon trout. Betty Allen does a Champagne sauce for this and uses only Mumm. Roast loin of lamb was perfectly cooked and presented, and the house wine, a 1986 Sauvignon Blanc, was just fine. Dessert choices included mango mousse and two chocolate offerings, a warm cake served with cream and a walnut fudge tart.

Samuel Johnson spoke wisely when he advised that, wherever you choose to sup, you should breakfast in Scotland. The first meal of the day is taken seriously at Airds, so you can start with fruit and progress to the best imaginable porridge, soaked all night; eggs, bacon, and sausage; and even black pudding. After having tasted this last, I asked Eric Allen what it was made of. "*Ach*, you best no inquire," he warned. (In fact, it is a blood sausage made with suet and oatmeal.) Lunch is not often a requirement after the largesse of the morning meal, but the Allens do serve tray lunches of soup and sandwiches. A wonderful chicken liver terrine teamed with Eric Allen's fabulous toasted brioche bread is also available at midday. Lunches can be packed for the road, too, which will be of special interest should you decide to join twenty-six-year-old Graeme Allen, trained at Claridge's and the Capital Hotel in London, on one of his fishing expeditions organized for hotel guests.

Airds is not an easy place to leave, but we headed north to

our second stop, the ten-room KINLOCH LODGE, on the Isle of Skye. The car ferry for Skye covers the three miles from Kyle of Lochalsh, on the mainland, to Kyleakin, about a half hour north of the lodge, in all of five minutes. (Kyle of Lochalsh is a three-hour drive from Port Appin, and the ferry goes back and forth all day.) Kinloch, an impressive white-stucco building that was once a farmhouse on the vast Macdonald estates, has a somewhat bleak exterior. It was built in 1680, eventually became one of the family's shooting lodges, and in 1974 was turned into a hotel by the present Lord and Lady Macdonald. Claire and Godfrey Macdonald manage the hotel, she in charge of the kitchen and he, high chief of Clan Donald, the factotum. With their four children, they also make their home at Kinloch.

Fires crackling away in the two cozy drawing rooms of faded-chintz–covered furniture, books, family pictures, and plants instantly set the scene of a nice, old country house. Umbrellas, hats, and Wellington boots in the entrance hall say something about the prevailing vagaries of climate. The only thing missing is a muddy spaniel or two lying about. The views are spectacular in every direction: Kinloch's lawns sweep down to Loch Na Dal, and in the distance are the Sound of Sleat and the hills of the Scottish mainland. Bedrooms are comfortable, again most with breathtaking views, but they are small, simple, and sparsely furnished. Bathrooms are more than adequate, yet they too are not fancy. Don't expect luxury, but there is a hairdryer and an electric kettle for early-morning tea in each room. All rooms, save one, have private baths.

Meals are an important part of life at Kinloch Lodge, for Claire Macdonald has written ten cookbooks. The spacious dining room sets a pleasant scene for serious eating. Highly polished antique tables are laid with pretty flowered mats, shining silver, crystal, and candles. Walls, hung with family portraits, are dark green with white trim. Two massive sideboards display oversized soup tureens and covered vegetable dishes. Dinner is served at eight, but guests peruse the menu and wine list and gather for apéritifs beforehand. Menus change daily and generally offer a choice between two first courses, followed by soup, then either fish or meat as the main course, and of course dessert.

Our first night a dense and well-flavored chicken terrine was served with Cumberland sauce, and the soup was an intriguing blend of pear, Stilton, and celery. Roast haunch of venison in *sauce jardinière* (with carrots and peas) was hearty. Vegetables, here too, are brought to the table in serving dishes: Sautéed parsnips, riced potatoes, and cauliflower with tomato were the choices. Claire Macdonald admits to a sweet tooth, and *Sweet Things* is one of her more successful cookbooks, so we knew that dessert would be every bit as good as it was. Coffee and chocolate profiteroles filled with cream were light and delectable, as was an apricot *roulade*. The Macdonalds are also proud of their cheeses, which they have sent in by express mail. A Stilton made from unpasteurized milk was perfect, and a Somerset Curworthy, new to us, was first-rate. Cheeses are put out on the sideboard with biscuits and fruit.

Breakfast at Kinloch Lodge is a treat. In the introduction to her cookbook *Seasonal Cooking from the Isle of Skye*, Claire Macdonald says, "When it comes to food in the hotel, breakfast is as important as dinner. We try to provide the sort of breakfast that Scotland used to be renowned for. . . ." Pitchers of fresh orange juice; cold cereals, including home-mixed muesli; fresh yogurt; and prunes and lovely, tart rhubarb—both stewed—as well as dried figs in syrup are all set out on the sideboard. A hot, freshly baked scone is brought to each guest to savor with superb Kinloch marmalade and thick honey. Porridge is the next course,

followed by eggs, bacon, sausage, tomatoes, black and white puddings, and fried bread. After some thought, I decided upon the
white pudding, this time having been told the ingredients by
our waitress: suet, spices, oatmeal, and onions. Served with fried
bread, it was, in fact, delicious. My companion was enthusiastic
about his broiled Mallaig kippers, and granary bread—its coarse
flour is special to the area—accompanies the feast. Kinloch Lodge
will pack sandwiches for lunch, and on damp, overcast days Earl
Grey and a square of shortbread by one of the drawing-room
fires hit the spot.

A forest path behind the lodge affords fine views and is bordered by blooming gorse and wild yellow primrose. Clan Donald
Centre, a short drive from the hotel, is a preserve of forty wood-
land acres with gardens and nature trails on the grounds of
partly ruined Armadale Castle. Splendid views across the Sound
of Sleat make this well worth a visit. Clan Donald Land Trust
bought the Macdonald estate in 1972 and since then has been
restoring the castle and gardens. Dunvegan Castle, the seat of
Clan Macleod, is on the northwestern side of Skye, fifty miles
from Kinloch. Steeped in the history of clan battle legends, and
the rich inheritance of Highlands life, the castle is an integral
part of the island's past.

For our last dinner at Kinloch, we enjoyed leek and mushroom broth, three-cheese tart with tomato sauce, and a fresh and
flavorful fillet of hake breaded in oatmeal and served with tartar
sauce. Roast pork was much enhanced by an apple and horserad-
ish glaze as well as prune and red-wine gravy. Chocolate cream
cake with toasted coconut was sinfully rich. Pouilly-Fuissé was
just the right wine with dinner, and a glass of vintage Port with
cheese made the evening a celebration.

The drive north from Kyle of Lochalsh to the fishing village of Ullapool, our last stop, took us through the northwestern Highlands, where the roads are narrow but good. Life is sparse here; the towns of Stromeferry and Achnasheen are small; and sheep, contendedly munching the rugged hillsides, seem to far outnumber residents. ALTNAHARRIE INN is on the southern shores of Loch Broom, just opposite Ullapool. When you arrive in Ullapool, call the inn and then walk to the pier, where you will be collected by *Mother Goose*, the inn's launch, for the ten-minute, one-mile journey ending at Altnaharrie's dock. The road to the inn is rough, and a four-wheel vehicle is required to negotiate the track.

Gunn Eriksen and Fred Brown turned this circa 1745 drovers' inn into a very special spot in 1980. As their brochure states, "We have no neighbors, the waves lap at the edge of the garden, and the surrounding heather-clad hills offer magnificent walks and the chance of spotting a variety of wildlife." Chickens and guinea fowl greet guests as they walk the path to the welcoming inn. Two sitting rooms—a small one downstairs with a fire in the hearth, books, and scatter rugs; and a handsome new, larger one upstairs—afford pleasant spots for reading, predinner gathering, and after-dinner coffee.

Altnaharrie has the feel of a country house in Scandinavia, something out of Carl Larsson. Gunn Eriksen is, in fact, from the town of Grimstadt, in Norway. A ceramicist and weaver in Inverness when she met Fred Brown, a veterinary surgeon, Gunn does the cooking at Altnaharrie and has gained celebrity status throughout the British Isles: Guests told friends about her extraordinary cooking, and then, in the television series "Take Six More Cooks," she was featured as one of Scotland's most talented chefs. Since then the world has been beating a path to her door. Meanwhile, Fred takes care of the 101 details of day-to-day hotel life, doing much to make guests who occupy Altnaharrie's seven bedrooms happy.

We were in the annex cottage, across a rushing stream from the main house. Our room was large, with two double beds and an oversized armoire instead of a closet. Every comfort is provided: down-filled duvets with covers to match printed sheets, good bedside lamps, bottles of mineral water, and even a flashlight. (A generator supplies Altnaharrie's electricity, and lights go out a decent interval after the last guest has turned in.) Yellow primroses in a vase were still wet with dew. Outside our door, a cherry tree had grown up between the porch floorboards.

The heart of the inn is the whitewashed dining room, with windows that overlook the lawn and Loch Broom. Mahogany tables are set with tatted white mats; wild flowers are folded into the napkins; and the glasses and silver flatware are of Norwegian design. Lunch is not served at Altnaharrie. The dinner menu changes every day, and, as is the case at Airds and Kinloch, apéritifs are served in either of two lounges. Fred, too, does request that wine be ordered earlier in the day. He has a good cellar of about two hundred well-chosen wines. Glasses in hand, we whetted our appetites on mussels from the half shell and puff pastry topped with caviar.

Dinner started with an intensely flavorful hawthorn and cucumber soup, which was pale green with a swirl of cream and a hawthorn leaf for decoration. Gunn Eriksen is not one to adhere to strict gastronomic conventions, so game was next and then the fish course. Thus, medallions of Sika deer, flambéed in

Armagnac and served with a sauce of juniper and dill, were followed by an elegant presentation of monkfish, halibut, turbot, and sole in Champagne sauce, encircling strudel pastry filled with prawns and leek. Gunn has had no professional training, but her cooking is sophisticated, evidence that she enjoys experimenting with tastes and textures. Livarot; Brie; Valençay, a goat cheese; and Epoisses made up the all-French cheese course. (Cheeses are a house pride, and one's selection can be made from between twenty and thirty, with the United Kingdom well represented.) Desserts were a crumbly rhubarb tart, lusciously rich chocolate cake, and sliced peaches in Port. A half bottle of Saint-Véran from Domaine Marcel Vincent and a very good Graves from Château Respide-Medeville were good complements to the extraordinary fare. Chocolate-covered strawberries, addictive chocolate truffles, and almond *kransekaker* were served with after-dinner coffee.

For a delightful day trip from Altnaharrie, drive from Ullapool down the western coast road to Inverewe Garden, a pleasant jaunt of about fifty miles. You will pass verdant pastureland, with the sea never far off. The garden, now managed by the National Trust for Scotland, was the singular achievement of one Osgood Mackenzie, whose dream was to create a garden on this headland of dark acid peat and rock. He brought in soil, set out trees for protection from fierce prevailing winds, and relentlessly planted. The project occupied him from 1862 until his death in 1922. Mackenzie's book, *A Hundred Years in the Highlands*, tells how the proximity of the Gulf Stream provides the temperate climate required for certain species of rare subtropical plants. One hillside, in fact, duplicates the weather conditions of New Zealand's South Island and has many of the same trees and shrubs.

It is easy to see why Inverewe receives over 140,000 visitors a year now. Walks here are of infinite variety. There is a charming walled garden with purple columbines, aconites, hostas, and bleeding hearts hedged by well-trimmed box and espaliered apple trees, abloom in spring. A splendid rhododendron walk leads to the impressive herbaceous border in front of Inverewe House. Big lily pads flourish with fiddleheads in the pond garden. We were lucky enough to arrive in time for a tour with head gardener Peter Clough. Inverewe has changed much since Osgood Mackenzie's day, he told us, but the single most extraordinary thing about it is, still, that it is here at all.

We drove back to Ullapool and the *Mother Goose*, happy at the prospect of another Gunn Eriksen dinner. Nor were we disappointed. We started with an ethereal crab soup, garnished with lobster and dotted with an intense basil and olive blend. Then came a mousseline of asparagus and chervil encased in pastry with a lemon sauce. Sauces here are an inspired balance of intensity and delicacy. Wonderful fresh bread also comes from this kitchen, as do freshly baked croissants each morning at breakfast. Our main course was fillet of grass-fed calf, accompanied by foie gras and sweetbreads. Two sauces, one of juniper and cream, the other natural juices flavored with Burgundy, were perfect foils. Sweets again were an embarrassment of riches: lemon and pistachio tart garnished with a dollop of whipped cream; *krumkaker*, or cloudberry ice cream in a pastry shell topped with spun sugar; and individual apple tarts.

Mother Goose ferried us back to Ullapool the next morning, as we made firm resolves to return to these inns in the Highlands. Possibly the best part of the trip had been the absence of frenetic sightseeing; there had been little that had to be done. Our sojourn seemed to epitomize Samuel Johnson's prescription for a pleasant holiday: "Turn all care out of your head as soon as you mount the chaise. Do not think about frugality, your health is worth more than it can cost. Do not continue any day's journey to fatigue. Take now and then a day's rest. Cast away all anxiety and keep your mind easy."

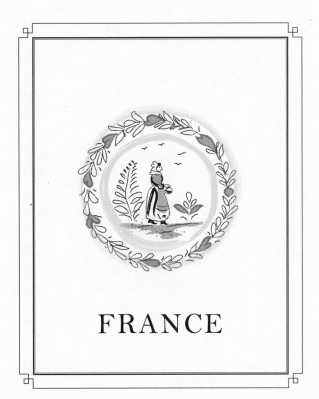

FRANCE

Quimper

HE TOWN OF Quimper is located in southwestern Brittany in a valley at the junction of the Steir and Odet rivers: Its name derives from the Breton word *kemper*, meaning "confluence." There is much in the architecture, customs, and ambiance of Quimper that makes it most distinctively Breton and thus quite separate from the rest of France. The chief town of the county of Finistère, Quimper encompasses an area of seventeen square kilometers of urban, agricultural, and maritime landscape and activity. Its aura of solidity and permanence derives largely from the indestructible Breton granite of its buildings. Huge, pink-blossomed chestnut trees bloom along the quay of the Odet, and medieval gables and carved wooden figures adorn the city's squares and the charming streets that link them.

The cathedral of Saint-Corentin is the oldest example of Gothic architecture in Brittany. Although most scholars consider Saint-Corentin to be an essentially fourteenth-century edifice, construction on the cathedral was actually begun in 1240 and was not completed for another six hundred years. The nave, built in 1424, is a few degrees out of line with the choir, creating a somewhat curious effect but one entirely in keeping with many of the town's other aging structures, well settled and mercifully undamaged by the wars of modern times.

Saint-Corentin was named for Quimper's first bishop, who, legend has it, ate the flesh of a single miraculous fish for years: He would consume the fish each morning, throw the remains back in the river, and then find the fish whole again the next day. The cathedral itself became "whole" only in 1856 with the addition of its two spires, which dominate the townscape and look down upon the square, where Breton ladies in handsome high headdresses sell lace gloves, doilies, and blouses.

Two museums provide glimpses into Quimper's cultural heritage. The Musée des Beaux-Arts, located at Place Saint-Corentin, has photographic exhibits in monthly rotation on the main floor, its permanent collection on the second floor. This latter contains some fine examples of Dutch, Flemish, and French painting of the seventeenth and eighteenth centuries, but it is only with its nineteenth-century works that local artists and local scenes come to the forefront of the museum's offerings. One monumental canvas by Lemordant depicts men and women in full Breton costume walking on a beach, and there is a charming view of the port at Quimper by Eugène-Louis Boudin, a precursor of Impressionism and one of the first painters to work in the open air directly from nature. One room is devoted to a large exhibit of watercolors by, and memorabilia about, Max Jacob (1876–1944), a writer and semimonastic convert to Catholicism who was associated with Cubism and Surrealism and is one of the better known of the town's native sons. The Musée Breton, next door to the cathedral, displays elaborately carved wooden furniture and decorations, costumes from the 1800s, and artifacts detailing the history of the evolution of Quimper's faience industry.

The indoor market at Place Saint-François is open every day save Sunday and Monday, but it is at its best each Wednesday and Saturday, when—even if one is not keeping house—a visit is an experience not to be missed. Long wooden tables are covered with bunches of red and white radishes, wild strawberries not much larger than peas, artichokes from small to gigantic, and tiny new potatoes. Everywhere are pink petunia plants and buckets filled with cut flowers: magenta sweet williams; yellow, white, and blue irises. There are melons from Cavaillon (near Avignon) as small as oranges, perfect pineapples from the Ivory Coast, and innumerable varieties of wild mushrooms. Separate shops sell eggs and blocks of Breton butter stamped with flower imprints, dozens upon dozens of cheeses, and a vast selection of *charcuterie.* Just a glance at the butcher's window, where chickens are still in possession of their heads and feet, makes one realize how far most of us are from the genuine article.

On Wednesdays and Saturdays outdoor markets flourish, too, specializing not in food but in jewelry, leather goods, brasses, and antiques, as well as clothing and shoes. The streets around the market are for the most part off limits to automobile traffic but draw a steady stream of pedestrians to their attractive shops. Rue Astor and Rue Saint-François abound in what you will for the well dressed, and Rue Kéréon is a mecca of leather and jewelry stores picturesquely ensconced in half-timbered houses decorated with carved Breton figures. Rolande Lingerie on the Quai du Steir has pretty cotton and silk nightgowns; Art de Cornouaille at 12, Place Saint-Corentin has probably the town's largest selection of Quimper ware for sale; and Héoligou at 16, rue du Parc is the only shop in town where one can buy any or all locally made woolens and textiles, among them Breton sweaters, hats, jackets, and fishermen's striped shirts. They are beautifully made and virtually indestructible.

CAPUCIN GOURMAND at 29, rue Réguaires is a serious

eating establishment. Periwinkles are placed on the table to help one stave off hunger while perusing the menu. Lunch one day consisted of a *pot-au-feu* of fish: turbot, sole, oysters, and scallops, each cooked separately and served en masse with an herb sauce, white turnips, spinach, and tomatoes. Another entrée was a delicious sole with asparagus. Six beautiful *belon* oysters on the half shell, redolent of the sea, preceded the main course. Sorbets of mango, passion fruit, and lemon followed it.

For a quick and simpler meal, the CAFÉ DE GRANDE BRETAGNE, on the Rue du Parc, is just the thing. At the bar or, on a fine day, at sidewalk tables one can have a sandwich; in the brasserie one can choose anything from an omelet, a plate of hors d'oeuvres, or *moules marinière* to the plat du jour, usually a roast or fowl with accompanying vegetables. Wine is served in pitchers, and beer is offered in three sizes: *demi, sérieux,* and *formidable,* depending on the imbiber's capacity. There are several *crêperies* in town where a buckwheat crêpe with ham, cheese, egg, or a variety of other fillings makes an abbreviated but satisfying lunch.

Faienceries de Quimper, a large white factory on the Route de Bénodet, is one of the chief reasons for a visit to this part of Brittany. Faience is a type of pottery made of fine-grade painted and glazed earthenware that has become Quimper's claim to international fame. The story of the growth of this industry is a convoluted one, spanning three centuries, and is perhaps best summarized as the rise, fall, and resuscitation of three family enterprises.

In 1695 Jean-Baptiste Bousquet, a master craftsman in the faience factory at Moustiers, in southern France, decided to start his own workshop, The Grande Maison HB, at Locmaria, Quimper. His son inherited the factory, which was expanded, flourished, and in fact remained in the hands of the Bousquet family until the death of one Guy de la Hubaudière during World War I. The house then was bought by Messieurs Verlingue, Bollari et Cie.

A rival *faiencerie* had been started in 1776 by François Eloury, a former thrower at the original factory, and was inherited in the early nineteenth century by a family son-in-law, Charles Porquier. Under his directorship the pottery was systematically marked for the first time—a practice carried forth by subsequent owners and a crucial guide to historians and collectors. The business was greatly expanded under Porquier's son, Adolphe, but it was Adolphe's widow, Augustine Carof, who struck the partnership that became the well-known shop of Porquier-Beau. It was Alfred Beau who introduced peasant figures as designs on dishes and as figurines, a decision that has had as much as anything else to do with the local ware's great popularity. The Porquier-Beau introduction of expanded floral and Breton scenes, its unusually delicate colorations, and its particularly fine glaze make the pottery of this house and period some of the most cherished produced in Quimper and won Beau a silver medal at the Paris Exposition of 1878.

About the same time the Eloury enterprise was initiated a third competitor emerged, under the ownership of Guillaume Dumaine, a thrower from Normandy. This factory, which produced mostly stoneware, was of little importance until 1886, when Jules Henriot (of Maison Henriot) bought first it and then, in 1913, the trademark, drawings, and molds of Porquier-Beau, which had closed down a decade earlier. Then, in 1968, the Henriot company went into liquidation and the surviving original firm, the Grande Maison HB, took on Henriot's work force and its new name, Faienceries de Quimper.

Sarah and Paul Janssens, an American couple who are importers, wholesalers, and—with a small shop in Stonington Village, Connecticut—also retailers of Quimper, naturally had a close association with the Faienceries. When the factory came on hard times and, in fact, closed down in July, 1983, the Janssens stepped in, formed a corporation, and bought the property. They hold fifty-one percent of the stock, and twenty-nine investors—one Dutch, the rest American though three are of Breton extraction—hold the remainder. The Janssens reside in Quimper part of each year, but the place inhabits them year round, for they eat, sleep, and even dream their factory. The town, too, seems to be delighted that the charming plates with the traditional peasant figures, roosters, and flowers are once again being manufactured, preserving an important feature of Brittany's cultural and economic life.

Tours of the factory, given every day, allow one to see the plates, bowls, cups, and pitchers being shaped, fired, and—most interesting of all—painted. The artists (about forty of them) sit according to their seniority and experience, master painters positioned at the far end of the large, bright studio, and paint freehand with special brushes that are changed every three weeks. They spend an average of a half hour on each plate and, of course, because the work is done by hand, no two are exactly alike. A master painter may very well spend a full day working on one of the special commemorative plates and several days on the exquisite pottery violins that are a popular product of the Faienceries. Perhaps the smocks have been updated and more sunlight now streams into the studios, but the methods used in the factory are much the same as they have always been.

The museum at the Faienceries is a veritable treasure trove. It belongs to the town of Quimper and details the history of the manufacture of pottery in this area. Of particular interest is a ceramic model of an entire town: wineshop, hotel, church, and townspeople, all designed around 1929 by the painter Mathurin Méhuet, perhaps best known for his frescoes for the famed French ocean liner *Normandie.* Vases from the 1930s in black and deep terra-cotta resemble lacquer. Handsome old plates marked HB and HR with such sayings as *Vivre libre ou mourir* and *Je vous annonce le bonheur* are displayed along with huge vases decorated with vibrantly colored scenes depicting an afternoon game of *boules.*

On the second floor of the museum the treasures continue, almost too much to take in. Figurines of saints are among the most charming items in the collection: Saint Anne, a great Breton patron saint; Saint Rigolar, really a joke, taking his name from the verb *rigoler,* "to giggle"; and the Virgin holding the solemn Babe. There is a display of curiously shaped pieces made by Porquier-Beau around 1898: These "fantasy" pieces, as they are called, include foot warmers, chickens, and airplanes. A beautiful and delicate violin that was made in the late 1800s and serves as a model for those produced today is also on view. Sarah Janssen is the museum's curator, and it is her great interest. She plans to open a museum shop in Quimper later this year and another in Paris in early 1986 and is anxious to involve individual artists in the factory's production, as was the practice in the early days. One of her projects is to have the artists choose a pattern, old or new, on their birthdays and then to create a one-of-a-kind signed piece for the museum shop.

Days on end could be spent exploring Quimper's pottery works, museums, and faience shops alone; days more investigating the town itself and the surrounding countryside. And not far from Quimper are any number of really very special places from which to base your peregrinations.

Set in a vast park, the MANOIR DU STANG, in La Forêt-Fouesnant, sixteen kilometers from Quimper, is a marvelous sixteenth-century country house turned hotel. The grounds are impressive, beginning with the approach: a long driveway leading to the gates and a stately courtyard planted with yellow pansies, mignonettes, and clipped evergreens. Only slightly farther along is a fine stone wall, a grove of magnolias, and in back two ponds presumably inhabited by trout. The bedrooms, either in the old walnut-paneled wing or in the more modern part of the hotel, are attractively furnished with antiques and extremely comfortable. The salon, where one can have a drink before meals or coffee afterward, comes alive with a blazing fire when the weather provides enough of an excuse, and there are always flowers about, regardless of the season.

The dining room overlooks hydrangea bushes and the ponds. It is a cheerful room, painted white with gray trim, the neutral palette complemented by pretty chintz curtains in a robin's-egg blue print. The young waitresses are dressed in blue uniforms and traditional Breton headdresses. Dinner is a pleasant affair in the soft, long twilight. *Coquilles Saint-Jacques* in Port and Cognac sauce, chicken with Muscadet sauce, and a delectable pastry called a *religieuse* (nun's cake) were served one night, and on another evening turbot, tournedos Choron with potato croquettes, and *grille à l'estragon* (tarragon lobster flamed with Cognac). The choices were varied and delicious, ranging from a prix fixe dinner to the temptations of a large à la carte menu.

The hotel LA BELLE ETOILE, which is at Le Cabellou-Plage, twenty-four kilometers from Quimper and just outside Concarneau, is a typically Breton whitewashed building with a slate roof. It overlooks a quiet harbor, the rooms are charming, and tables and chairs dotting the lawn provide a very pleasant perch from which to enjoy all the nautical goings-on.

The seventeenth-century MANOR DE MOËLLIEN, north of Quimper and near Locronan, is set high on a hill amidst verdant farmlands. Constructed of blocks of gray and buff stone that are often exposed inside, it is very much what one imagines a rustic and substantial ages-old residence to be. Over-sized fireplaces and beamed ceilings highlight the public rooms, including the dining room, which is much frequented by local residents. The bedrooms are simple, clean, and comfortable.

For visitors who would prefer not to rent a car, there is the HÔTEL LA TOUR D'AUVERGNE in Quimper itself on Rue Réguaires. It is small but pleasant, with completely adequate rooms and baths and its own restaurant, although the Capucin Gourmand is just down the street.

The Aigrette steamboat line and the French National Railroads provide a river trip on the Odet that goes back and forth between Bénodet and Quimper. The round trip takes three hours, and the schedule varies with the tides. A very commodious launch glides smoothly along the river past manor houses with lawns that slope to the water. Bushes of purple rhododendrons and yellow broom line the riverbank, and one slips gracefully by the small Lanroz Château, once the property of Madame de Sévigné, and Deianniron, the former residence of the bishops of Quimper. Most hotels and the tourist office in Quimper can provide the timetable, and tickets can be purchased just before sailing, in both Bénodet and Quimper.

Dinner in Bénodet at LA FERME DU LETFY is a high point of the river trip. Monsieur and Madame Guilbault are the personable proprietors, and their son, Jean Marie—Lenôtre and Plaza-Athénée trained—is the chef. Specialties during our visit were the freshest, reddest of *langoustines* (Norway lobsters), served with a perfect mayonnaise; a delectable dish of curried sole; and salmon topped with a *mousseline* of sole. The chef is, of course, an accomplished pastry cook, and Madame turns her hand to some of the cakes too, so desserts are a special event. Excellent Sancerres and Muscadets complement the seafood admirably, and the owner serves an unusual and particularly delicious version of a "Kir Royal" as an apéritif: Champagne flavored with orange liqueur instead of the traditional *crème de cassis.* The atmosphere is inviting and rustic: stout wooden tables, checked napkins, and dinner plates in a colorful floral Quimper pattern.

Two restaurants in Pont-Aven, thirty-two kilometers southeast of Quimper, are most assuredly worth the journey. In the center of town LE MOULIN DE ROSMADEC, a fifteenth-century mill on the Aven River, is thoroughly engaging. Contributing to the charm are a large fireplace, pink napery, flowers everywhere, and, at the door, the babbling brook that once served the mill. The owners, Monsieur and Madame Sébilleau, see that the food is up to the surroundings. A memorable salmon charlotte with asparagus started dinner one night. Fillet of sole *beurre blanc* and *pigeonneau avec chou,* quartered squab on a bed of the youngest, freshest cabbage imaginable, were first-rate. A warm *galette* of apples was the perfect finishing touch.

LA TAUPINIÈRE, a thatched-roof inn on the road from Concarneau and four kilometers outside Pont-Aven, serves both lunch and dinner in style. The pride of the restaurant is broiled *langoustines* and a fragrant local ham grilled on a wood fire and served with white beans. The dining room is soft and pretty, with pale peach walls and bright yellow and blue lamps on the tables. As is the custom in many of the restaurants in Brittany, petits fours and luscious chocolate truffles were put on the table with after-dinner coffee.

All in all, this corner of France is a thoroughly pleasant place to tour, with present-day comforts serenely nestled in the gardens and manor houses of past centuries. And at its center historic Quimper and its artistic heritage endure, offering much to instruct and delight.

A Tour in Lorraine

ORRAINE IS AN almost forgotten province, always paired with
and much less frequently visited than Alsace. It is basically
rural, with expanses of flat farm- and pastureland divided by avenues of trees. Large dairy herds and a profusion of orchards
dominate the scene, and on two-lane roads traffic is anything but
a problem. At the beginning of our stay we made our headquarters in Nancy, a pleasant, two-plus hours' train trip from Paris's
Gare de l'Est. The GRAND HÔTEL DE LA REINE, on the
elegant Place Stanislas, is, hands down, the place to stay. Legend
has it that Marie-Antoinette, on her way to be crowned, stopped
here. The square, a remarkably beautiful eighteenth-century
town-planning achievement, was conceived by the great builder
and twice-deposed king of Poland, Stanislas Leszczynski. Louis
XV of France, married to Stanislas's daughter Maria, made his
father-in-law duke of Lorraine in 1737 with the understanding
that upon the elder's death the duchy would become a part of
France. Stanislas was much loved by the Lorrains and left many
splendid monuments in remembrance of his nearly thirty-year
stewardship.

The Grand Hôtel de la Reine is small, with fifty rooms, and
comfortable. All the amenities that one would expect are avail-

able, the service is smooth and thoughtful, and the public rooms are attractively furnished. The dimly lit bar's paneled walls are decorated with bunches of glass grapes, which also show up as table lamps. Our bedroom, done in understated beiges, overlooked the square.

LE STANISLAS, the hotel's dining room, painted a pale apricot and brightened with silver candelabra and colorful still lifes and landscapes on the walls, is a delightful spot for lunch or dinner. Chef Michel Douville specializes in foods of the region and game cookery. We started dinner our first night with an *amuse-bouche* of salmon tartare on thinly sliced black radishes. Next came rich and smooth *crème de homard* (lobster cream soup) and *brouet Stanislas* (*brouet* is a Lorraine rendition of a classic *petite marmite*, a clear, flavorful meat broth with pieces of chicken, carrot, and zucchini). Veal kidneys on slivers of artichoke hearts and a breast of pheasant in shallot cream accompanied by pears poached in Burgundy were our main courses. A selection of farm cheeses and an excellent Münster with cumin were the proper final touch. On another occasion, we sampled the game menu, enjoying *marcassin* (baby wild boar) flambéed at the table, venison Rossini (with *foie gras* and truffles), and an excellent chestnut mousse for dessert.

Nancy is an appealing city in which to walk. The glorious main square, masterpiece of Emmanuel Héré, Stanislas's architect, is adorned with delicate grillwork by Jean Lamour, two magnificent fountains, and a fine statue of Stanislas. From the square, the Rue Héré leads through a triumphal arch to the Place de la Carrière. Four rows of linden trees set off eighteenth-century dwellings that once served as quarters for cavalry officers. Place Stanislas culminates in an imposing palace, the façade of which incorporates a grand row of Ionic columns. The nearby Basilica of Saint-Epvre was constructed in the Gothic style between 1864 and 1871 and boasts three handsome rose windows.

Near the arch off the Place de la Carrière is the Rue des Maréchaux, which is made up almost exclusively of restaurants—fourteen to be exact. We had been told to head straightaway to LA GENTILHOMMIÈRE, on the premises of a house where Victor Hugo's father once lived. A comfortable, countrified ambiance reigns within the restaurant's stucco walls and beamed ceilings; a fireplace and displays of antique faience add to the effect. Chef Alain Masson produces good, solid country food. We feasted first on a *galette* of potatoes and wild mushrooms, and for our main dishes we chose *émincé* of rabbit and *coq au vin*. The latter dish was authentic—the rooster's drumstick was nearly the size of a turkey leg—and had clearly been simmered for hours in wine to produce a dense sauce that also contained *lardons* (diced thick bacon) and very slightly pickled white onions. For dessert we sampled perfect *oeufs à la neige* (poached egg whites in vanilla custard) and dark chocolate mousse. An Alsatian Pinot Noir was just right with such hearty fare.

In the rues Gambetta, Stanislas, and des Dominicains, all near the Place Stanislas, are attractive shops sporting the fashion names that one would expect in France, and more besides. The Grande Rue, which runs through the center of Nancy's old town, is sprinkled with antiques shops of all descriptions, selling curios, jewelry, books, stamp collections, and bits of faience. On the same street is the Palais Ducal, which houses the Musée Historique Lorrain, an impressive and vast collection of archaeological relics, statues from the Middle Ages, handsome faience stoves and fire-backs, apothecary jars and tapestries. We spent nearly an entire very rainy day here and found it a treasure trove as well as a great source of information on the region's cultural history.

Next door the Chapelle Ducale, construction of which was begun in 1607 under Charles III, stands over the burial caves of the dukes of Lorraine. Shaped octagonally with sixteen columns, the handsome building contains six black-marble sarcophagi. The church cloister and part of an ancient monastery have been restored to house the delightful Musée des Arts et Traditions Populaires, where rooms from Lorraine residences are reconstructed; built-in bunks, bed warmers, kitchen utensils, and faded photos give a vivid picture of yesteryear in the province.

Two other museums—the Musée des Beaux-Arts, on the Place Stanislas, and the Musée de l'École de Nancy, in a residential section of town near the Parc Sainte-Marie—should be seen. The fine-arts museum's collection includes Delacroix's *The Death of Charles the Bold at the Battle of Nancy* and Rubens's huge *Transfiguration*. A startlingly realistic canvas by Emile Friant depicts a family, dressed in mourning and carrying flowers, stopping on the way to a cemetery to give a beggar alms. Vlaminck, Dérain, Utrillo, Monet, and Manet are all represented. The School of Nancy Museum is located in the former residence of one Eugène Corbin, a businessman who was a patron of the school, on the Rue du Sergent-Blandan. It is a truly extraordinary collection of furniture, glass, screens, and wall panels, all in the Art Nouveau style, which had originated in the 1880s and was initiated here in 1901 by Emile Gallé, a leading glassmaker and designer. Many other artisans, cabinetmakers, ironworkers, architects, and furniture designers were part of Gallé's group, and examples of their work can be seen in buildings throughout the city. The museum has to be seen to be believed. A large, elaborately carved wooden construction contains a bench, desk, and cabinet, the whole taking up one entire wall of its exhibition space. Massive leather furniture was popular early in the century, and frosted and colored glass is used in profusion throughout the house.

An attractive example of Art Nouveau is the brasserie FLO EXCELSIOR, a member of the Paris-based Brasserie Flo group, just off the Rue Stanislas and across from the train station. Stained-glass windows executed by Jacques Gruber, brown velvet banquettes, and shining brass railings serve as a stage set for a devoted clientele who pack the place at both lunch and dinner for typical, delicious brasserie fare. Waiters in black vests and long white aprons maneuver around, often at a dead run, with tiered tin platters heaped with shellfish. Shared by two or more happy diners, selections of sparklingly fresh oysters, clams, crabs, mussels, sea urchins, *langoustines* (Norway lobsters), and cockles are deposited in the middle of already crowded tables. Melted butter, mayonnaise, and thin brown bread are the usual accompaniments. We observed this ritual with fascination as we enjoyed a salad of *frisée* (curly endive) with *lardons*, croutons, and a warm poached egg. A gratin of plump mussels, puréed spinach, leeks, and mushrooms was napped in delicate curry sauce.

The GRAND CAFÉ FOY, on the main square, is another café-brasserie, this one a good choice for a creditable chef's salad, omelet, *croque-monsieur* and *croque-madame* sandwiches, and the house white. The restaurant, a fixture on the *place* for twenty-five years, is owned by Jacqueline Rollier (called J.R. by her regulars), who used to own the restaurant upstairs also. When running both got to be too much, she sold the grander upstairs establishment, which has since gone *nouvelle*, and stayed with the early-risers and night owls who appreciate her simple food and the 7 A.M. to 2 A.M. hours.

A visit to Nancy's very special covered market on the Place Henri-Mengin is a memorable experience. In fall, yellow and purple chrysanthemums bank the large main building and the stalls where toys, clothes, and household items beckon. Indoors is a feast for all the senses: tables of shiny black prunes from Agen, figs, golden raisins, and tiny walnuts alongside bunches of perfect leeks, radishes with milk-white tips, *cèpes*, chanterelles, and every variety of lettuce imaginable. Glass cases are filled with spinach ravioli and *gnocchi*, and the seafood section overflows with a dizzying choice of fish and shellfish. Scallops can be bought still in the shell with their pink roe, and on the day I visited I saw fourteen boxes of different types of oysters on display.

Michel Marchand, *maître fromager-affineur-volailler*, has the most lavish shop in the market. On one side of its central aisle is game—pheasant, quail, venison, boar—so beloved by French chefs and available from October to February, which is purveyed to a large percentage of Nancy's restaurants. Farm-raised chickens, ducks, and roosters are also for sale along with fresh whole and tinned *foie gras.* Across the aisle is an awesome selection of cheeses, all made *au lait cru* (with unpasteurized milk) because, according to the Marchands, pasteurization kills flavor in cheese. Goat cheeses (I counted sixty-five), produced by private cheesemakers in very small quantities, are a Marchand specialty, and more than two hundred other cheeses from all over France are available, too. We tasted an aged Beaufort from a herd of cows that grazes in mountainous pastures three thousand meters high in the Haute-Savoie; the cheese is actually made *sur place* before being brought to market. The Marchand family has scrupulous standards when it comes to food, and its knowledge and experience ensure that excellent quality will be passed on to clients. Beginning this month, the cellars where the cheeses age will be open to visitors who want to look and taste products that are harder and harder to find in this world.

Nancy is a great city for sweets, too. Madeleines, the lovely scallop-shaped cakes put on the gastronomic and literary map by Proust, are frequently served here, and Nancy's macaroons are as well known throughout France as her specialty citrus drops, called *bergamotes*. The yellow bergamot was first brought here from Italy by René, duke of Anjou and Lorraine and titular king of Naples. Oil extracted from the rind of this sweet-smelling fruit was used strictly as a perfume until the middle of the nineteenth century, when a confectioner in Nancy, Lillig, made a delicious hard candy from the fruit's essence. Today third-generation *maître confiseur* Roger Lalonde—his shops are at 20, rue Héré, and between the Place Stanislas and the covered market, at 32, rue Saint-Jean—makes these *bergamotes* along with jewel-like chocolate bonbons, macaroons, and two other special sweets: *craquelines*, assorted fruit-flavored almond-paste candies covered with a clear sugar glaze; and *charlestines*, which resemble sugar-coated almonds but have semisoft praline centers.

The RESTAURANT DU CAPUCIN GOURMAND, on the Rue Gambetta, is one of the best-known eateries of Nancy. Gérard Veissière, the chef-owner, runs a highly professional and welcoming establishment. The décor is formal and, in the style of the Ecole de Nancy, comfortably Old World, with Oriental rugs and green fabric on the walls. Service here is traditional and correct, and flowers grace impeccably set tables. Beginning one evening with tiny warm cheese pastries and fricassee of *girolles*, the pale-orange forest mushroom perfectly teamed with cream and white wine, we went on to standout main courses: a wonderfully satisfying fillet of sole, roasted with crispy potatoes; and fillet of lamb cooked in a salt crust with thyme. Each dish was accompanied by *ratatouille* in little zucchini baskets. There is a note on the Capucin Gourmand menu to the effect that "whether our guests order a large meal or one simple dish, we will do our best to please them." Having amply sampled Lorraine's bounty, we felt no qualms about passing on dessert—but, in accordance with French custom, we were nevertheless presented with a lovely assortment of candied orange peel, chocolate truffles, and cookies to enjoy with our coffees.

We had heard glowing reports of the restaurant AU BON ACCUEIL and so decided to stop in for lunch on our way from Nancy to Lunéville. Fourteen kilometers due south of Nancy in Richardménil, it is an unpretentious family affair that specializes in *"cuisine vieille France."* Since 1960 Adrien Kruch and his wife, Marie-Louise, have been serving enthusiastic clients hearty, fresh regional food. Now their three children, two sons and a daughter, assist in the kitchen and dining room. The proprietor is justly proud of his wine cellar. Though hesitant to commit himself to an exact count, he admits to having in the neighborhood of thirty thousand bottles, among them some rare and prestigious vintages from every region of France. Of note, too—he loves to give tours. Small wonder that he calls the cellar *la chapelle.*

We were served a fine meal. *Sandre,* a local river fish resembling perch, was served with homemade noodles in a light *beurre blanc. Choucroute* (from the German for "sour cabbage") with pheasant, smoked goose, and *boúdin noir* (blood sausage) followed. Our cabbage, the first of the autumn season, was so slightly pickled that my companion, who generally behaves as if sauerkraut were the enemy, cleaned his plate. We then sampled some excellent farmhouse Münsters, and for dessert we had bowls of mirabelle *sorbet* with whole mirabelle plums and caramel sauce flavored with the same plum's liqueur. *Eaux-de-vie* are widely produced in Lorraine, and the one made from the small, sweet yellow mirabelle is most prized. With our earlier courses, we had sampled some extraordinary wines; a white Graves, a 1984 Clos

Vougeot, and with the *choucroute* a 1987 Rouge de Marlenheim, a very good Alsatian Pinot Noir.

Our next stop was Michel and Bernadette Million's delightful country hotel LE CHÂTEAU D'ADOMÉNIL, just five kilometers from Lunéville, in Rehainviller. Built in the seventeenth century and restored in the nineteenth, the château, where the Millions opened their restaurant in 1980 and guest rooms in 1986, stands in seven *hectares* (about 17 acres) of tree-shaded park in the midst of a working farm. Cows graze on hillside pastures while ducks and swans meander around the front lawns and swim in the nearby pond. The seven bedrooms and one apartment are named for the fruits that contribute their flavors to the local *eaux-de-vie*; ours was *Prunelle*, meaning blackthorn. Its warm earth tones, setting off decorative touches of pastel chintz, and a large window overlooking the nearby hills made for a welcoming chamber. The guest rooms' bathrooms are well-appointed, even luxurious; and there is no shortage of closets. After the singular pleasure our first morning of being awakened by the crowing of a rooster, we settled down to breakfast, brought up to our room on a large tray, next to one of the windows. Coffee, fresh orange juice, tiny *madeleines, pains au chocolat,* croissants, toasted baguettes, Münster, the château's own honey, and mirabelle jam were all served on flowered Lunéville faience.

Three richly paneled rooms with parquet floors make up the dining area of the hotel. Comfortable armchairs, commodious tables set with white napery and white Rosenthal china, and flowers arranged by Madame Million create an elegant, timeless style. The food is in keeping with the surroundings. Succulent fresh *foie gras* came with tiny cubes of aspic, toast, and coarse salt. Lobster ravioli in shellfish butter sauce were exemplary. Main courses were a fillet of delicate smoked rabbit with *girolles*, and more *sandre*, served with *lardons* (clearly a popular flavoring in these parts), mushrooms, and a sauce made from a local rosé, Gris de Toul. Desserts were a souffléed *crêpe aux mirabelles* and a crisp, light pastry filled with red fruits and caramel sauce. Jossmeyer Tokay Pinot Gris '86 was our wine. On another evening we sampled an intriguing scallop salad with figs, veal kidneys in a fragrant *diable* (white-wine and mustard) sauce, and boned pigeon in a crepe. *Pain perdu* was our dessert choice. The slightly crisp bread, served here with luscious Calvados-soaked apples, added a whole new dimension to my experience of bread puddings.

Lunéville is an agreeable small town dominated by its eighteenth-century château, built to the specifications of Léopold, duke of Lorraine. Germain Boffrand, pupil and nephew of Hardouin-Mansart, who designed Versailles, was the architect. By 1723 Léopold and his wife, Elisabeth-Charlotte d'Orléans, a niece of Louis XIV, had established their court at the chateau. Following the example of Louis XIV, Léopold encouraged artists and writers, and soon the social life of the Chateau de Lunéville was nearly as glittering as that of Versailles. Alas, Léopold died prematurely, in 1729. His son and heir, Francois III, left Lorraine to marry Marie-Thérèse of Austria and share with her the Hapsburg throne. Elisabeth-Charlotte, François's mother, was regent until her retirement to the Château de Commercy in 1737, when Stanislas Leszczynski arrived as the newly appointed duke of Lorraine. For the next three decades, the Château de Lunéville was the scene of court life at its best; men of letters, aristocrats, and nobles visited the benevolent, *bon vivant* duke-philosopher.

In the central part of the château, three arches join the courtyard to the gardens, called the Bosquets. Beds of blue salvia, yellow marigolds, and red begonias line gravel paths, fountains, and pools. Designed by Yves des Hours, the gardens were later embellished by Stanislas with the addition of kiosks, small guest cottages, and pavilions. The Lunéville Museum, in a wing of the chateau, houses a fascinating collection of faience from the Far East as well as the Strasbourg rose pattern and prized specimens from the nearby Lunéville/Saint-Clément manufactory. One room is filled with nothing but apothecary jars. For enthusiasts of French faience, this museum is a must.

The best way to see the old section of Lunéville is to walk along the cobbled Rue du Chateau; on the street named for Elisabeth-Charlotte are some particularly fine stately houses. The baroque Church of Saint-Jacques, built between 1730 and 1747 by the aforementioned Boffrand and Héré, has a fifteenth-century Pieta of polychrome stone and some works by Stanislas's court painter, Jules Girardet. On Tuesdays till noon and Saturdays till four, the market is held in the Place Léopold. Cheeses, flowers, brioches, pâtés, and innumerable intriguing household articles are available. The Saint-Clément faience factory is eleven kilometers away, but only a very small quantity—specifically copies of the old Réverbère line (a reference to the reverberating furnace used for its firing)—is hand-painted. A few pieces of the reproduction Réverbère and other types and patterns are available at the factory store (1, rue Trouillet) on the outskirts of town and at Lun' Faiences (18, rue du Général Leclerc), a small shop with somewhat erratic business hours. No visits to the factory in Saint-Clément are permitted, and the factory store will not ship.

A pleasant place for lunch after appetites have been whetted at the market is FLORÉAL, on a second floor overlooking the Place Léopold. Cheerful and bright, with pink tablecloths and a lively local crowd, the restaurant is run by a young couple, Gilles and Christiane Demonet. Small rounds of bread with finely chopped tomatoes and herbs were brought to the table before we happily consumed our bowls of mussel soup, the special of the day. Vividly yellow with saffron, the creamy base contained diced carrots, celery, and zucchini as well as a generous quantity of tiny mussels. It was delectable, one of the best mussel soups I have tasted. With this plus a pitcher of local white wine, good bread, and a fine green salad, we lunched like royalty.

On the northern outskirts of Lunéville is LE VOLTAIRE, where Elisabeth and Jean-Marie Pothier oversee their ten simple guest rooms and a good dining room. We began a most satisfactory meal one night with a pigeon terrine and *salade de caille*, which came as small pinwheels of boned quail on mixed greens. Turbot with a heady Sauternes sauce and a split, boned chicken breast stuffed with spinach and served with a sauce enriched with *foie gras* came next. A tricolor vegetable terrine—pumpkin, spinach, and cauliflower—and crispy crescents of potato pancake were the accompaniments, and mirabelle *eau-de-vie* was our dessert.

Nearly equidistant from Nancy and Lunéville is the town of Saint-Nicholas-de-Port, where the basilica of the same name is to be found. Flamboyant Gothic in style, the church, built from 1481 to 1560, is said to have been constructed on the site where Joan of Arc knelt for a blessing before her fateful mission. Local lore has it that, in former times at least, no inhabitant of Lorraine would consider embarking on a voyage without coming to pray at the basilica. The enormous, light-filled interior is indeed impressive, as are the stained-glass windows by the Lyonnais Nicole Droguet.

A mere nine kilometers southeast of Nancy is the Château de Fléville, one of several handsome châteaux that dot the countryside hereabout. Built on the site of a fourteenth-century fortress, it is its sixteenth-century incarnation, complete with Renaissance façade, that the visitor sees today. I missed viewing the interior with its Louis XV and XVI furnishings due to the rather limited open hours during the off seasons (only weekend and holiday afternoons from April 1 to June 30 and then September 1 to November 15); for the high season in between, the château can be visited any afternoon of the week.

Approximately thirty kilometers southwest of Lunéville is the handsome Château d'Haroué, often referred to as Lorraine's Versailles. Its dark grayish-blue slate roof and red chimneys give a colorful first impression of this castle designed by Boffrand in the 1720s on the site of an ancient fortress. Built for Marc de Beauvau Craon, then chancellor of Lorraine, the castle is still occasionally inhabited by his descendants. A conducted tour reveals a charming faience stove, an impressive collection of Sévres and Delft porcelains, and delightful paintings of the four seasons represented by animals: Rabbits recall spring, monkeys summer, squirrels autumn, and weasels winter. Part of the château is furnished with pieces that belonged to Louis XVIII. The Château d'Haroué is open daily from April 1 to November 15, but again only in the afternoon.

Outside the village of Portieux, about forty kilometers southeast of Nancy, is the nearly three-hundred-year-old Cristallerie de Portieux. Visitors are welcome in the factory, where handsome lamps, decanters, vases, bowls, stemware, and purely decorative objects are made. A small operation but a prestigious one, the manufactory counts among its clients the Hôtel Crillon and the Jules Verne restaurant in Paris, Le Crocodile in Strasbourg, and the Grand Hôtel de la Reine in Nancy. A samples shop next to the glassworks is most accommodating, takes *"plastique,"* and will ship abroad. We could not leave without sending off a pair of handsome candlesticks in the shape of dolphins and a beguiling blue crystal candy dish. They arrived a month later in perfect condition. Baccarat is, by the way, only sixty kilometers from Nancy. We did visit there but were somewhat overwhelmed by huge quantities of glass in several large shops and busloads of people shopping for dear life.

We decided to spend our last night in Lorraine at LE PRIEURÉ, a small hotel and restaurant owned and run by Joelle and Joel Roy in Flavigny-sur-Moselle, sixteen kilometers south of Nancy. The four guest rooms, decorated in a light, spare, but comfortable style and with new bathrooms, face a pretty terrace and small garden. Our expectations of the restaurant were high, for we had heard of the chef's talents, particularly with fish. The dining room, where Madame Roy reigns, is elegant yet cozy, with period vernacular furniture, pewter-ware, and on chilly nights a blazing fire in the hearth. Smoked salmon wrapped around *langoustines* and a stew of fresh *cèpes* and *langoustines*, fragrant in a heady sauce, were our starters. A truffle ice cream, curious but delicious, accompanied them. *Pieds-paquets* made with *sandre* and *cuisses de grenouilles* followed. The reference to the classic Provençal dish normally made with sheep's feet and tripe had only to do with its purse-like form. In this version pike-perch fillets enveloped slivers of tender boned frogs' legs and were napped with goat cheese sauce. My companion exclaimed over scallops wrapped in a gossamer crêpe with a sauce redolent of truffles from the valley of the Meuse. From the tempting dessert menu we chose coffee crème brûlée with a *coulis* of mangoes; and a pyramid of bitter chocolate sheets filled with chocolate mousse and garnished with pistachio cream. From the Roys' considerable cellar, we drank a half bottle of Meursault from Louis Jadot and another of Tour Martillac, a red Graves.

Breakfast the next morning was fresh fruit, yogurt, *pains au chocolat,* croissants, and café au lait. We bade Le Prieuré *au revoir,* feeling we had experienced a glorious end to our visit to Lorraine—no longer to be, for us at least, a forgotten province.

Moustiers

OUSTIERS-SAINTE-MARIE was one of the "Cinq Grands" in the eighteenth century, a title referring to the "big five" of faience production and thus ranking this tiny town in the Alps of Haute-Provence alongside Marseilles, Nevers, Rouen, and Strasbourg. Moustiers's second claim to fame is surely its dramatic setting: Overlooking the valley of La Maire, the town is set at the bottom of a five-hundred-foot ravine against a great wall of rock at one end of the spectacular Gorges du Verdon, or Verdon Canyon. A mountain torrent rushes through one of the crevices in the rock, giving the impression that the little squares, arcades, and houses of the village are hanging on for dear life. Between the two highest peaks a gilded star is suspended on a seven-hundred-foot iron chain. Legend has it that the star, dedicated to Notre-Dame de Beauvoir, was originally secured in place by the crusading duke of Blacas after his joyous release from Saracen captivity. Golden stone buildings with red tile roofs cluster around a handsome medieval bell tower. And high above the village two cypresses stand watch over the fifth-century chapel of Notre-Dame de Beauvoir, which can be reached by a scenic small path.

Every Friday morning a market of stalls displaying the products of the region is held in Moustiers's diminutive main square.

Cakes of lavender, honey, and olive oil soap are stacked next to plump hams and sausages. Dozens of bottles of luminescent green olive oil sit alongside variously shaped goat cheeses. It is overwhelming to see such bounty in a town of but six hundred inhabitants. Moustiers is, of course, chockablock with shops selling faience. Plates, platters, bowls, soap dishes, lamps—almost anything that could conceivably be made of earthenware—are available here; some of it is decorative and delicate, some of it in regrettably poor taste.

Whether you're interested in shopping, sight-seeing, or both, a visit to the Musée de la Faïence, housed at Place du Presbytère in a medieval crypt built by cloistered Lerins monks, is a good way to acquaint yourself with the town. According to the guidebooks, the museum is open daily, save Tuesdays, from nine to six April through October, and till seven in July and August. I found reality to be somewhat more inventive. Daily opening schedules appear to be influenced by some mysterious greater power unknown to me. And the museum is, like everything else in southern France, firmly *fermé* from noon till two in the afternoon.

But if you are lucky enough to obtain entry—it's worth a bit of perseverance—you will find a comprehensive history of faience production in Moustiers, starting with the first factory, owned by the Clérissy family, in the 1670s. The story goes that Pierre Clérissy acquired the secret of *grand feu* faience from an Italian monk in the nearby Servite convent. He started production with his son Antoine. Their repertoire consisted of monochrome blue armorial designs and copies of mythological etchings from the Italian artist Antonio Tempesta. But in the middle of the eighteenth century, by which time the grandson, Pierre II, had taken charge, the less exacting *petit feu* method had been developed in Strasbourg and initiated in Moustiers by the Ferrat brothers.

This process called for a third firing, or baking, at lower temperatures and made possible the use of reds, purples, and pinks, which had not withstood the higher temperatures of the *grand feu*. Production continued, in the Moustiers ateliers of the Olérys, Laugier, Féraud, and Ferrat families, until the beginning of the nineteenth century, when the industry, basically created for the rich, began to suffer from economic and political change.

The first blow dealt it was the Treaty of 1786, which among other provisions allowed English creamware into France, glutting the market and undercutting French faience. And then the Revolution cut deeply into aristocratic clients' attention to decorative matters. Factories were shut down and did not reopen until the mid-1920s, when Marcel Provence revived the industry, which thrives today. The museum, which moved to its present vaulted-ceiling premises in 1978, has a good collection from all the Moustiers periods: huge armorial platters that resemble Chinese export ware; charming *pots de crème*; and a handsome *raffraîchissoir à verre*, a large scalloped-edged receptacle in which glasses were rinsed and chilled. The museum also provides instructive charts and pictures delineating the steps involved in the production of faience.

It takes a bit of doing to sort out all the faience shops, piled with mountains of plates and cups, and to find the best-quality work. Across from the museum, Le Cloître has a relatively modest display of some attractive patterns, among which are reproductions of antique pieces. Alas, Le Cloître neither ships nor accepts credit cards. Bondil, on the Place de l'Eglise, has a particularly good selection of lamps and attractive grape (or berry) servers, the top dish with small holes through which excess water can drain to the plate beneath. Bondil accepts all credit cards and will also ship. J.M.V. Fine, situated where the road from Riez enters town, is the only atelier that makes a concerted effort to highlight faience designed by contemporary artists, although styles representative of every period of production are also available, and all can be paid for with credit cards and shipped. On the main street of town, Faïences Féret has charming fountains for the garden and pretty soap dishes and toothbrush holders that would dress up anyone's bathroom. Its factory, directly across the street, offers tours from June through September.

Two of the most interesting ateliers are, however, outside town: Simonne Favier in Riez, eight miles west on the Moustiers road, has some high-quality faience. Extraordinarily delicate full dinner services decorated wih birds, flowers, and intriguingly grotesque figures are made to order on the premises by three potters and two painters. Mademoiselle Favier, trained at the Ecole des Beaux-Arts in Marseilles, opened the atelier with her sister in 1943. She will ship, and you may pay with, as the French say, *"plastique."*

On the same road, a couple of miles from the center of Moustiers, is the Atelier de Ségriès, probably the town's best-known company. It is Ségriès that produces the faience tableware that one is most likely to find in such specialty shops in this country as Pierre Deux: Patterns feature barnyard animals, wild flowers of Provence, and the Ferrat rose, and a particularly stunning one depicts hot-air balloons. Candlesticks, shapely pitchers, and elegant serving plates with deep scalloped edges are only a small part of the stock.

At four in the afternoon, Monday through Friday, tours are conducted of the Ségriès atelier. Here visitors can see production in progress. Plaster molds for vases and bowls, for example, are filled with liquid clay, which sets for several hours and is then poured out, leaving a "skin" behind. The mold is removed from around this skin, which is allowed to dry naturally and completely during two to three days. Then the shape is fired over a twenty-four-hour period at temperatures that gradually reach 1,040° C. The resulting "biscuit" is submerged in a glaze solution, which dries almost instantly, and a design is traced in charcoal. One of eleven decorators at Ségriès paints the article, which then undergoes its second twenty-four-hour firing, this time reaching a temperature of 970° C.

Quality control is the next step: Each item is meticulously examined for even the slightest flaw; if the item is not perfect—and this, alas, is the fate of seven to ten percent of production—it is sold in the seconds shop in town, at a reduction of one third. Because even the slightest blemish is considered to render a piece unacceptable for such tony establishments as Hermès, Christofle, and Pierre Deux, it is easy to pick up some nice buys. Ségriès has another in-town shop, where its stock is sold at full price and where, naturally, there is a far wider selection. Tonia and Claude Peyrot have owned and operated the Atelier de Ségriès for more than ten years. They will ship anywhere and take charge cards. Georgette Buckner, the Peyrots' American partner, runs the atelier's U.S. distribution operation, Solanée, at 138 East 74th Street in New York City.

We found the time, between a visit to the museum and explorations of the ateliers, to squeeze in a delicious lunch. RESTAURANT LES SANTONS, on the Place de l'Eglise in the middle of Moustiers, is perched high above the town's rushing mountain stream and has a pleasant, sunny indoor dining room that seats about twenty as well as a picturesque terrace for lunching or dining on fine days. Olive rolls and eggplant butter were put on the table soon after we were seated, which staved off hunger pangs, for everything is cooked to order and there is bound to be a slight wait. Our patience was rewarded with perfect first courses: a *mille-feuille* filled with sautéed red mullet and onion *confit* and served with an olive purée; and lobster ravioli with *sauce américaine*. Free-range chicken in a honey sauce spiced with cloves, thyme, cinnamon, and coriander seed, among other surprising tastes, was delicious, and the other main course of kidneys with wine mustard sauce was cooked to a turn. Dessert was a really extraordinary crème brûlée in which the caramel that in most renditions coats the surface had been gently folded into the custard, leaving no crisp topping but a caramel taste permeating all. It was a memorable lunch, enhanced by a bottle of light white Château Minuty from the Côte d'Azur. Reservations are advisable at this little gem, which is closed from November 15 to March 1.

As for accommodations, we found two country hotels well worth the detour from Moustiers proper, both about thirty miles away. Route D6, going west from Moustiers, leads past acres of lavender fields and fruit orchards through Valensole to Manosque and, not far outside this attractive town, HOSTELLERIE DE LA FUSTE. A member of the Relais du Silence association, La Fuste is very much a family affair. Daniel Jourdan, the chef-owner, is seconded by his son-in-law, Ritz-trained Dominique Bucaille, and Madame Jourdan and daughter Lydia take charge of creating the friendly ambiance of a French country house. Bedroom walls and furniture are covered in flowered fabrics, and deep-pile carpets and immaculate bathrooms complete the cozy picture. Public rooms are small, for in this gentle southern climate life is lived mostly out-of-doors. The terrace and gardens, shaded by fine plane and chestnut trees, accommodate guests for apéritifs or for lunch when the weather cooperates. Next to the kitchen are flourishing herb and vegetable gardens, and beyond is a swimming pool. High-backed chairs upholstered in cut velvet and walls adorned with tapestries and with a collection of Moustiers plates make the opulent dining room the perfect setting for a quite splendid evening meal.

We started dinner one night with cold tomato soup flavored with fresh mint and a gratin of summer *cèpes*, a luscious dish of wild mushrooms that had been creamed, dusted with Parmesan, and glazed. *Tranche de broutard*, sliced lamb from the hills near Valensole served with *foie gras* and a creamy Port sauce, was my companion's main-course choice. Tiny artichokes, beets, and carrots were the colorful garnish. My choice was the *coquelet*, a free-range chicken halved and stuffed with a rich mixture of livers, gizzards, and truffles, and this was accompanied by slightly crunchy zucchini. Afterward we sampled the region's famous Banon goat cheese, which is traditionally washed with eau-de-vie and wrapped in chestnut leaves; the combination of creamy cheese and assertive liqueur is a memorable one. *"Les desserts La Fuste"* consisted of a delectable praline mousse with raspberry purée, a tiny cold lemon soufflé, and pear *sorbet*. And then, when we felt that another morsel would be *de trop*, a dish of miniature fruit tarts, paper-thin lace cookies, and *calissons* (the almond confection from Aix-en-Provence) appeared—and we succumbed.

We were awakened the next morning by the crowing of a rooster and a tempting breakfast tray: freshly squeezed orange juice, glistening green grapes, individual brioches as well as warm brioche bread slices, thick apricot jam, and a block of butter. Before leaving we visited the shop on the ground level of the inn, where foods prepared in the kitchen of La Fuste are sold. Game *civets* (stews) of boar and hare are displayed in liter jars along with *coq au vin* and the traditional Provençal dish *pieds et pacquets*, or tripe with lamb trotters cooked in tomato and wine. Every imaginable jam and preserved fruit is available, all put up by the staff during the slower, winter season under the watchful eye of Madame Jourdan.

LA BONNE ETAPE, located in Château-Arnoux, north of Manosque, is another fine stopover. Though situated off a well-traveled main road in a somewhat unprepossessing town, the hotel itself is secluded and quiet. Huge terra-cotta pots of marigolds and geraniums in the shaded car park set a welcoming tone. Behind the hotel is a pretty pool surrounded by chestnut, cypress, and pomegranate trees. Indoors, beamed ceilings and stucco walls and arches recapture the days when La Bonne Etape, a *relais de poste*, was a station stop for coaches. Like Hostellerie de La Fuste, this hotel is a family affair; Arlette Gleize is the official greeter, and Pierre Gleize and son Jany take care of the kitchen. Under their expert supervision the young staff makes guests feel not just welcome but pampered. Rooms here are furnished with dressy chintzes and every amenity.

No matter how inviting the rooms and atmosphere, however, it soon becomes apparent that the really serious business here is conducted in the dining room. Well-spaced tables, commodious dining chairs, starched white napery, and waiters dressed in dark uniforms all indicate a no-nonsense establishment. We feasted one evening on mushroom ravioli and zucchini blossoms stuffed with vegetables and set on a *coulis* of tomato with coriander and lemon. Lamb sweetbreads and kidneys were served side by side on the plate, the sweetbreads enhanced with cream, the kidneys in a juniper and mint sauce. And we sampled here Sisteron lamb, raised in the herb-scented hills just north of Château-Arnoux that Pierre Gleize likens to the Scottish highlands; the meat is renowned throughout France for its delicate flavor. Three perfect chops and a rich brown sauce were exquisitely teamed with a crisp potato gratin served in a minute copper pan. Desserts were a chestnut mousse cake, satisfying yet not overly sweet, and *tarte au potiron et aux amandes*, a pumpkin "pie" to end all others. Pumpkins proliferate in Provence, as do almonds, so this tart appears often on local menus and, in addition, is served traditionally on Christmas night. The tart was flat and almost caramelized, the taste extraordinarily concentrated, and the texture dense, almost dry, by comparison to the classic American pumpkin pie. An aromatic red Palette from Château Simone, near Aix, was a fine choice to accompany dinner. Given the culinary standard set here, we were not surprised to learn, long after our trip had ended, that Pierre and Jany Gleize were the chefs chosen by President Mitterrand to prepare the Bastille Day dinner for the heads of state visiting Paris for the economic summit.

The following morning two *cafés complets* included *pains au chocolat*, tiny croissants, and the establishment's own jams: a red-fruit one of cherries, red currants, raspberries, and strawberries, and another, yellow-fruit one of pears, peaches, apricots, and melon. *Toutes fleurs* honey and butter were the finishing touches.

We look back on our excursion into and around Moustiers as a perfectly balanced few days. We had visited the unique and lovely hilltown itself, satisfying our acquisitive urges along the way; driven through the foothills of the Alps and the northern reaches of Provence, some of France's loveliest countryside; and been impeccably coddled and fed in two flawlessly comfortable *relais*.

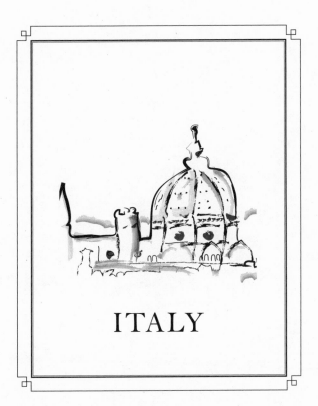

ITALY

GOURMET | JULY 1985

Lake Garda

AKE GARDA IS the largest of the Italian lakes and certainly the most varied. Along its thirty-two-mile length the
scenery changes from palms, olive trees, vineyards, and cypresses in the southern part to dramatic evergreens and mountains
to the north. Geographically it has the distinction of belonging
to three regions—Veneto on its eastern shore, Lombardy on the
south and west, and Trentino-Alto Adige in the north—and ad-
ministratively it comes under the jurisdiction of three separate
provinces. Some say that Garda is Italy's most beautiful lake.

Sirmione, a slender peninsula often described as resembling
a cat's tongue, reaches out into the lake at its southernmost point
and divides the gulf of Desenzano from that of Peschiera. The
old part of the town of Sirmione, at the tip of this peninsula, is
dominated by the castle of the Scaligeri, with its turreted towers and wide moat, an oft-visited landmark. Built in 1200 by the
Veronese Mastino della Scalla, the castle has weathered many a
bloody battle and even served as a place of exile for Dante when
he fled Florence. In the shadows of the castle, on the Piazza Cas-
tello, a fruit vendor sells slices of coconut kept fresh in a trickle
of water from a miniature fountain. His cart is resplendent with
ropes of lemons and displays of melons and oranges.

The whole town is most agreeable. No cars, save those of residents, are permitted in the center, and, in fact, Sirmione's charm is much enhanced by the fact that one need not have an automobile to enjoy a visit. Everything is within easy walking distance. The main Piazza Carducci, bordered by three cafés and the maritime dock, is the focal point and a perfect spot where one can see and be seen. There is a variety of small restaurants, and those who enjoy shopping will find good choices: linens and leathers (Pratesi and Céline), ceramics of all descriptions, and plenty of knickknacks to carry back to envious stay-at-home friends.

Sirmione is very much a spa. The Terme, exuding a pungent odor of sulfur, is a large and busy stone edifice just beyond the old town. It is surrounded by palms and oleander, and at the entrance the day's date is written out in red begonias. Past it, the Via Catullo is an elegant byway lined with stately cypresses and leading to the ruins of a Roman villa at the tip of the peninsula. The villa is popularly reputed to have been the dwelling place of the Latin poet Catullus, who died in 54 B.C., but serious archaeologists, notorious killjoys, tend to date it later. Whatever the period, the views of the lake from its crumbling arches are magnificent. As one looks out toward Salò and Gardone on the western bank, the lake steamer appears to be a child's toy sailing on a piece of glass. A short walk from the villa is the tiny ninth-century church of San Pietro in Mavino. It is set in a peaceful grove of olive trees, and across the way, behind an iron gate, a private garden boasts huge roses, staked five feet high, dahlias, and giant rosemary and sage bushes.

The GRAND HOTEL TERME is set at the entrance of the old town, next to the Scaligeri castle and directly on the lake. It is old-fashioned and spacious, with wide marble halls and stairways and comfortable balconied bedrooms. There is a spa right in the hotel, for those who have come to take the cure, and a swimming pool, complete with wooden deck and chaises, where one can enjoy the sun or the aquatic goings-on. (Lake steamers, hydrofoils, sailboats, single-man sculls, and a variety of seabirds are but a few of the sights one is apt to see.) The dining room is an indoor-outdoor affair, two sides of which are sliding glass doors that are open in fair weather.

The chef, Augusto Terruzzi, sees that the food lives up to the surroundings. A truly perfect lasagne and fettuccine with fresh *porcini* were two of the pasta delights; and, whether it was risotto with snails, roast turkey, veal, or kid, or grilled fresh fish, everything was prepared with utmost care. One lunch, enjoyed on a sunny day as we sat overlooking the lake, came close to perfection: prosciutto with a flawless melon, *vitello tonnato* decorated with little lemon baskets holding capers, and fresh figs for dessert. It occurred to me that were I a condemned man choosing a last meal it might very well be this one. The menu changed daily, and the consistently high quality of ingredients made selecting a difficult exercise. The cheese tray always boasted first-rate Gorgonzola, Parmesan, and Bel Paese, to name just three, and a wide choice of salad greens and fruits was available. Although there are restaurants in Sirmione, when the menu at the hotel was posted in the front hall every morning it seemed impossible to tear oneself away. The food was enhanced by the wonderful white Lugana and red Bardolino made just a few miles away, and the hotel's entire staff, under the watchful eye of the courtly director, Gianfranco Bianchi, add immeasurably to the happy ambiance. The Hotel Terme is open from Easter until about the third week in October.

Five kilometers from Sirmione, the TRATTORIA VECCHIA LUGANA is one restaurant that is worth a visit. In an informal yet sophisticated setting wonderful fare is produced. Just past the entry one is greeted by a vast display of antipasti in pottery dishes set around a grill, where meats and fish are done to order. In an adjoining loggia the best produce available—waxy red and yellow peppers, tomatoes, eggplants, and symmetrical little white onions—is set out in baskets next to dozens of wine bottles. The ceilings are vaulted and the floor is tiled, but the atmosphere is quiet and leisurely because tables are set far apart. The note on the menu under antipasto reads "self-service," and, with fresh anchovies in oil, pink salmon trout with *pesto*, pungent *frittate*, proscuitto wrapped around a delectable cream cheese, and shrimp and celery root napped with mayonnaise, the diner's main problem is one of restraint. When such a delicacy as *pasticcio di melanzane* (a casserole of eggplant, tomato, and cheese with a sublime white sauce) or *crema di porcini* (an individual pie of wild mushrooms) is to follow as a second course, moderation is advised. Meat and fish, as fresh as can be, are done simply and deliciously on the grill and accompanied by whatever vegetables are most choice. Dessert might be tiny strawberries or raspberries with *gelato*, and little pastries of fruit and *crème pâtissière*, a signature of the restaurant, automatically appear with the coffee. The wine list is exemplary and extensive. A Custoza, again from this prolific region, was a fine complement to our meal, and a sweet Recioto di Soave with our fruit dessert was unusual and delicious. All in all, Vecchia Lugana is an outstanding dining adventure.

Proceeding up the eastern shore of the lake, one comes to Lazise, a delightful walled town filled with history. It was once an important port for warships of the Republic of Venice, and the ubiquitous stone lions of La Serenissima are testament to that connection. Cafés ring a picturesque harbor where fishing and pleasure boats cohabit. The town was enlivened by the local itinerant market, which was in residence on the day of our visit.

Primarily for clothes, the market also offers linens and other household effects. The stalls appear in a different town on the lake each day of the week: Wednesdays in Lazise, Thursdays in Bardolino, Fridays in Sirmione, etc. There are many wares, and it is sobering to think of the effort involved in setting up and moving these shops every day.

Bardolino, just north of Lazise on the Riviera Orientale, positively exudes wine. The town is in a fertile valley that has for centuries been famous for its vineyards, and the well-known red is sold everywhere. Be it a shoe shop or bookstore, every window has a display of bottles. There is a long quay by the lake bordered by neat little hotels and cafés and a pleasant walk shaded with palms. Bicycle carts are available for visitors who enjoy sight-seeing while pedaling. The town has a decidedly more cosmopolitan and commercial air than its neighbor Lazise.

At the end of a small peninsula between the busy town of Garda and Torri del Benaco is Punta di San Vigilio. It is a beautiful and unspoiled spot with a horseshoe-shaped beach on the lake, the stately, private sixteenth-century Villa Guarienti, and the small LOCANDA SAN VIGILIO, with just six bedrooms and a simple bar. Spaghetti with tomato sauce followed by a delicious grilled trout from the lake was served for lunch by the water's edge. Rumor has it that Vivien Leigh and Laurence Olivier spent their honeymoon in this romantic and idyllic setting.

The HOTEL GARDESANA in Torri del Benaco is an ideal stopping place. It is small—thirty-four rooms—and has a welcoming street café and second-floor dining terrace that overlook the port and the town square. One of the upstairs lounges has a display of pictures and memorabilia from some of the famous guests who have stayed in the hotel since the early part of the century: Winston Churchill, André Gide, Gabriele D'Annunzio,

Max Ernst, and Stephen Spender. A day or two in residence, and it is easy to see why this has traditionally been such a popular spot. We dined happily on the terrace, by the light of a full moon and candles, on *spaghetti alla Gardesana* made with a paste of black olives, basil, and virgin olive oil; *risotto mari e monti* with tiny shrimp and mushrooms; calf's liver with onions; and a chicken redolent of fresh herbs. The chef, Roberto Finanzi, is young and enthusiastic, and the rest of the staff, from the desk clerks to the bartenders to the young chambermaids, are all accommodating as can be.

There are attractive shops in the little town: several boutiques selling bathing attire, ceramics, and souvenirs. Picnic supplies are available from two good *alimentari*, and it is a treat to drive up into the hills above Torri armed with lunch. At Albisano, five kilometers directly above Torri, the view from the belvedere of the parish church, San Martino, is spectacular. San Zeno di Montagna is another five kilometers up the mountain; here, at an altitude of seven hundred meters, the terrain and flora take on a decidedly Alpine feeling. Across the valley to the east the country changes once again, and Lumini is surrounded by some of the lushest pastureland imaginable, complete with grazing cattle. There is no point in hurrying, as it is commonplace for traffic to be halted by a herd of cows with sonorous bells being driven at a leisurely pace back to their barn.

The most pleasant way to visit Lake Garda and the towns on its shores is by boat. There is an extensive timetable (somewhat less so in the winter months) for the steamers and the speedier but less atmospheric hydrofoils; with a little study and planning, one can travel all over the lake. The dock at Torri is the hub of the town, and the steamers are the lifeline of the lake. In the evening many of the inhabitants stroll on the jetty and occupy benches shaded by chestnut trees, always taking a lively interest in the comings and goings of the boats. There is a *traghetto* (car ferry) that plies its way regularly back and forth across the lake to Maderno, and in the morning one can board a steamer for the two-and-three-quarter-hour trip to Riva at the head of the lake. The steamer stops at such intriguing ports of call as Malcesine, where yet another Scaligeri castle rises perpendicularly from the lake, and Limone, on the western shore, surrounded by the deserted lemon houses that so intrigued D. H. Lawrence when he lived there in the early 1900s. In "The Lemon Gardens," an essay from his book *Twilight in Italy*, Lawrence says, "I sat and looked at the lake. It was beautiful as paradise, as the first creation. On the shores were the ruined lemon-pillars standing out in melancholy, the clumsy, enclosed lemon-house seemed ramshackle, bulging among vine stocks and olive trees. The villages, too, clustered upon their churches, seemed to belong to the past. They seemed to be lingering in bygone centuries." Torbole, almost at the top of the lake, was visited in 1786 by Goethe, who was taken with the scenic splendor of the area.

The last steamer stop is Riva, well into the province of Trento and set between two mountains, Rocchetta and Brione. The atmosphere here is definitely northern, and it was, in fact, only after World War I that this part of the lake was annexed to Italy from Austria. The trees are predominantly willows and evergreens now, and Monte Rocchetta casts a vast and almost eerie shadow over most of the town. There are pleasant places to lunch on the lake, and, in case there was any doubt of the dramatic change in settings here, on the day of our visit an Alpine oompah band, complete with lederhosen, played at dockside. After lunch there is time to visit Riva for an hour or two before the steamer heads back down the lake.

Gargnano is a particularly agreeable town about halfway up the Riviera Occidentale (western shore). Mussolini and his family stayed here in the massive Villa Feltrinelli, which now belongs to the University of Milan, and language courses for foreigners are conducted at the villa in the summer months. The lakefront promenade and the central square are worth a visit as is LA TORTUGA, a small restaurant on the main street. A lunch of *pappardelle* with *porcini* and tomatoes, *lavarello* (a simple and excellent local fish), and veal with truffles, accompanied by a Lugana bottled especially for the restaurant, was first-rate. The owner-chef, Dani Filippini, takes great care with all the details of his restaurant.

High above Gardone Riviera is the villa where the poet Gabriele D'Annunzio lived in splendor from 1921 till his death in 1938. His house is now part of a national monument, the Vittoriale, which also includes a huge mausoleum and relics of a ship, an airplane, and antique cars. A tour of this bizarre villa is an experience. It contains a library of over thirty-five thousand volumes and, in the poet's bedchamber, a separate collection of works by Dante, Stendhal, Shakespeare, and Verlaine. It appears that every article of clothing, every bibelot, and every memento this gentleman possessed has been preserved here, including even a half-empty bottle of mineral water in his study.

D'Annunzio had three idols: his mother, Eleonora Duse, and Saint Francis, and there are remembrances of all three throughout the house. The door to his study is so low that even a short person must bend down to enter. It was apparently constructed at the poet's behest so that anyone entering the room, including himself, would by virtue of having to stoop be rendered more humble. On the wall of a writing room is the pithy inscription, "There is no house so small that it cannot be made great by a magnificent inhabitant." D'Annunzio died at his desk on the evening of March 1, 1938. The guides are painstaking and almost reverent when they point out the smallest details, and the house is preserved as though the poet had just walked out the front door to stroll in his garden. And, on the subject of gardens, the Giardino di Gardone is a well tended botanical garden, just across from the Vittoriale, where one can pass a pleasant hour or two.

Just down the hill in Fasano di Gardone Riviera is the VILLA DEL SOGNO (Villa of Dreams). A hotel of twenty-four rooms housed in what used to be a private residence, it has a large and pretty veranda overlooking the lake with shaded gliders and tables and chairs. Massed bunches of petunias and geraniums in pots, lush bougainvillea and jasmine fill the surroundings with color and fragrance. The bedroom and baths are commodious and decorated in a style that, for lack of a better description, we shall call twentieth-century or neo-Italian Art Deco. The dining room is light and cheerful with immaculate white napery and pretty blue-and-yellow pottery. *Gnocchi alla romana*, roast pork accompanied by tiny roast potatoes, a green salad, cheese, and a Pinot Grigio to go with it all made a more than satisfactory lunch. Villa del Sogno has a pool, is high above the bustle of the lake in summer, and is open from Easter until October 1.

Garda is beautiful. Seventy years ago D. H. Lawrence, presumably looking down from the hills above Limone, wrote, "The four o'clock steamer was creeping down the lake from the Austrian end, creeping under the cliffs. Far away, the Verona side, . . . lay fused in gold. . . . The little steamer on the floor of the world below, the mules down the road cast no shadow. They too were pure sun-substance travelling on the surface of the sun-made world." Much has changed in those seventy years, and, as is the case in many areas of scenic beauty, man does not improve its condition. Lawrence would probably not recognize Limone were he to appear there today. But when I registered a guarded complaint about an excess of visitors to a gentleman who is a native of the region, he shrugged in a very Italian manner and answered me thus: "*Signora*, Garda is so beautiful. You want to keep it for you, and I want it for me. It has always been so."

Winter in Venice

*V*ENICE IN THE OFF-SEASON—November to April —is a relatively undiscovered phenomenon. Emptied of giddy
summer crowds, the city in winter is rich with the bittersweet
nuance and somber beauty of the once-was. Half a century after Thomas Mann wrote *Death in Venice* winter visitors still
search for something elusive in the misty labyrinthine water-
ways. Though they will probably neither bask in sunshine nor
eat alfresco, off-season sojourners will find that the freedom
from crowds in museums, churches, and shops is more than a
fair trade off. And the winter sky cloaks La Serenissima with
an eerie mystery: The fog is often so dense that all water traffic
is brought to a halt, and a dusting of snow makes the city indescribably lovely. Only the absence of galleons in full sail on the
lagoon reminds us that we are not wandering through one of
Turner's canvases.

Cafés and restaurants are warm, cozy, and uncrowded during a Venice winter, and visitors can leisurely stroll the byways
of the city unjostled. There is time to examine this façade or that
rooftop and even to linger before paintings in the Accademia and
Ca' d'Oro. Tables are available in the cafés of Piazza San Marco,
and early risers can see this enchanting square perfectly empty

and silent. Venice—even at the height of the tourist season—has a peace that only a city without automobiles can know; in the wintertime this quietude is even more pronounced. And the light! Natives of Venice speak to visitors so often of the winter light. I was told by one Venetian that to see the early morning sun reflected on the roof of the Sansovino library across from the Doges' Palace is to be certain that the architect positioned this fine building precisely with sunrise in mind.

Apart from aesthetics, there are practical reasons for visiting Venice in the off-season. An association called Promov, Venice in Winter, organized by the management of twenty-seven hotels, offers all manner of benefits to their guests. Some of these include fifty percent off hotel prices—just as a starter—complimentary entrance to many museums and churches, discounts on Venetian crafts, seats at the fabulous La Fenice, and even an invitation to tea at the grand Palazzo Mocenigo. Venetians are accustomed to visitors; theirs is a city that thrives on tourism, and they handle it well.

Walking is one of the lures of Venice—and at no season is it more delightful than in winter—thus four winter strolls are suggested: first, Piazza San Marco and its environs; second, Isola della Giudecca and the Accademia on the mainland opposite; third, the exuberant Rialto, Ca' d'Oro, and the Ghetto back across the Grand Canal; and fourth, northeastern Venice around the Arsensale and Campo Zanipolo.

There is no better place to start a stroll—winter, spring, summer, or autumn—than the Piazza San Marco, which with its bustle of shops and cafés is the veritable core of the city. It has been called the most beautiful square in the world; it has been called the largest drawing room in Europe; but superlatives pale beside the reality. On the east end the Piazza faces the truly extraordinary marble-clad Basilica San Marco, and, on the north, the Torre dell' Orologio's mechanical men have been hammering out the hours to the delight of visitors for five centuries. Enter the magnificent gilt Basilica, note the Byzantine relief carvings and dome mosaics, and walk up the murderously challenging flight of stairs to see the original Roman bronze horses (Crusaders' booty from the sack of Constantinople in the thirteenth century), moved inside for protection from the elements.

In the sunny Piazza jewelry, glass, and linen shops abound. GIOIELLERIA MISSIAGLIA—founded in 1839 and owned ever since by the same family—enjoys the distinction of being one of the finest jewelers in Italy. On the opposite side of the square S. NARDI, a jeweler of similar caliber, is respected particularly for precious stones, coral, and jade. Its designs also come from its own workrooms. Glass from the factories of Murano is known the world over, and the choices are a real embarrassment of riches. On the Piazza, too, is PAULY & C., with table glass and splendid shimmering bead necklaces, marvelous fakes not meant to fool. The shop also has a vast showroom nearby filled with chandeliers and other large decorative pieces. Speaking of beads, ARCHIMEDE SEGUSO, just off the Piazza, offers handsome crystal and opaline necklaces in stunning colors: green and blue, black and white, and tortoiseshell and black, very chic and just the thing for a simple jersey dress or suit. INDUSTRIE VENE-ZIANE DI B. BATTISTON, next door to Harry's Bar nearby, has the charming pitchers that are used at Harry's famous Venetian venue and one of the best assortments of goblets and glass. It is reliable and will ship.

Before one becomes overly occupied with philistine pastimes, it might be nice to take a breather at the Correr Museum, which displays fine art as well as Venetian relics. Its entrance is under the Piazza's Portico dell'Ascensione, built by Napoleon in 1807. At the Correr important loaned exhibitions are shown during the winter months, and there is a fine permanent collection that includes Carpaccio's "Two Courtesans" and three of Canova's earliest statues. After this timely brush with culture stop by FLORIAN'S, the legendary café on the right of the Piazza, for hot chocolate and whipped cream or steaming pots of China tea. Here, seated on red velvet banquettes at marble-topped tables, one can't help wonder what sights these smoky, gilded mirrors have reflected for more than 250 years. Rumor has it that during Austria's reign Venetians favored Florian's but boycotted Quadri's, where the Austrians drank. A window seat brings us back from the past with a view of contemporary passersby bundled in furs and lodens.

HARRY'S BAR has become almost a cliché: There one goes to see and be seen—and to eat extremely well. It is jammed in tourist season, but in the off-season Venetians gratefully reclaim it for themselves. The décor is virtually nonexistent, but the food! Start with the Tiziano cocktail—white grape juice with sparkling white wine—and go on to *Carpaccio*, shrimp cocktail, or any of the really wonderful smooth and creamy soups, including mushroom, artichoke, and fish. Pastas, too, are fresh and delicious, and for the main course Veronese chicken sautéed with red bell peppers, calf's liver *alla veneziana* with *polenta*, and all the curries are splendid choices. Desserts are without equal: Chocolate cake, zabaglione cake, and lemon meringue pie are always favorites. In other words, cliché or not, Harry's Bar is still *de rigueur*.

Behind the Basilica is the charming Diocesan Museum of Venice. One enters a quiet brick cloister distinguished by an old wellhead and relics of friezes and columns. Upstairs is a collection of artifacts from the city's religious past: wood panels of pudgy *putti* suspended in midair and mannequins of the Madonna. One Virgin, dressed in red and silver brocade with a string of pearls around her neck, holds the Christ Child in her lap, and, for a stopper, the babe wears a wig. There are thirty-one portraits of church patriarchs who inhabited the cloister and four massive organ doors from the Basilica. Most of the art has come from de-sanctified churches and collections and is now all in one place for the first time.

Another small and unique museum is the Palazzo Fortuny, home of the Spanish fabric designer and painter, at Rio Terra della Mandorla. The palace, approached by a long, outdoor staircase, still has the feel of a working atelier, with hangings of the well-known brocade and paintings of Fortuny's studio and models. Antique dresses and capes are preserved behind glass, and painted stage backdrops hang in a pleasant state of confusion. Not far from Palazzo Fortuny on the Salizzada San Luca is FRETTE'S linen shop, which sells luxurious terry robes and table, bed, and bath linens, many of which are the same designs as those sold by Frette in the States, but available in Venice at more reasonable prices.

RISTORANTE ANTICO PIGNOLO, a block or so from Piazza San Marco, is a pleasant place to lunch or dine. It is so dark that one strains to see across the table—but never mind. In this attractively rustic spot the old copper pots that give the restaurant its name hang from beams above stained-glass windows. Venetian cooking is well represented: *Granseola* (spider crab) is served simply in its shell with lemon and oil on the side, risotto with *scampi* arrives steaming and fragrant, and a veal chop is grilled to perfection. For dessert the waiter whips up a refreshing fruit *sorbet* with liqueurs.

Heading west away from the Piazza along Calle Larga XXII

Marzo, one of the main pedestrian streets, one finds LIBRERIA SANGIORGIO, with many English books, including guidebooks to Venice. On the same walkway is MARICLA, a shop with lovely handmade baby clothes and stunning wool and cotton bathrobes. It is almost impossible not to go in. Many of the city's better-known hotels are in this central location, too. The LUNA on the Grand Canal and EUROPA E REGINA—almost next door, with a dramatic view of Santa Maria della Salute—are both large and comfortable, while the tiny FLORA, with just forty-four rooms, is set in from the water on a quiet court. Closer toward the Campo Francesco Morosini the legendary GRITTI PALACE faces the Grand Canal as well. The public rooms are luxuriously ornate and old-world, and the bedrooms are equally sumptuous, newly refurbished with gesso and marbleized walls and antique furniture. During the off-season, meals are served in a little dining area in the bar at tables covered in pink linen. A leisurely lunch of San Daniele prosciutto, *osso buco*, and fillet of sole was beautifully served and thoroughly enjoyable. The Gritti, as an added winter attraction, conducts a lecture series during January, February, and March on cultural topics that pertain to Venetian history and life. In the past these lectures have included "Opera at La Fenice," "Venice in Imaginative Literature," "The Passionate Sightseer: Berenson and Venice," and "Titian: The Early Years."

A stop at LEGATORIA PIAZZESI, where hand-printed papers and fine bookbindings are the specialty, is a must. One enters the tiny shop to be greeted by an explosion of colors and patterns—and everything is made of paper! Waste baskets, desk sets, notebooks in marbleized papers of soft pastels. Of particular interest are those items bearing the emblem of the Venetian lion, in red on white or deep blue. Rolls and rolls of paper are available, whether for lining drawers or for extravagantly papering a closet or small room. The latest addition to the shop's treasures is Il Quanderno di Venezia, a lined notebook with sketches of the buildings along the Grand Canal etched in an exquisitely delicate hand across the top of each page.

As you approach Campo Morosini you will pass PASTI-CCERIA MARCHINI, where the sweet temptations are irresistible: marzipan shaped into ears of corn, bananas, lemons, and apples and chocolate eggs that would rival Fabergé's creations. Sundays offer a typically Venetian scene: Parents and their children line up to buy Marchini's special tarts and cakes.

The spacious Campo Morosini, with its nineteenth-century statue of Nicolò Tommaseo, is a pleasant place to catch the rays of winter sun and sip coffee or Campari. The fourteenth-century church of Santo Stefano is quiet and empty at this time of year. There are three apses with pillars of red Veronese marble, but the real sight is the roof, built of elaborately carved massive beams that form an upside-down ship's keel. On the opposite end of the Campo is the Palazzo Pisani, once one of the largest privately owned palaces of the city, now home of the conservatory of music. Stroll in just to see the open-arched *loggia* separating the two courtyards with their Istrian-stone pillars. Parts of the façades in the courtyards have been cleaned, making a startling contrast. Be sure to inquire about the conservatory's music programs: Concerts open to the public take place all year.

A ceramics shop, RIGATTIERI, between the Campo Morosini and the Campo Sant' Anzolo, has a vast stock of pure white platters, pitchers, vases, dishes, picture frames, and handsome Della Robbia plaques for a garden wall or terrace, and the shop will wrap packages and also ship abroad. Walk through the Campo Sant' Anzolo to the Teatro La Fenice, one of the most beautiful and well-known opera houses in Europe. It was built in

1790, then rebuilt in 1836 after a fire. The gilt and pink velvet interior echoes with musical history, for such classics as Rossini's *Tancredi* and Verdi's *Rigoletto* and *La Traviata* premiered here in the nineteenth century. The charming hotel LA FEN-ICE ET DES ARTISTES is next door. Though small, the rooms are attractively furnished, with individual terraces opening onto a lovely courtyard. Reserve well ahead, as the Fenice enjoys a full house of regulars.

For one of the best—and most economical—sight-seeing tours, Venice's *vaporetti* (aquatic buses) can't be beat. On a brisk winter day bundle up and catch Line One or Two from San Zaccaria next to the Doges' Palace up the Grand Canal to the railroad station. Take in the rich canvas of the canal's right bank— the Piazetta, the hotels Bauer Grünwald, Europa, and Gritti; fantasize about the golden era of *palazzo* life, about Mann's or Wagner's or Ruskin's Venice; and look closely at the palaces on the bank—Pisani, Contarini, and Barbarigo, the magnificent frescoed ceilings of which can be seen, chandelier-lit, through the tall windows on clear evenings. The *vaporetto*, accompanied by the chimes of church bells along the way, glides under the wooden Accademia bridge and then under the busy Rialto bridge, affording its passengers the greatest seventy-cent tour in the world. In fact, many of the *palazzi* are currently being restored, making the ride even more spectacular. Take the boat back to San Marco and enjoy the other side of the canal: the Rialto markets, such palazzi as the Ca' Foscari and the Ca' Rezzonico, and, finally, the monumental church of Santa Maria della Salute. Timetables of the various lines are available where tickets are sold.

Our second walk begins at the HOTEL CIPRIANI, moored like a magnificent ship at the tip of the island of the Giudecca. When guests alight from the motorboat that runs back and forth between San Marco and the hotel, they are greeted with tranquil luxury and an exclusive atmosphere where the smallest detail is supremely important.

While visiting the Giudecca take a Number Five *vaporetto* from Le Zitelle church to the church of San Giorgio Maggiore one stop beyond. This stately Palladian landmark occupies a magnificent position on a small separate island facing San Marco. The immense and austere interior, impressive enough structurally, is highlighted by two Tintoretto masterpieces—"The Last Supper" and "The Gathering of Manna." And the view from the campanile is breathtaking. From here Venice seems to be laid out in all its extraordinary beauty like a fine old-world map. Back on Giudecca, one can stroll the length of the island on the Fondamenta Giudecca. A stop at the Franciscan church of the Redentore will explain why it is considered one of Palladio's finest churches. The church was constructed from 1577 to 1592 in honor of the city's deliverance from the plague of 1576. The Doge of that day made a vow to visit the church annually, in a ceremonious procession of boats that would bridge the Giudecca to the Zattere on the mainland. Venetians uphold the tradition each year, on the third Sunday of July, with the feast of the Redentore. Every floating vessel in the city is out on the water, where fireworks and celebration continue into the night.

HARRY'S DOLCI, owned by Arrigo Cipriani of Harry's Bar, is Giudecca's chic new spot. Venetians love this place; they all seem to know each other and table-hop as if playing a game of musical chairs. Sunday lunch is usually a cacophony of three generations of Venetian families Almost stark in appearance, with white-tiled walls, terrazzo floors, and a mirror cleverly positioned to reflect the canal, Harry's Dolci is a place to come for a light lunch or dinner. There are usually one or two pastas, excellent soups—as at Harry's Bar—main courses that vary from day to day, a selection of sandwiches, and savory salads. Desserts, though, are the *pièce de résistance*, hence the *dolci* in the name. Pies and cakes can be eaten in or taken out; lovely packages of chocolates are impossible *not* to take out. And the ice cream—hazelnut, orange, chocolate—is *meraviglioso*. Harry's Dolci, where one can eat as little or as much as one likes, is a splendid addition to the Venetian culinary scene.

Catch a *vaporetto* just outside Harry's Dolci and cross the canal of the Giudecca to the Zattere to visit the church of Santa Maria del Rosario, known as the Gesuati. The glorious ceiling, painted by Tiepolo, depicts in three large panels the life of Saint Dominic. Near the church, RISTORANTE AND PIZZERIA DA GIANNI is a delightful place for a pizza or full meal. Nothing fancy here or next door at the popular *gelateria* Nico. If the weather is fine both of these establishments will serve outdoors, and it is sheer joy to watch the boats while consuming the divine *gelato*. In from the canal of the Giudecca on the Fondamento delle Eremite, LOCANDA MONTÍN is another simple but comfortable *trattoria* that has served Venetians well. Paintings cover the walls of the two dining rooms, and a small garden in the rear accommodates alfresco diners. Try the antipasto of salami, prosciutto, and *pancetta* and the pastas, including *rigatoni* with four cheeses and *tortellini* with meat sauce. Grilled fish is fresh and well cooked, and the salad crisp. Something to remember: Venice does not go in for dressy restaurants; décor is generally of minimal interest except in hotel dining rooms.

Peggy Guggenheim's Palazzo Venier dei Leoni stands nobly—though incomplete—on the Grand Canal across from the Palazzo Corner. Built by the powerful Venier family, who claimed to be descended from the Romans, it was designed to be as high and grand as the Corner. No one knows why it was not finished—perhaps lack of funds—but its one-storey façade presents an attractive contrast to the massive edifices surrounding it. The Venier dei Leoni has been a museum since 1949, when Peggy Guggenheim opened to the public a collection of sculpture in her garden. Since her death the collection has been operated by the Soloman R. Guggenheim Foundation. Although traditionally open only for the six months of the Venetian season—beginning with Easter and continuing into the autumn—the museum features loaned exhibitions at other times as well.

A leisurely visit to the Galleria dell' Accademia—one of the world's great galleries—can be accomplished in the off-season with a minimum of aggravation. Indeed, there is much to see. The structure itself is noteworthy, particularly its gilded wood ceiling carved by Marco Cozzi in 1484. In the second room two huge altarpieces by Carpaccio and Bellini are the preface to a veritable surfeit of masterpieces that include canvases by Giorgione, Tintoretto, Tiepolo, Titian, and Veronese as well as an entire gallery of Longhi. It's a good idea to take a break for lunch or coffee and come back for more.

Another wonderful museum is the Palazzo Rezzonico, one of the grandest of the Baroque Venetian palaces, with frescoed ceilings by Tiepolo, an immense frescoed ballroom with a grand staircase leading to it, a collection of unusual furnishings, and in the second-floor gallery a delightful collection of Longhi. The palazzo has enjoyed a number of famous tenants in its day: Byron, Browning, and Cole Porter all once lived in the Rezzonico's luxury.

A few short streets from the Rezzonico, on the Calle dei Nomboli, is the fifteenth-century Palazzo Centani, where Carlo Goldoni, the prolific playwright, was born in 1707. Now a theatrical museum, the Casa Goldoni is open to the public. It features a particularly picturesque Gothic courtyard with a wellhead and an open stone staircase with stone finials carved in the shape of lions decorating the banister. Upstairs are mementos from performances of the Cloldoni comedies and a library containing scripts and *libretti* of plays and operas, which theater students use for reference.

A short distance west of the Casa Goldoni the Gothic Santa Maria Gloriosa dei Frari, known as I Fran, soars. Finished in the 1400s, it is one of Venice's largest churches and contains real treasures. Visit early in the morning because the afternoon light during the winter is brief, and most churches close at noon and do not reopen until three or four, if then. Built for Franciscan friars, the church is plain in accordance with their ideal of poverty; embellishments were kept to a minimum, and the structure remains basically unadorned. Two of Titian's famous Madonnas grace the walls: On the left as you face the main altar is the 1526 Madonna of Ca' Pesaro, surrounded by the family that commissioned the painting; and over the high altar is Titian's glorious Assumption of the Holy Virgin, painted in 1518. The colors are vibrant and rich, and one has only to compare Titian's canvas to Bellini's 1488 triptych of the Virgin and Child on the sacristy altar to see how truly innovative Titian's masterpiece was. Bellini was Titian's teacher, and only thirty years separate these two works, but there is a world of difference between them: Bellini's style was formal and staid; Titian's, fiery and turbulent. In the first chapel on the right of the Assumption is a powerful wood statue of Saint John the Baptist by Donatello. Everyone who has seen his unique Magdalen in the museum of the Duomo in Florence will recognize Donatello's Renaissance-style realism.

An appropriate place to start the third of our walks is the

main market of Venice—the Rialto—on the site of the fourteenth-century fish market next to the Rialto bridge. It is a
wildly tumultuous place when boats laden with produce dock in
the dim early morning to unload their bounty. Clementines the
size of large olives are in season, and tiny, pale-green artichokes
sold with their edible stems are also plentiful in late winter, as
are potatoes in all shapes and sizes and a flat white onion that is
delicious served *agrodolce* (sweet and sour). Just walking among
the bustling vegetable stalls whets the appetite. The provender
from the sea will delight too: tiny, glistening-silver whitebait;
bags of ebony mussels; scallops still claiming their delicate roes;
little clams the size of acorns; huge, pink-shelled crabs; *granseole*;
beautiful sides of dark-meat tuna; and both fresh and salted cod.
Cheese shops display *taleggio*, Bel Paese, *grana*, and smoked mozzarella. Just a step in from the canal, on Calle della Madonna,
the TRATTORIA MADONNA, a thoroughly Venetian establishment, will satisfy the appetite. This busy no-nonsense place,
with the usual dearth of décor, displays the specials of the day:
fish *antipasto*, the fresh catch from the market, and generous platters of spinach and luscious brown-sauced onions. *Minestrone*, a
favorite staple of Venice, arrives hot and delicious, and the white
house wine goes well with just about everything.

The church of San Salvatore beckons from the other side
of the Rialto bridge, just off the Mereerie. In 1982 a tomb
was discovered under the floor in the center aisle of this sixteenth-century Baroque church. It was opened to reveal frescoes
by Titian's brother, Francesco, which are now covered with glass
and illuminated. This patch of light emanating from the dark
floor is startlingly beautiful. The organ doors were also painted
by Francesco. Other masterpieces in San Salvatore include two
statues by Vittoria, the painting "Supper at Emmaus," attributed

to Bellini, and two paintings by the master Titian, an "Annuncia-tion" and a "Transfiguration."

The Ca' d'Oro, built in 1424, and one of the finest of the Gothic palaces, has been *in ristoro* for the past few years. It is now open and restored to within an inch of its life. Inside are many medieval paintings beautifully hung. Van Dyck's stunning eight-foot portrait of a man in black, for example, Mantegna's Saint Sebastian, and two splendid, small Guardis of the Salute and of the Piazza San Marco make a visit worthwhile. Now behind the Ca' d'Oro, walk the delightful Strada Nuova, a wide thoroughfare lined with clothes shops, food stores, and bars. Take shelter in one of the busy bars, fragrant with brewing coffee, that offer de-licious little sandwiches, which Venetians consume to tide them over between meals: tuna, sliced egg with anchovy, prosciutto, or chicken on moist white bread. The Strada Nuova will lead into the Rio Terra della Maddelena and eventually to the Ghetto. Ghetto comes from the word *gettare*—to cast, as in metal—and the name was given to this area because there was a foundry here in the late fourteenth century. In 1516 Jews were granted per-mission to live in this part of the city, and the word *ghetto* was forever after used to designate communities inhabited primarily by Jews. A series of seven impressive bronze plaques cast by the artist Arbit Blatas graces the island of the Ghetto Nuovo. Com-pleted in 1979, they "commemorate the Jews of Venice who were deported to the Nazi concentration camps on December 5, 1943, and August 17, 1944."

Our final walk begins at the Via Garibaldi, in the eastern section of the city near the Arsenale, far removed from the cen-tral markets and tourist traffic. Innumerable bakers sell delicious flat *cuabate*, olive bread and rolls, the dough made from a special flour and then baked with whole olives, and small pizzas, both the traditional round ones and square-cut Genovese. Vegetable and flower stalls abound with fresh produce, yellow mimosa, and deep crimson primrose. Pasta and butcher purveyors sell their wares from shops along the way, displaying a fine variety of fresh noodles in intriguing shapes and a large selection of game that includes quail, pheasants in their plumage, ducks, and rabbits. One candy store exhibited a tray of marzipan porcupines in the window, their backs stuck with pine-nut quills and their nails sporting bright red polish. If the day is pleasant the park next door has benches where one can sit in the sun with some fresh mortadella, cheese, and olive bread and enjoy a picnic.

If you prefer lunch in a restaurant, walk back to the Riva degli Schiavoni and turn right on the Calle del Pescaria. You will stumble in a block or two on the Calle del Pestrin and the CORTE SCONTA (the hidden court). Bare and simple, Corte Sconta has terrazzo floors, wooden tables set with paper place mats and red paper napkins, and lamps hanging from the ceiling. The cooks and waiters are all young, the air crackles with energy, and the food is like the surroundings: simple yet generous. The freshest available shellfish make up an antipasto, and spider crabs are served in their shells with roe. *Fritto misto* of squid, octopus, whitebait, and small shrimp is fried perfectly crisp. Daily menus vary according to the vagaries of the fishermen, and the pasta might include minute clams still in their shells. A salad of greens comes next, dressed at table by the waiter, and for dessert an unusual, quite liquid zabaglione exploding with Marsala is served with cookies that are *brutti ma buoni*—ugly but good. The meal is, in fact, close to perfect and demonstrates why Corte Sconta is one of the few restaurants in Venice that is crowded all year. Reservations are a must.

On the Rio della Pieta and the Calle dei Furlani is Scuola di

San Giorgio degli Schiavoni, the old guildhall of the Dalmatians. It contains a series of paintings done by Carpaccio, circa 1500. The walls of the small room are covered with scenes from the lives of three Dalmatian saints: Jerome, Tryphon, and George. Saint George slaying the dragon and Saint Augustine with his little white dog in his studio are just two of the extraordinarily appealing murals. Another treasure is the church of Santa Maria dei Miracoli just off the Campo Santa Maria Nuova. Designed by Pietro Lombardo and completed in 1489, this Renaissance masterpiece is said to be built of the surplus marble from the construction of the San Marco Basilica.

Two more churches—as different from each other as they can be—must be seen. First, the church of San Giovanni e Paolo, known in Venice as San Zanipolo, is a huge, Gothic brick edifice in one of the city's finest squares. The square contains the well-known equestrian statue of Bartolomeo Colleoni, a mercenary general who fought for the Venetian republic. It was designed by Andrea Verrocchio in 1483 but cast by Alessandro Leopardi after Verrocchio died. The vast interior of the church—101 meters long and 46 meters between the transepts—is sparse and simple and compares in size to the Frari.

Second, Santa Maria Assunta, the church called the Gesuiti, is in Campo dei Gesuiti near the Fondamenta Nuove. The church has an absurdly elaborate Baroque interior with green and white marble intarsia that looks for all the world like Fortuny brocade, and the pulpit is "draped" in heavy folds of porcelain-like marble. In the last century the Gesuiti was thought to be unspeakably vulgar and was much maligned by visitors and critics alike. It is still just as vulgar, but now we seem to have come full circle and react with wonder and amusement to the excessive decorations. Religious it is not.

Back in San Marco, the Piazza is radiant and nearly deserted in the brief winter twilight. The pigeons seem to own the square. We head toward the warmth and comfort of our hotel to say farewell to one more bittersweet winter's day in Venice.

Shopping in Florence

*F*LORENCE IS TODAY, as it has been for centuries, a center for artistic handwork. Since the twelfth century, when the Arte di Calimala, the earliest of the merchant guilds, literally controlled trade in Florence, some of the world's most elegant goods have been produced there. Fine craftsmen of all types flourished, and the skill and talent clearly have been handed down from one generation to the next. Even in the twentieth century, when meticulous handwork has given way to an age of volume and merchandising and bottom lines, quality of craftsmanship is still to be found in abundance in Florence.

The fact that beautiful things are so readily available is not all that makes this city a first-rate shopping place, however. Florence itself makes it easier, for it is manageable. With a good map one can soon get one's bearings. Moreover, the Florentines are gracious. Whether one is shopping, partaking of the glorious museums, or just exploring, Florence is a good place to be, and her population seems universally bent on showing the visitor her best side.

A shopping spree requires a headquarters, and a more comfortable and attractive one than the HOTEL REGENCY would be difficult to find in Florence or, for that matter, in any city.

Situated on the tree-lined residential Piazza Massimo d'Azeglio and formerly a villa, the building has been converted into a thirty-one-room deluxe hotel. A member of the Relais et Châteaux association, the establishment was completely done over three years ago. No expense or effort was spared, and this is reflected in the cozy lounges and the small but delightful bedrooms, where fresh fruit and a bright primrose are touches that do much to dispel that impersonal feeling prevalent in many hotels. Bold colors and fabrics have been used with success, and the whole place has the feeling of a well appointed private house. Because the Regency is somewhat away from the center of Florence there is a real air of tranquillity, and the taxi system in the city is so efficient that the location does not present an inconvenience. The hotel will call a taxi, and it is generally at the door within two or three minutes. Restaurants and even shops are happy to do the same. The taxis, incidentally, are not only immaculately clean, but their drivers are as gallant as can be.

The Regency has a good dining room where one can lunch or dine either in a handsome paneled room or in a bright winter garden with large windows and potted plants. Such delicacies as *risotto vin santo* (rice cooked in the local sweet wine), calf's liver with sage, or a perfectly grilled veal chop appear on the menu. When the rigors of touring become a little too much or if the weather is such that one would choose to stay near the hearth, it is pleasant to dine in. The hotel staff, from the personable young women at the front desk to the equally pleasant young waiters, are all extremely helpful and courteous.

Where to begin with the treasures that are in store for the shopper in Florence? Of course, the Ponte Vecchio, where goldsmiths, silversmiths, and jewelers have populated the stalls along that bridge and its environs since the end of the sixteenth century.

G. SETTEPASSI, at number 1-3r, the first shop on the left as one crosses, is among the city's most elegant jewelers. The windows display gold necklaces studded with diamonds, sapphires, and amethysts, a diamond and sapphire pin with matching earrings, and various gold necklaces with semiprecious stones. Handsome silver articles include picture frames, an unusual boxlike ice bucket, and a silver stapler—a charming conceit for the well appointed desk. The store contains dozens of beautiful items and will make almost anything a customer might fancy. GIOVANNI DEL BONO, at 2-4-6r just across from Settepassi, exhibits in addition to jewelry silver objects in the shape of various vegetables such as artichokes, carrots, and radishes. We were also intrigued by a clever tea set with wooden handles, the tea caddy of which carried the inscription "the Duchess of Devonshire's tea."

For those who are not in the market for precious gems and metals BIJOUX CASCIO offers the excellent alternative of stunning costume jewelry, cast as if it were real gold, with the same precision and care. There are compelling chokers with replicas of old coins in the center, pendant earrings with a variety of colored stones and pearls, and a wide choice of chains. They have two shops in the city, one at Via Por Santa Maria 1r, the street that leads to the Ponte Vecchio, and the other at Via de' Tornabuoni 32r. The Tornabuoni, *the* center of fashion in Florence, runs due north six blocks from the Ponte Santa Trinita and has some of the finest stores in Italy.

Leather stores abound and offer the shopper a stunning selection of handbags, wallets, luggage, and shoes. S. LUTI & SON, at Via Parione 28-32r, west off the Piazza Santa Trinita, is a well established conservative concern with an extensive collection of leather goods, stylish umbrellas and briefcases, folding leather wastebaskets, and a good choice of gifts for stay-at-home relatives and friends that include a key chain with striped ribbons and a bold brass initial and a Luti shopping bag in felt or indestructible plastic.

SALVATORE FERRAGAMO, well-known outside of Florence, warrants a visit to its headquarters—the impressive Palazzo Ferroni at the head of the Tornabuoni—where a boutique sells skirts, women's shirts, the classic sweater-blazer in almost any color one could require, and, of course, shoes for both women and men. The variety of sizes and lasts is so vast that if one is endowed with what euphemistically might be called a "problem foot" this is the place to come. Not only is there much from which to choose, but the staff is unfailingly interested. Ferragamo and Luti are both open year round, unlike many of the shops in Florence, which close for two weeks in August, usually from the tenth to the twenty-fifth. Magnificent leatherworks—handbags and shoes—by Franco Pugi are also available in Florence, and my advice is to keep an eye out for them.

Luncheon can do much to recharge a shopper's flagging spirit, and because the shops in Italy close from twelve-thirty or one until about three-thirty in the afternoon, it helps to find a restaurant where one can eat lightly and linger. CANTINETTA ANTINORI in the Palazzo Antinori on the Via de' Tornabuoni is such a place. Hearty soups such as *pappa al pomodoro* (tomato soup thickened with bread) or chickpea and pasta as well as omelets and salads are served with a selection of the fine Antinori wines in an attractive, atmospheric setting.

Also on the Tornabuoni is the popular BAR GIACOSA, which, though advertised as tearoom, American bar, and *pasticceria*, exudes the cheerful albeit frenetic atmosphere of an Italian *bar*. One can sit at small tables and partake of delectable chicken or ham sandwiches, genteel pizzas, and luscious pastries with wine and/or coffee. Across the street is PROCACCI, a Florentine institution where *panini tartufati* (soft rolls with truffle paste inside) are consumed with a glass of wine or a Campari and soda. Regulars there prefer to stand and seldom seem to linger over their midmorning or afternoon treats. The bar stocks jams, fruit juices, crackers, and Sherries to take home.

Linens, too, are justly famous in Florence, and much embroidered handwork is still done there. TAF, with two shops across the street from each other at Via Por Santa Maria 17r and 22r, can provide just about anything in table linens, towels, blouses, handkerchiefs, and baby clothes. The proprietor of Taf also owns vineyards in the Chianti region, and, while the men work in the fields, their wives and daughters embroider. The linens are kept select by virtue of the fact that no more than ten or twelve of each tablecloth or set of place mats and napkins are produced. The colors and designs are changed constantly and might include such combinations as bright blue linen mats with an orange border and an iris or daffodil in the corner or a huge tablecloth embroidered with birds and berries in a variety of hues. Special designs are created for such diverse establishments as the Gallo Winery in California and Grande Maison de Blanc in France. And what baby clothes! Any doting grandmother would go home happy with a blue and white linen suit piped in red and embroidered on the front with a full-scale barnyard complete with a flap on the chest (the barn door) that opens to reveal a small yellow chick. Christening dresses, long and beautifully embellished, are a specialty of Taf.

LORETTA CAPONI, Borgo Ognissanti 12r, in just a couple of days will make small pillowcases or for that matter virtually anything to specification. Items with elaborate hand embroidery, of course, take longer but can be ordered and shipped. On a rather dreary gray day Caponi's windows were positively aglow with yellow—long nightgowns in white linen appliquéd with bunches of mimosa and dotted swiss bedspreads and pillow slips festooned with bright yellow ribbons. The shop also has an impressive collection of antique linens, including hand towels, bureau scarves, and oversized pillowcases. Mothers or grandmothers-to-be will find here a charming tiny silk baby shirt that, according to Italian tradition, will bring *buona fortuna* to any newborn who wears it.

Surely one of the most unique pharmacies in the world, the OFFICINA PROFUMO-FARMACEUTICA DI SANTA MARIA NOVELLA at Via della Scala 16n, just northwest of the church of Santa Maria Novella, was originally the pharmacy for the church's convent and was opened to the public in 1612. Dominican friars manufactured the herbal remedies that were and still are sold there. The present store, dimly lit and with a high vaulted ceiling, is a far cry from today's drugstore and is, in reality, a chapel that was built by a member of an aristocratic Florentine family who, when deathly ill, vowed that were he to find a bunch of Ursina grapes, purported to have miraculous therapeutic powers but not in season at the time, he would build a chapel by way of thanksgiving. He found the grapes, was restored to health, and built the chapel for the Dominicans.

The pharmacy sells shampoos, perfumes, soaps, potpourris of dried wild flowers from the hills in Fiesole, and delicately scented talcum powders. The story goes that when Maria de' Medici went to France to marry Henry IV she took her *capo maestro profumaio* (master perfume-maker) with her and with him went all the secrets for making perfumes. (The secrets eventually made their way to Cologne, Germany, and from there to Grasse in the south of France, which would become the center of the French perfume industry.)

Medicines that have been manufactured over the centuries are also sold at the pharmacy: elixir of rhubarb for the digestion, an elixir from China to stimulate the appetite, and Acqua di Santa Maria Novella, antihysteria water. The graceful flask of clear liquid comes in a neat cardboard tube, can be carried in a handbag, and might, at any time, prove to be a lifesaver. All the products are beautifully labeled and packaged by hand by one of the shop's five employees. Like so many of the Florentine concerns the Santa Maria Novella pharmacy is based on tradition and on the premise that articles made by hand and in small quantities tend to be infinitely more satisfying than goods that are mass-produced.

A sweater shop with the unlikely name of LA CASA DI HOGG, at Via de' Tornabuoni 24, 26, 28r, has an opulent display of lamb's wool, cashmere, and Shetland sweaters in such dramatic colors as electric blue, shocking pink, and magenta. Argyle knits of every conceivable hue, Fair Isle sweaters with garish yokes, and knee socks giddy enough to satisfy the most flamboyant taste are also available, as are stylish shirts on display in cotton and silk.

For ladies and gentlemen who are only happy with shirts that are made to order there is BIANZINO at Piazza San Giovanni 11-12r. The plaza is directly in front of the Baptistery, world-renowned for its exquisite doors and magnificent interior mosaics. Bolt after bolt after bolt of shirting material is neatly stacked from floor to ceiling. There are stripes, checks, and solids in all colors, and the choices are exhilarating. Shirts can be made up in ten days to two weeks, only one fitting required. The firm also carries woolens in a staggering variety of tartans and will make up kilts, skirts, and other custom orders.

Not far from Bianzino, CAFFE RIVOIRE, on Piazza della Signoria, is another very engaging spot for tired shoppers to refresh themselves. There is a bar at the entrance where sandwiches and pastries are set out and a large room in the rear with tables. Light lunches include whole-wheat Tuscan bread grilled with mozzarella, tomato, and rosemary, soft rolls with artichokes, prosciutto, and sliced hard-boiled egg, and croissants filled with ham and cheese. The cappuccino is delicious and the sweets are sublime.

Use an afternoon to visit the EMILIO PUCCI boutique at Via dei Pucci 6, the street that runs north from the Piazza del Duomo to the Piazza San Marco. There scarves in Pucci's extraordinary colors, blouses and dresses of silk, and wallets in leather and velvet await. Costume jewelry and handbags in the famous prints are also knockouts, and to keep up with the times there are even trendy cotton T-shirts. For men there are neckties, robes, belts, and a special cologne.

Next door to that store is the wineshop, where wine, honey, and oil from the Pucci estates are sold. The Marchese's flair for imaginative yet traditional design is evident in the unusual wine bottles. The *fiasco*, the traditional straw Chianti bottle, became too costly to manufacture so he produced a bottle copied from a twelfth-century fresco. Honey from Pucci bees in a terra-cotta jar would be a welcome present as would luminescent green extra-virgin olive oil.

The choice of household effects is also astonishing in Florence. RAFANELLI, manufacturers and purveyors of brass and copper items, is located at Via del Sole 7r and can be reached by going west off the Tornabuoni on the Via della Spada to the intersection of Via delle Belle Donne. Everything here is handmade: The store is chockablock with brass doorknobs and knockers, light brackets of every description, and lanterns that would enhance any hall or doorway. They also make brass bedsteads, towel racks, elaborate soap dishes, and a beguiling sunburst to dazzle a garden wall.

Back to the Tornabuoni and a short walk east along the Lungarno Acciaiuoli to the Piazza del Pesce 2r, where the intrepid browser will find MENEGATTI, a particularly choice ceramics shop. Majolica from Florence and from neighboring Umbria includes plates depicting the four seasons and pretty apothecary jars in blue and orange. Pottery bathroom glasses and toothbrush holders are but a few of the items also for sale. Sets of plates and cups with saucers can be ordered in different patterns, and this shop will ship anywhere.

Fringed tassels, frequently seen in Italian houses on tiebacks of curtains, window shades, or just dangling gaily from a door key or the handle of a drawer, are a thoroughly Florentine bit of froufrou. Still and all, they make excellent presents for that certain someone who "has everything" and can easily be tucked into the suitcase to be taken home and put away for Christmas. ANTICHITÀ DI ALBERTO PIERINI, Borgo Ognissanti 22r, has a good choice of these tassels made by Mr. Pierini's mother, which are on display along with his lovely antiques.

On the Via Porta Rossa 53r, east from the Piazza Santa Trinita, VALMAR is surely the definitive tassel emporium with sizes ranging from a tiny one suitable for a dollhouse door to one for a house key to one immense enough to pull a heavy drape. Every inch of the small shop is neatly packed with braid, roping, tufts, and fringe, and as a reminder of a more gracious era the store still carries elaborately embroidered bellpulls.

On the Pitti Palace side of the Arno are countless artisan and antiques shops. The Via Maggio and the Via Santo Spirito positively teem with them, and on the Via Guicciardini, the street straight off the Ponte Vecchio, a microcosm of Florentine products—leather, linen, ceramic, and silver—exists. Across from the Pitti is a charming establishment called GIULIO GIANNINI

E FIGLIO, a thriving little paper concern that has been owned by the same family and housed in the same building for 136 years. A variety of printed papers cover address books and scorepads for cardplayers, and pencils match cylindrical containers. Balls of twine in decorative holders and kaleidoscopes there would delight a child of any age. Desk clips in all patterns and colors have been fashioned into sea horses, turtles, butterflies, and sunbursts and undoubtedly would alleviate some of the onus from a stack of unpaid bills. The workshop is over the store, and, of course, everything is made there by hand. Also on this side of the river MAIOLI-PANDOLFINI, Via Guicciardini 43r, is a popular and well established bar serving sandwiches and wine or coffee.

Candy is much beloved by the Florentines and is sold in many of the places one would stop for coffee or pastry. DONEY on the Tornabuoni and Giacosa and Rivoire, both previously mentioned, all sell beautifully packaged chocolates, marzipan, and hard candies. But MIGONE CONFETTI on the Via Calzaiuoli 85-87r, the street that runs due north off the Piazza della Signoria, is one of the few enterprises involved primarily in candymaking and selling confections. The shop was started in 1918 by the Migone family, who are still very much in evidence. It is a mouth-watering experience to amble in and select a piece or two of cream-filled chocolates. Jars of gum drops, jelly beans, and hard candies cover the shelves, and all the chocolates are made in Florence expressly for the shop. The sugared chickens and lambs come from Bologna and the stock of *panforte*, a type of nougat, hails from Siena. The real specialty of the house, though, is to provide all sorts of sweets for occasions such as baptisms, first communions, and weddings. The presentation, tiny white boxes with minute ribbons and colored flowers, is a visual delight.

BM LIBERIA, at Borgo Ognissanti 4r off the Piazza Goldoni, is a first-rate bookstore carrying a good selection of titles in English, both hardcover and paperback, and a comprehensive supply of travel, history, biography, and art books in English about Italy. BM is a helpful address as traveling and suitable reading matter go hand in hand.

Two gift shops on the Via della Vigna Nuova, southwest off the Tornabuoni, are filled with finds. PAOLI, Via della Vigna Nuova 24-26-28r, has straw items, baskets, frames, and even furniture painted in dazzling high-luster colors. It is amazing how the brightest pinks, purples, and greens can transform everyday straw into stunning additions to a house or garden. Trays fashioned in the shapes of vegetables are interesting and decorative, and shellacked frames in bamboo are also available in various sizes.

Just a few doors down the Vigna Nuova, on the same side of the street at 58r, is BICCHIELLI, which advertises itself as a gift shop, silver shop, and jeweler. It has a fascinating array of items that one never knew one needed but suddenly cannot live without. Fine handmade enameled and wood frames in rich colors, enameled nutcrackers, and cheese and butter knives are among the choices. There are also pretty bottles to hold bath salts, powder, or cologne. At Via Cerretani 7r is another gift shop, BONGI, a small establishment that specializes in games—chess boards and the like and sets of poker chips in pastel colors not usually associated with gaming. tables. Mr. Bongi stocks a wide variety of fine pipes, tobacco boxes, and pipe holders as well. All are made locally and have that elegant air of most Italian designs. Last but not least Mr. Bongi carries barometers and thermometers for weather buffs.

No discussion of shopping in Florence would be complete without a word about some of the city's markets. The MERCATO

CENTRALE, as the name indicates, is the main marketplace. Near the church of San Lorenzo in the northern part of the city, it occupies an entire piazza and much of the surrounding area. There are two floors in a huge building, and, if one enjoys gazing on some of the most splendid fruits and vegetables in the world, to say nothing of the hams, sausages, and enormous wheels of cheese, this is the place to spend a happy hour or two. The housewives of Florence seem to know exactly which stall to patronize, not an easy decision it would seem as there are four or five right next to each other selling nothing but mushrooms. For those whose main source of comestibles is the modern supermarket this is an illuminating experience. All around the main building are stalls that sell everything from gloves to shoes to linens to pots and pans, and with patience some bargains can be had. The food market is open every day but Sunday, and the surrounding stalls are closed Sundays and Mondays.

In Le Cascine, a park west of the city, there is an extraordinary happening on Tuesday mornings known simply as the MERCATO CASCINE. On either side of a wide walkway stalls bursting with a prodigious variety of goods—antique linens and dresses, baby clothes, sweaters for men, women, and children, shoes galore, and squares of designer scarves that are rolled off a bolt and cut—stretch for over a mile. Here nobility and ordinary mortals rub shoulders, all bent on acquiring exceptional purchases. The market provides a fine morning's entertainment.

Closer at hand but not nearly as diverting is the much frequented straw market just off the Via Por Santa Maria in the Piazza del Mercato Nuovo. Known as the MERCATO DEL PORCELLINO, because of the well-known statue of the bronze boar that keeps watch over the comings and goings, the market offers linen, leather, and, of course, straw items. There is much less selection here than at the Cascine, and the local color does not compare.

One could spend weeks exploring the dozens of fine small shops in this enchanting city. The possibilities are boundless. In a world where quality is on the wane Florence is a happy, beautiful reminder that style and excellence have existed and have transported us for many centuries. The more things change, the more some things remain splendidly the same.

The Subtle Charms of Florence

*T*HESE DAYS, for obvious reasons, the small hotel is coming into its own. The search is on to discover comfortable lodgings that are well situated and low pressured—but still with good service—for, one hopes, much less than the price of deluxe hostelries. Experienced travelers now have their favorites, and they tend to guard those names like deep, dark secrets. The city of Florence has more than its share of these charming finds, however, and to add to the pleasure there are innumerable *trattorie* where one can feast for what today is still a bargain.

The Hotel Principe, on the Lungarno Vespucci, a bit outside the heart of the city, has distinct old-world appeal, with just twenty-one rooms. The lobby with its high ceiling, crystal chandelier, and brown, black, and white *terrazzo* floor is furnished with large upholstered chairs and tables where coffee or drinks are served. As with most of these small hotels the Principe has no formal restaurant, but breakfast and snacks are available in one's room and in the bar. The bedrooms, although not large, are comfortably appointed, and those on the second and third floors, with balconies overlooking a lovely garden, are particularly desirable. Be warned: Rooms on the north bank of the Arno (the front of the hotel) are noisy. The Italian's long-standing love affair with his motorcar makes noise a fact of life here, and, unfortunately, in the evening the *lungarni* turn into veritable speedways for *macchine*, Vespas, and the like. One must choose either the romance of gazing out over the Arno and the Ponte Vecchio or the pragmatism of a room in the back and the possibility of a sound sleep.

Behind the Principe, toward the Piazza Santa Maria Novella, on the Via del Porcellana, is one of the city's characteristic *trattorie*. The word *trattoria* comes from *tratto*, way or byway; thus, a *trattoria* is a spot that one finds "on the way." And though the ways may change, the spots remain remarkably the same: To describe one *trattoria* is to describe them all. There is no decoration; the walls are usually white tile, the floors stone or dark tile. The tables are covered with either plain white cloths or no cloth at all; the chairs, often benches, are designed simply in wood and rush. Due to all the tile and stone and the high spirits of many Italians, the decibel count verges on barely controlled pandemonium. Tables are frequently shared, so don't be surprised if you end up dining with *la nonna, il nonno, mamma, papa,* and numerous *ragazzi*—the family. If you speak Italian, you will most certainly be included in the conversation, and, if you don't, you will be sure to have your menu decoded for you. But sometimes there are no menus, in which case the waiter recites the choices of the day. The ceremonies may be minimal, but the results can be superlative.

A bit of looking is needed in order to find Sostanza, for it is totally indistinguishable from any of the other buildings on the narrow street, and the name, on a faded menu tacked up by the door, is barely legible. The menu presents not a vast choice— *tortellini al sugo* and *al burro*, spaghetti, a soup or two, boiled chicken or *bistecca alla fiorentina* (T-bone steak broiled over charcoal or wood)—but all of the seven or eight tables were taken the evening of our visit, and the entrance was filled with patient diners awaiting their turn. The plate of the day was tripe, simmered long and lovingly with tomato and stock, a great favorite of Florentines. For dessert there was meringue tart or cheese and fruit.

Just a few blocks east of Sostanza and still in the neighborhood of the Principe is another *trattoria*, also undistinguished from the outside but worth a visit, Coco Lezzone, which is on the corner of the Via del Parioncino and the Via Purgatorio, right near the Via dell'Inferno. Trying not to dwell on the metaphysical dangers implicit in our surroundings, we ventured in for lunch one bright day. The meal started with *pappa al pomodoro*, a Tuscan specialty of stewed tomatoes with basil that is served with the saltless bread of Florence and a spoonful of pungent green olive oil. This was followed by *stracotto* (pot roast) and *osso buco* (veal shank) accompanied by turnip greens and *fagioli*. Enamoured of beans, Florentines are known as *"mangia-fagioli"*—bean eaters— by the rest of Italy, and one does not have to be there long to see why. The white bean, we are told, was brought to Florence from North America in the sixteenth century. It appears with meat and chicken dishes, usually with a bit of oil added from a cruet on the table, and is also served cold at the beginning of the meal with tuna and sometimes even caviar. Our lunch ended with *biscotti di prato*, hard, almond-flavored rusks that were served with a small glass of blackberry liqueur called *morellino*. One dips the cookie into the drink, then eats it as it begins to soften.

The Via Tornabuoni is Florence's most fashionable shopping avenue. Here are Gucci, Fendi, Caine, Saint Laurent, Giorgio Armani, plus countless others, and on the Piazza Antinori, where the Tornabuoni ends, is the charming Hotel de La Ville Florence. With seventy-one rooms it is one of the larger of the so-called small hotels and also a bit more expensive. The mirrored lobby with its fresh flowers and Murano sconces and the reception desk manned by a most accommodating staff in impeccably tailored blue suits give the impression that guests are well taken care of. The bedrooms are not large but of more than adequate size, and the furnishings are comfortable. In each room there is a small refrigerator well stocked with Fiuggi, the exhilarating Italian water, splits of Champagne, white wine, and soft drinks—a nice touch that must also simplify the hotel's room service. The tiled bathrooms are modern and satisfactory. This hotel does have a restaurant.

Next to the De la Ville, in the Piazza Antinori, is the Cantinetta Antinori. Do not be fooled by the sign outside that advertises "snacks," for this establishment is not really a *trattoria* but an elegant wine bar that serves wine and produce from the Antinori estate, Santa Cristina, in the hills outside Florence. In addition to the red and white Villa Antinori, well known and available outside Italy, the Cantinetta offers a white Santa Cristina, dry and full of bouquet, and a new wine, Galestro, fruity and fresh. The menu, mostly soups and such dishes as *vitello tonnato* and tomatoes with basil and mozzarella, provides a pleasant change from a full meal. Highly polished wooden tables, tulip glasses, a display of grapes in bunches, and bottles of Antinori vintages create a stylish atmosphere in which fashionable Florentine ladies often take a bite of lunch.

It is an easy walk from the Via Tornabuoni to the Piazza del Mercato Nuovo. There, under an arcade, is Florence's famous straw market—Mercato del Porcellino—guarded by the much photographed statue of the bronze boar. There one sees not only straw baskets, boxes, and bags but table linens, silks, and elaborate woodwork. Bargains are still to be had there as well as in the outdoor stalls of the leather merchants in the *loggie* of the Uffizi. For those who enjoy bartering, it seems to be an acceptable pastime.

In this neighborhood, between the Corso and the Piazza del Duomo on the Via Sant'Elisabetta, is Ottorino, a large, busy, and popular trattoria. The first thing to catch one's eye is a table laden with starters such as octopus, squid, tiny clams, snails, mussels in oil, and a mix of cold vegetables. Farther into the room is a trolley heavy with pears, grapes, cheeses, and fruit tarts. The waiters, in shirt sleeves, are deft at avoiding collisions as they carry trays with plates and plates of steaming pasta, and the clientele, seemingly oblivious to the confusion, look as if they know that they will be well fed. There are few tourists at Ottorino, rather businessmen, families, and the occasional solitary Florentine aristocrat.

The menu here is vast. On the day of our visit *paglia e fieno* was prepared with cream, white wine, and a sprinkling of truffles. *Scaloppine Ottorino*, a heady combination of veal, Emmenthal, prosciutto, and Cognac, was also difficult to pass up. Tripe and *bollito misto* (boiled meats) with *salsa verde* (herbed green sauce) are favorites, and of course the selection of Chianti in this, the heart of the wine region, is staggering. These remarkable wines are from the small area from Pisa to Pistoia in the north and Arezzo and beyond Siena in the south. How glorious they can be! We sampled an Antinori Tignanello, and the aroma and bouquet rivaled that of many Bordeaux.

The Hotel Continental and the Augustus e dei Congressi stand side by side on the Piazzetta dell'Oro. The Continental has few frills. The lobby is small, and the rooms and bathrooms, too, are less spacious than those in the other hotels of this category. However, the hotel has a particularly agreeable lounge and bar on the second floor where a view of the Arno and the activities around the jewelry shops on the Ponte Vecchio can be enjoyed over a cup of coffee or a drink. The bridge, one of Italy's best-known landmarks, was rebuilt in 1345 after a flood and at that time it was decreed that henceforth its shops would be reserved for the goldsmiths of Florence. The goldwork done there today is renowned for its sophisticated craftsmanship and excellence of design.

The Augustus is set slightly back from the Lungarno so that it looks out on the little square and a side street. Its lobby is grander than that of the Continental, with vases of bright anemones, deep couches, and low, glass coffee tables, and the bedrooms, many with canopied beds, are furnished with antiques. The atmosphere exudes comfort and serenity. Both hotels have about sixty-five rooms.

Almost next door, but well hidden down the Via dei Girolami, is the Buca dell'Orafo (the goldsmith's cellar). This restaurant seats only forty, and there never seems to be an empty table. The same frenetic feeling that pervades all the popular *trattorie* exists here, and the noise level is such that it is difficult to know how the two or three waiters who take care of all the guests manage to keep their sanity. The clientele seems to be made up of regulars, and visitors soon learn that Florentines are faithful to their favorite *trattorie*. To engage one or two locals in a discussion of the merits of various eating establishments is to become involved in a highly controversial debate that has precious little chance of being resolved.

There are almost as many good *trattorie* as there are Florentines, and Buca dell'Orafo is certainly one of the better ones. We dined happily on a pungent salami from Siena, *tagliolini* (ribbonlike pasta topped with a little oil and grated truffles), and a marvelously fragrant *stracotto* served with the ever-present beans.

The house Chianti, the ideal accompaniment, was drunk *al consumo*, a system whereby the straw encased vessel is placed on the table and the imbibers are charged for what they drink.

Leather goods are still one of the great bargains in Florence, and around the church of Santa Croce on the Via Anguillara and Borgo dei Greci the leather "factories," as they are called, abound. Every sort of wallet, handbag, and Piazza della Signoria suitcase is available, and the shopkeepers will gladly initial any purchase. While in the area don't miss a small bar and *gelateria* called Vivoli, on the Piazza San Simone, which can be reached by taking the Via Torta from the Piazza Santa Croce. It has without question some of the world's finest ice cream. Cups of this heavenly concoction can be bought in any size and price, from thirty cents to a dollar or two, and the flavors are sublime—coffee, chocolate (the darkest, lushest I have ever tasted), hazelnut, raspberry, blueberry, blackberry, lemon, banana, and rum crisp, to name a few. It is like ingesting the pure, exquisite essences.

Across the Ponte Vecchio, on the south side of the Arno, is the Lungarno hotel on the Borgo San Jacopo. It is a delightful place to stay. There are seventy-one rooms, and because the hotel abuts the river the rooms that overlook it are the choicest. From them one can see patient fishermen, casting from the bank hoping to hook lord knows what in the murky mustard-colored water, and a scull or two gliding by gracefully. There is also a perfect view of the Ponte Vecchio, the dome of the Duomo, and Giotto's Campanile. The rooms are comfortable, simply but well appointed, the lobby with chintz and deep carpeting is warm and inviting, and the service is efficient and friendly.

There is a plethora of good *trattorie* on this bank of the river, with Mamma Gina and Cammillo, two standbys, right on the Borgo San Jacopo, and Celestino a block or two away on the

Piazza Santa Felicita. A Florentine friend told me that some Italians are suspicious of any restaurant that is too richly decorated, feeling that the effort and money spent on trappings could be far better spent on food. This concern is not germane to any of the just-mentioned establishments: They are plain to the point of being Spartan, and the food cannot be faulted. Celestino's serves *scampi alla pescatora* done deliciously with oil, garlic, tomato, and lemon and a very fine ravioli with cream. A specialty at Mamma Gina's is *valigette della nonna,* or grandmother's little suitcases, which turns out to be first-rate stuffed cabbage. Here the house Chianti Fattoria dell'Ugo is an excellent choice.

Cammillo's has curried shrimp and rice, a curious item to find on the menu of a Tuscan *trattoria* but, in fact, admirable. One evening perfectly ripe figs and fine prosciutto proved an auspicious starter. All *trattorie* in Florence are required to close one day a week, and all must post the closing day outside their doors. In these three restaurants reservations are necessary but are also sometimes meaningless as we found to our sorrow after having waited at Cammillo's for a full hour one Sunday night. You soon learn in Florence that the *trattoria* that is not crowded is probably the *trattoria* that is also not very good.

Fine shopping is available on this side of the river. The Via Guicciardini, which runs from the Ponte Vecchio to the Pitti Palace, abounds in fashionable possibilities: knits, silks, umbrellas, handbags, and gloves and every sort of bibelot for the house. A charming shop across from the Pitti that sells boxes, notebooks, and desk accessories covered with beautiful Florentine papers has been in the same building and in the same family for 134 years. Everything is done by hand, and the workshop is over the store. The Via di Santo Spirito, near the Pitti, is the antiques center of the city and a pleasant place to wander and perhaps to buy.

But when lunchtime comes, Angiolino's is the place to be.

The kitchen is open in the back of this *trattoria*, and the vault-ed ceiling, black ironwork lights, and hams swinging reassuringly from the rafters suggest a serious eating place. The specialty is grilled meats—all done to order and all of the highest quality. To start, we had a wonderfully pungent *soppressato*, similar to a *mortadella* or salami but spicier and available only during the colder months. The coarse Tuscan bread was a perfect foil for the aromatic meats, and a Fattoria Montellori Chianti provided the finishing touch.

To the south of the city, high in the hills on the Via Castelli, is the Villa Belvedere. A spacious old house with twenty-seven rooms, a tennis court, and a swimming pool, this hotel is set in a park with spectacular views of the city from its broad verandas. There is no restaurant, but breakfast and light lunches are served in the bright, commodious lounges. The bedrooms are spacious and airy, with a few suites to accommodate families. This is an ideal place to stay in the summer, when Florence, sheltered by hills in the Arno valley, can be unbearably hot. There is a bus stop just past the gate of the hotel, and one can be at the Piazza Pitti in ten minutes. The hotel is closed during December, January, and February.

A short ride from the Belvedere, on the Via Pian dei Giullari in the town of Arcetri, is Omero. To reach the dining room of this trattoria one has to walk through a small food shop, passing along the way an enormous wooden vat of local olive oil, a wheel of Parmesan, prosciutto, and sausages—all of which are for sale. The dining room is bright and large with straw mats on the ceil-ing that have a special use in the preparation of Chianti wine. Lunch began with mortadella and *crostini della casa*—a pâté of chicken livers with anchovies, capers, and whatever else the chef sees fit to add. (*Crostini* appears frequently on menus in Florence and is served warm on toast at the start of the meal.) A grilled steak followed, with *fagioli al fiasco*, beans cooked in a flask over coals as they have been for centuries in Tuscany, and a salad of *radicchio*. We drank a Fattoria di Scrafana and ended a thoroughly satisfying lunch with Gorgonzola and a perfect pear.

An eating excursion that is well worth the twenty-minute ride from Florence is the Trattoria Le Cave in Maiano, three kilometers from Fiesole. It is a simple white stucco country inn where, on fair days, lunch is served on stone tables overlooking the olive groves and vineyards. Indoors the dining room is unadorned and utilitarian. There is no menu and choices are limited, but the produce and the manner in which it is prepared result in a meal as well orchestrated as any fine piece of music.

Lunch starts with a series of small platters brought to the table—one with an ideal salad of peas, carrots, and potatoes lightly napped with a velvety mayonnaise, another with country-cured prosciutto, mortadella, and *crostini*, and another with juicy green and black olives and bright yellow and red peppers. The pastas of the day when we were there were green *tortellini* filled with chicken and sauced with cream and grated Parmesan and ravioli with a fragrant tomato sauce. Our main course consisted of *pollo al mattone*, grilled chicken flattened with a brick as it cooks so that it is crisp without becoming dry. There were also veal, pork, and beef possibilities, grilled or roasted. All the choices were served with fried potatoes, fried artichokes, polenta, and white beans. Dessert was a pear cooked in wine or a crisp apple tart. Now all of this may sound quite ordinary, but the high quality of each ingredient made the meal memorable. The cooking of Italy, and, most particularly of Tuscany, does not depend on embellishment or ornamentation; at its best it rests on the pure tastes of

its fine produce, and that is why it is extremely difficult to repro-
duce anywhere else. The *trattorie* of Florence and its surrounding
countryside might well spoil one's palate irrevocably and make
one long, in far distant lands, for the joys of the Tuscan table.

The Amalfi Coast

*T*HE AMALFI COAST begins officially six kilometers west of Positano on the road between Sorrento and Salerno with a sign that reads: Costiera Amalfitana. As early as the fourteenth century Boccaccio in *The Decameron* described it thus: "Few parts of Italy are reckoned to be more delightful . . . a strip of land known as the Amalfi coast, dotted with small towns, gardens, and fountains." The Amalfi Drive, the road that services this coast, is truly an extraordinary engineering feat. Designed by Luigi Giordano and completed in 1852, the Drive, a twisting byway often too narrow for two cars to pass and always too narrow for two buses, is carved out of perpendicular cliffs and offers vistas that— indeed—defy the imagination.

When driving, one logically approaches the Amalfi coast from Sorrento, a pleasant city of about seventeen thousand inhabitants mainly given over to hotels and tourists. For years the mild climate and lush vegetation have made Sorrento a popular spot with visitors from the north, always hungry for Italian sunshine. The list of luminaries who have spent time in these parts is legion: Richard Wagner, Goethe, Lord Byron, Sir Walter Scott, Alexandre Dumas, Henry Wadsworth Longfellow, James Fenimore Cooper, Friedrich Nietzsche, and Henrik Ibsen, who completed

Peer Gynt in Sorrento in 1867. They were attracted by what visitors find here today, for one of the great joys of the Amalfi coast is that in a rapidly changing world it has changed little.

The drive from Sorrento is spectacular almost as soon as one leaves the town proper. Olive and palm trees, umbrella pines, oleander in varying shades of pink, and lantana that looks positively out of control make up the local landscape. By the roadside, vendors display their wares: bags of hazelnuts and almonds, chains of fiery red peppers, and citrons the size of grapefruits. Ideally there should be two drivers in the car so that each can take a turn at the wheel, allowing the other to look at the incredible scenery. The road needs the driver's complete attention, and under no circumstances should one both drive and sight-see. The Drive winds in an unbelievable succession of serpentine turns, which would be totally blind were it not for strategically placed mirrors along the way. The views over the Tyrrhenian Sea change with every turn, and the color of its waters is a blue beyond one's wildest notions.

The first town of any real size is Positano, long a favorite of artists and writers. It is easy to see why, for one could not conjure up a more evocative sight. Positano is clustered on a hillside above a pebbly shore, where beach umbrellas coexist with dozens of colorful fishing boats that make up the town's active fleet. On fine nights the sea is dotted with lights from these little vessels as they pursue their catch of seafood—the main staple here. Positano is literally built on steps. Every thoroughfare is an ascent or a descent; therefore all movement is vertical rather than horizontal. Purple bougainvillea proliferates on walls and balconies, and there are boutiques everywhere with clothes, sandals, and ceramics, making the town an enjoyable place in which to stroll.

Down on the beach are two excellent restaurants: BUCA DI

BACCO, where some of the delights are fresh anchovies, which have never seen salt or the inside of a tin, lovingly marinated in oil and lemon juice, *zuppa di cozze* (mussel soup), and perfectly grilled swordfish; and, next door, tiny LA CAMBUSA, which serves up unusual and delectable *bruschetto* (toasted bread spread with a fragrant tomato concoction) to hungry diners while they peruse the menu. One evening a dinner at La Cambusa included *linguine* with *scampi* and *fritto misto* composed of deep-fried anchovies, sardines, squid, and *gamberi*, the large, flavorful shrimp of the region, all accompanied appropriately by a local white, Greco di Tufo. Up the hill from the beach is the perfect stop-off place, LA ZAGARA, where the pastries are tempting and the hazelnut and pistachio ice creams can be enjoyed on a vine-shaded terrace overlooking the town and seashore.

On the main road into Positano is LE SIRENUSE (the sirens), a charming eighteenth-century house converted into a hotel that boasts a view of the majolica-tiled dome of Santa Maria Assunta. Green-tiled floors, jade plants in terra-cotta pots, and hanging baskets of geraniums contribute to the pleasing décor, and the bedrooms, which include balconies, are furnished with old white wrought-iron furniture. An outdoor terrace with a pool and bar overlooks all of Positano, and the dining room is an indoor-outdoor arrangement, common in this gentle climate, where the chefs can be seen skillfully stoking the pizza oven and tending the open hearth.

Dinner at Le Sirenuse one balmy night started with a subtle risotto made with zucchini, carrots, parsley, basil, and Parmesan and *penne alla vodka*, fat quill-shaped pasta napped with a sauce of ham, tomato purée, cream, and vodka. *Bocconcini al gorgonzola* was an intriguing combination of veal, Gorgonzola, and brandy. Twice a year the talented chefs at Le Sirenuse present a pasta festival in which up to forty kinds of pasta are served. The last time this event took place 250 souls were expected, but 400 actually appeared. The capable management, under the watchful eye of Luigi Bozza, somehow coped.

Two kilometers east of Positano at a sharp bend in the drive is the entrance to the HOTEL SAN PIETRO. Nothing can be seen from the road but a sign and a three-hundred-year-old stone chapel dedicated to the fisherman saint for whom the surrounding land and the hotel are named. A path planted with jasmine, red salvia, and hibiscus leads discreetly past the doors of two suites to an elevator that carries guests down to one of Italy's finest hotels.

The main lobby of the San Pietro, always filled with flowers, is an airy, open room, with terra-cotta floors, comfortable sofas, and a statue of San Gennaro, patron saint of Naples and Campania. Bougainvillea vines have taken root on the ceiling, and when they are in bloom the room is a bower of pink. The loggia, where one can sit for coffee or drinks, is decorated in autumn with piles of pumpkinlike squash and ropes of small tomatoes, strung together and preserved for use in cooking. Here, a splendid multicolored parrot named Don Pedro says hello to passersby and calls the headwaiter, Peppino, by name. His cage and that of Federico, a myna, and two parrakeets swing from the vines on the ceiling.

Beyond the loggia is the dining room, which is, again, both indoors and out with a terrace that overlooks Positano and the neighboring town of Praiano. The tables are set with crockery made nearby at Vietri, and the dozen or so different bold bright patterns are mixed with striking effect. At dinnertime, with the flame of the pizza oven casting a reassuring glow, flowers and candles on the tables, and a piano playing in the background, the ambiance is close to perfection.

The San Pietro is Carlo Cinque's special achievement. Mr.

Cinque, who was born in Positano, first opened the smaller Miramare hotel (which he still owns) in his family house in Positano. In 1960 he built a flat for himself on the crest of a hill in San Pietro and spent the next ten years overseeing the rock blasting and construction required to complete the hotel. Elegant and spacious, the building melds unobtrusively into the landscape.

An old Spanish proverb contends that "the greatest fertilizer is the master's footsteps," and Mr. Cinque is proof positive of this aphorism. He walks about the gardens, his passion, with a keen eye. Every spare inch is planted with giant double yellow and red hibiscus, pink and white geraniums, coral roses, magenta bleeding heart, and masses of marigolds, all interspersed among pines and lemon trees heavy with fruit. On these tours Mr. Cinque is always accompanied by Pietro, his German shepherd, and usually by Paolo, an English sheepdog, and Betty, a boxer.

Many of Mr. Cinque's guests are close friends, and, because eighty percent of his clientele are returnees, those he does not know at first he soon gets to know. His taste permeates the hotel; each suite and bedroom is different, with fine antiques, brass beds, and colorful tile floors. There is a spot in each room—often a balcony—which takes maximum advantage of the view, where one can breakfast, and the rooms all come with small refrigerators well stocked with mineral water, wine, and Champagne, as well as stronger spirits. The closets are commodious, and the bedside lamps are just right for late-night reading—often not the case in Italian hotels. There is air conditioning in the bedrooms, but it is a delight to fall asleep with just the curtains pulled, listening to the gentle sea lapping the rocks, and to be awakened by the roosters sounding their daybreak call.

Mr. Cinque's niece, Virginia, has much to do with the smooth running of this incredibly civilized establishment, and Virginia's brother, Salvatore, has the almost impossible task of assigning the sixty-five rooms. Because so many of the guests have strong preferences when it comes to their accommodations, sorting out the reservations is a veritable Chinese puzzle. Luckily Salvatore retains his good humor throughout.

In exactly 1 minute and 23 seconds an elevator from the lobby transports one literally through the rocks to the "beach." It is, in fact, a rocky promontory where there is a hard surface tennis court and where one can bathe in the stunningly clear, clean water. A bar has been cut into the cliff, and a wonderful lunch of mozzarella, prosciutto, tomato, and basil sandwiches on thick slices of bread can be ordered here. Elephant's Milk, the deliciously refreshing drink of the house, is also served. It consists of lemon juice, mineral water, and, allegedly, a splash of elephant's milk After serious detective work, however, we discovered that the last ingredient was in fact almond milk. But don't spoil Mr. Cinque's fun.

The food at the San Pietro is a happy adventure and an opportunity to savor the local produce. There is a vast á la carte menu, and each day a suggested lunch and dinner. One can sample everything from a perfectly cooked omelet to a hearty *pasta e fagioli* (pasta and white bean soup). Risotto simmered with squid, octopus, mussels, clams, and *gamberi* is addictive, and individual pizzas with various toppings are made every evening. Lunch one day brought mozzarella wrapped in lemon leaves and grilled over coals. Mozzarella in this area of Campania is made from the milk of the sad-looking dark gray *bufalo*, a descendant of the Indian water buffalo, and is unlike most mozzarella with its fine texture.

Fish and shellfish at the San Pietro are always at their peak, and fruit is abundant: melons, peaches, pears, and, joy of joys, figs! Eaten with prosciutto or alone, these ripe green figs are a treat of which one never tires. A dessert of the region is *torta di mandorle,* a chocolate almond cake that is rich but light.

On our last night at the San Pietro there was a magnificent display of fireworks, much beloved in southern Italy, set off in nearby Praiano to celebrate the feast of San Gennaro. From the hotel's terrace there was a perfect view of the show, the deafening explosions mercifully muted by distance. The church in Praiano was decked out in colored lights, and all in all it seemed a celebration worthy not only of the venerable Neapolitan saint but also of this extraordinarily beautiful place.

Leaving San Pietro and progressing east on the Drive toward Amalfi, we passed through Praiano. After observing the town from a distance we were intrigued to walk through the main square and church of San Gennaro and to climb to the upper village, where flights of stairs connect the tiny houses.

The Drive, with views changing around each curve, continues its spectacular course for nine kilometers before reaching Amalfi, the largest town on the coast. Built into a deep valley and following the slope of the hills, Amalfi is ideally situated. From the beginning of the ninth until the end of the twelfth century, it was a powerful maritime republic rivaling Venice and Genoa. With a population then of fifty thousand (now seven thousand) Amalfi supplied the Western world with products of the East from as far as Constantinople and Alexandria. It was ruled, like Venice, by doges and produced the first maritime code, which governed conduct at sea. A citizen of Amalfi, Flavio Gioia, is credited with inventing the compass. In 1135 the republic was attacked by the Pisans, and, though Amalfi continued trading with the East, the town was never again to be a naval power.

Amalfi today is an active tourist center. The waterfront is a busy collection of souvenir shops and bars and includes a large parking lot, which, alas, when dozens of tour buses roll in, is not large enough. But a few steps from all of this confusion is the impressive cathedral of Sant' Andrea. With a dramatic geometric façade, the cathedral stands at the head of a broad and dignified stairway. Its fine bronze doors were cast in Constantinople, and the Baroque interior has been extensively restored. The Cloisters of Paradise behind the church are an unusual mix of Romanesque and Arabic. Across the piazza is a fountain and a statue of Saint Andrew, Amalfi's protector, standing in front of a cross and holding a bundle of fish.

A walkway near the cathedral leads under a stone archway to the diminutive Piazza dei Dogi, where the DA BARRACCA *trattoria* is located. A seafood antipasto, spaghetti with shellfish, and a splendid stewlike soup were happily consumed at noon on a sunny Sunday. The soup, or stew, consisted of mussels, octopus, clams, and three kinds of fish in a heady tomato garlic sauce served over a thick slice of bread that had managed to retain its texture. A house wine from a bottle without a label proved more than adequate, and by the time our lunch was over the little piazza was crowded with local folk eagerly awaiting tables.

Less than a kilometer from Amalfi is Atrani, a picture-book village built on either side of a sharp curve on the Drive. With its dining terrace located in Amalfi and its kitchen in Atrani, LA CANTINA DEL NOSTROMO is an unprepossessing but first-rate *trattoria*. *Bruschetto* came to table, warm and fragrant, while we awaited a sauté of seafood, which was a delicious blend of mussels, oysters, tiny clams, sea dates, sea truffles, and razor clams bathed in an aromatic sauce of oil, garlic, and wine. *Marmola*, a delicate white fish, and large, meaty *gamberi* came next, grilled to just the right degree of doneness over charcoal and dressed with a bit of oil and vinegar. This simple but memorable meal ended with pears and cheese.

The road to Ravello branches off the Amalfi Drive at Atrani and climbs steeply in a series of horseshoe turns for four or five kilometers through the Dragon Valley to a site twelve hundred feet above sea level, where this charming town perches. The air is rarefied in this quiet place, and the views toward the sea and the Capo d'Orso are indescribable. All around are vineyards (Ravello wine is choice) and groves of fruit trees, and the stillness is such that the tolling of church bells, the barking of a dog, or the crowing of a rooster constitutes a disturbance of the peace.

Ravello's main square, the Piazza Vescovado, is a peaceful setting for the cathedral, a few shops, and a pleasant café. On Sunday afternoons a solemn uniformed band faces the cathedral in military order and serenades it for an hour or so. No applause, no explanation. The cathedral, founded in 1086, has, like the one in Amalfi, a particularly beautiful pair of bronze doors, as well as an unusual marble and mosaic pulpit supported by six stone lions, which was commissioned in 1272 by a member of the rich Rufoli family.

The Rufoli family were merchants and traders who flourished with the town of Ravello from the tenth to the thirteenth century. The Villa Rufolo, with its wonderful gardens and views of the coast, is one of Ravello's main attractions. Richard Wagner is said to have found inspiration for the stage sets of *Parsifal*'s garden of Klingsor here. Each July a series of concerts is held at the villa, and a more divine location would be difficult to find.

The more contemporary but spectacular Villa Cimbrone, a half-mile walk from the Piazza Vescovado, offers a cloister and a belvedere, complete with statuary, that affords an incomparable view of Minori, Atrani, and the Gulf of Salerno. The garden, with avenues of giant cypress, hydrangeas, and oversize staked dahlias growing in beds of nasturtiums and blue salvia, is unabashedly Italian.

The HOTEL PALUMBO, owned and operated by Pasquale Vuilleumier and his son and in the Vuilleumier family since 1875, is housed in the twelfth-century Palazzo Confalone on a narrow street in Ravello. The hotel is situated around a courtyard with pointed arches supported by Corinthian-capped pillars and floors of handsome blue, red, and black tile. Wooden panels depicting benevolent saints and large terra-cotta planters filled with flourishing ferns give a comforting atmosphere to what is now the lobby-bar area. And of course everywhere are the views that one almost begins to take for granted in Ravello.

The hotel has twenty bedrooms (some in an annex across the street), and each is unique. One room in the tower of the *palazzo* has a huge terrace that overlooks both the valley and the sea and another, on the lowest level, is virtually nestled in the garden with casement windows that open onto lemon trees, impatiens, petunias, and an arbor heavy with grapes. Choice antiques fill the rooms, giving each a distinctive character. Flowers are everywhere—roses, Japanese anemones, carnations, and calendulas—arranged with care by Elena Gambardella, who has served as greeter and concierge for fifteen years.

The dining room at the Palumbo is first-class. We dined on various occasions on *crostini* (smoked salmon and mozzarella rounds), *gnocchi* (souffléed semolina and cheese dumplings), fish served whole with a pungent mayonnaise, and crêpes with pastry cream. (Lorenzo Mansi has been the chef here for twenty years.) This excellent fare was accompanied by the house wine, Episcopio, which Mr. Vuilleumier's family has been producing in Ravello since 1860. (It is available all over Italy and in the United States as well.)

Just down the street from the Palumbo in the Palazzo d'Afflitto is the hotel CARUSO BELVEDERE, where the rooms are comfortable, the view spectacular, and the dining room well worth a visit. *Linguine saracena*, a piquant combination of shellfish, red pepper, garlic, and oil, and a baked eggplant and macaroni dish were two outstanding dinner selections, and the lemon chocolate soufflé, presented in all its puffy glory with one side of the dish lemon and the other chocolate, topped off a superb meal. Mr. Caruso, too, has his house wine, and both the red and white complemented the food to the fullest.

The twelve hundred feet that separate Ravello from the sea have had much effect on life here. Not only is the vegetation different from that of the milder coastal regions (there is no hibiscus or bougainvillea), but there is a distinct sense that the town itself has somehow been fixed in time. Church processions and marching bands are weekly occurrences, and women dressed in black hurry along the cobbled walks with *finocchiona* (fennel salami) and bread in their market baskets. What really sets Ravello apart, though, is the quiet and the air; the feeling is unworldly, closer to the stars, truly magical.

The Amalfi Drive continues south and west from Atrani to Minori, a seaside town with palm trees lining the avenue adjacent to the beach, and to Maiori, a busy spot with a population of over six thousand. Maiori's character is somewhat out of tune with the rest of the coast, for there are unhappily some high rises along the waterfront. The road in this area is dotted with ancient stone towers bearing such names as Cesare, Normanna, and Torre di Badia, reminders of less peaceful days.

Erchie is a village situated among lemon groves and surrounded by vineyards. It started as a Benedictine convent around the year 1000 and was later devastated by the Saracens; a monumental stone tower commemorates this lugubrious event. Cetara, the next settlement, is a busy center for deep-sea fishing, where fishermen leave home for months at a time and return with catches that supply markets throughout the Mediterranean. Like most of the communities on this coast, Cetara has a history of constant change, governed at one time or another by the Saracens, the Dukedom of Amalfi, and the Turks. Regardless of the upheavals, life along the coast seems to have remained basically unchanged.

The last town on the Amalfi Drive is Vietri, famous for the manufacture of ceramics. The main street consists of countless shops where vases, plates, animal figures, and in fact most of the type of pottery one sees throughout Italy are displayed. The factories are here, and one, Solimene, on the Via Madonna degli Angell a kilometer or so out of town, manufactures the charming plates used at the Hotel San Pietro in Positano. Solimene will pack and ship anywhere.

Off the southwest shore of the Amalfi coast are the small Galli Islands, sometimes known as the Siren Islands. Legend has it that Ulysses had himself roped to the mast when he sailed past these islands so that he could resist the seductive call of the sirens who dwelt there. The sirens still call today, but happily one need not resist them. As Bernard Berenson once wrote of the area, "You have to see it to believe it."

SWITZERLAND—TICINO

Lugano's Vintage Festival

UGANO, A SMALL and attractive city, lies on the shores of the lake of the same name that forms the border between Switzerland and Italy. The city itself is Swiss but a real mixture—in language, custom, and general ambiance—of both Swiss and Italian. It has been said that the Ticinese, the inhabitants of Switzerland's Ticino, suffer from an identity crisis, that they themselves cannot decide who they are. But to a visitor the dichotomy provides a thoroughly pleasant atmosphere.

The Festa della Vendemmia, or the Festival of the Vintage, has taken place in Lugano since 1932. On the first weekend in October the city is turned over to a variety of traditional entertainments that for years have been synonymous with the gathering of the grapes. The philharmonic orchestra from neighboring Castagnola, a group of mandolin players from nearby Gandria, and innumerable folk groups who dance in costume, tossing bright flags in the air, are just part of the fun. The festival's pièce de résistance, a parade down the length of the lakeside boulevard, takes place two days into the festivities, on Sunday afternoon.

Our own enjoyment of the festival was enhanced by a stay at the HOTEL SPLENDIDE ROYAL, a little way out of central

Lugano, in Paradiso. The hotel, opened in 1888, is just what its name would indicate, both splendid and royal. An old guest list boasts such names as Vittorio Emanuele di Savoia; Maria, queen of Romania; and a plethora of princes, dukes, and counts. The surroundings equal the guests in grandeur: The lobby is gleaming and modern now, and new additions include an indoor pool and a wing of bedrooms and suites, but the main public rooms are as old world as one could wish. The hotel's pleasant restaurant, La Veranda, has tables overlooking the Riva Caccia, the quayside, and the lake. Flowers brighten every corner, and a large serving table temptingly displays treats in store. Service in the restaurant is impeccable, as it is throughout the hotel, and we dined happily on, dried beef from the Grisons, *penne* with *porcini* and tomatoes, veal cutlets with morels, and kidneys *alla Turbigo*—a wonderful concoction of kidneys with sausage and tomato. Accompanied by the white Merlot of the Ticino, it was a fine start for a visit to the wine festival. Bedrooms in the old part of the hotel are the ultimate in old-fashioned comfort, and ours, with its walls of soothing beige outlined by white trim, and a patterned blue carpet that blended with brocaded velvet on the chairs and chaise longue, had a balcony overlooking the lake. The armoire, dressing table, and bureaus are painted in the Venetian manner with sprays of roses, and the beds—complete with linen sheets, down comforters, and ample square pillows—are a delight. Large bathrooms and tubs, heated towel racks, and two sinks add to the comfort of guests. Our breakfasts arrived unfailingly promptly, accompanied by a newspaper, and the room staff was expert and, as a result, unobtrusive. Aniello Lauro is the hotel's dedicated director; his staff is proof positive of that dedication and of his professionalism.

High up the hill in Paradiso, on the Via del Boschetto, is the LOCANDA DEL BOSCHETTO. A huge grill with a fire so hot that it brought to mind a mini-inferno greets the visitor to this busy, noisy, and informal eating place. In front of the grill stands the stalwart and apparently ovenproof chef preparing meats and fish. The rustic, all-wood, no-frills restaurant accommodates patrons who have that unmistakable air of satisfied diners. Dinner was comprised of a delicious seafood salad followed by spaghetti with tiny clams in their shells, grilled swordfish, and *gamberi* (large shrimp) and was accompanied by an exemplary house white wine. The Locanda is a taxi ride from the Splendide, and a taxi ride in Lugano is a very pleasant experience. Most of the cabs are new or nearly new Mercedes, immaculately cared for, with a driver who invariably hops out of the cab to open the door and almost always bids one *"buon appetito."* This sort of courtesy is the norm here.

Clipped chestnut trees line the delightful lakeside walk from Paradiso to the Parco Civico beyond the center of the city. One strolls past neat, well tended beds of begonias, marigolds, red salvia, and canna lilies, watching the lake steamers cruise to and fro. Situated among sculptures by Arp, Max Bill, and Giacomo Genucchi that dot the park is a small rotunda with eight Doric columns and a bust of "Giorgio" Washington given to the city by Abbondio Chialiva, an engineer from Switzerland, who evidently was a great admirer of our first president.

Happily for visitors, most of the central city is closed to vehicular traffic during the festival, so walking and exploring become a real pleasure. A cluster of men's and women's clothing boutiques and jewelry shops (watches galore at the vast Bucherer's and at Gioielleria Steffen, to name just two) form the Via Nassa, Lugano's main shopping street. An authentic and colorful cuckoo clock can be purchased at Cleta Rossignoli, a tiny store at number 66, whose proprietress refers to herself as the oldest shopkeeper in Lugano's smallest shop. A little farther along the Via Nassa is Franz Carl Weber, a first-rate toy store. Innovazione, Lugano's biggest department store, has its main headquarters on the lake and a discount outlet in the center of town. Surely no one can resist the temptation of Vanini—a very special chocolate store. This is, of course, chocolate country, and, not surprisingly, bars, boxes, and blocks of every type are sold all over the city. Food shops show geographic trends, with large varieties of sausages and cold cuts that look more Swiss than Italian. Bally, the well-known Swiss leather concern, is located on the Via Pessina, near the Via Nassa, and, at Via Canova 7, Gusberti is a fine shop for porcelain, silver, and other household items.

Piazza della Riforma is Lugano's main meeting place. The spacious, open square, lined with cafés and housing the large town hall, also has its share of banks—thirty-five in all despite the city's population of a mere twenty-eight thousand. The top floors of these buildings are apartments and *pensioni*, whose balconies are ablaze with beautiful double pale pink geraniums.

On Tuesday and Friday mornings the food market is held in the piazza, where local farmers add their displays of fresh eggs, flowers, honey, and home-baked breads to the regular rows of large stalls selling vegetables and fruits and wagons laden with cheese. Every twenty minutes a small train runs from a corner of the piazza on a short turn around the city center. Small children climb on board enthusiastically, bidding farewell to their mothers as though departing on the trans-Siberian express. Squares of pavement just off the piazza form a huge chessboard complete with two-foot-high chessmen, where some of Lugano's male citizenry contentedly spend an afternoon of serious play.

Just behind the Piazza della Riforma on Via Pessina is BIANCHI, one of Lugano's oldest and most respected restaurants. Entering, one has the sensation that time stopped here fifty years ago: The setting is gold brocade and paneled walls, chandeliers, red carpet, and red upholstered chairs. Crisp white napery and brightly colored flowers grace each table. Signora Bianchi greets the guests just as her family did before her. *Trittico del Cenacolo*, a selection of three pastas, is a house specialty: *tagliarini* with cream and mushrooms, *ziti* with meat sauce, and a delicate ravioli with spinach. *Piccatina di vitello con funghi freschi* (small slices of veal with mushrooms, and one of the most delicious combinations imaginable) followed the pasta, and calves' brains with sage proved to be another first-rate entrée. Both were accompanied by small deep-fried rounds of mashed potato with pine nuts—also a house specialty. A fine white Pinot Grigio was well suited to the dinner, and raspberries with cream provided the grand finale. Kidneys *alla Bianchi* are flambéed at the table, and particularly recommended by the restaurant's regulars is the curried shrimp. Throughout the wine festival and the autumn a great selection of game appears on menus around the city, so one can feast on quail, pheasant, and partridge cooked a variety of ways. There is nothing *nouvelle* about Bianchi; instead one eats as in a more gracious era long past—at leisure and at peace.

A funicular goes from the Piazza Cioccaro to the railroad station high above the city. Walking down from the station provides the opportunity of a visit to the cathedral of San Lorenzo, a Gothic church with Baroque ornamentation and a stunning Renaissance façade. On a clear day the terrace in front of San Lorenzo offers a magnificent view of the lake and its environs. Via Cattedrale, lined with wool and linen shops and places to buy local souvenirs, is a walkway of steps that wends its way back down to the city. Here again we were aware of a distinctly Swiss influence in the knick-knacks and chalet-style buildings.

RISTORANTE OROLOGIO, on the Via Nizzola, north-east of the Piazza della Riforma, is another well established and traditional Lugano eatery. Run by Signor Vincenzo Campanile, the restaurant has the air of a no-nonsense *trattoria*. An Italian friend once told me that most of his countrymen are suspicious of restaurants with fancy décor. If they suspect that effort and money have been put into unnecessary embellishments rather than into edibles, they feel the owner's priorities may have been misplaced. Orologio would set these purist minds to rest. Dinner began with an interesting prosciutto *salmonato*. The waiter explained that this prosciutto, which is found only locally, derives its unusual flavor from being cured and hung along with salmon. Bizarre though this sounds, it was in fact delicious. The pasta course was *tagliarini alla nonna* with porcini, truffle paste, and cream followed by a perfect veal chop cooked simply with sage. A house specialty, *filetto Orologio* (filet mignon with Cognac cream sauce), is another extraordinarily tempting and satisfying dish. The filet is flambéed at tableside, a method that, in Lugano, is accomplished with frequency and flair.

The maritime authority provides a variety of pleasurable ways to explore Lake Lugano by boat, and we decided to take the grand tour. With Swiss precision our boat left the dock in Paradiso at exactly 2:38 P.M. and returned to Paradiso at 5:20 P.M. A stately cruise on the steamer reveals the charming fishing village of Gandria on the Swiss-Italian border, a favorite subject of visiting artists, and, on the lake's southern shore, picturesque towns that can be reached only by water. Campione d'Italia, an Italian enclave, is the next port of call; there the main attraction is a gambling casino. (Residents of the town, Italian citizens, are apparently allowed to play the tables only on the last day of each year, but the reason for this curious law was never explained to us.) Next we sailed under the railroad bridge that divides Italy from Switzerland. Monte Generoso towers over the lake at this point, at a lofty 5,605 feet the highest peak in the region. We docked briefly at Morcote, another quaint village, with house façades sporting colorful coats of arms and several pleasant places to lunch. A half-hour stop on the "grand tour" at Bissone allows the traveler to take in the small museum, Casa Tencalla. On view here are furnishings that convey an idea of the past way of life of patrician Ticinese. Restoration has preserved the house's original seventeenth-century construction.

If the Thyssen-Bornemisza collection at the Villa Favorita in Castagnola were the only attraction in Lugano, it alone would make a visit to the city worthwhile. The permanent collection is open on weekends from Good Friday to the second Sunday of October. (For special collections the hours may be different.) The villa can be seen from the lake, sepia-colored with elaborate trompe l'oeil scrolls, shells, and pomegranates around its casement windows and its neat gravel walks lined by magnolia trees and trimmed lawns. In the 1920s Baron Heinrich Thyssen-Bornemisza began collecting European paintings from the fourteenth through the eighteenth centuries. He acquired the Villa Favorita in 1932 and proceeded to have the gallery constructed. When the baron died in 1947, his son, Baron Hans Heinrich Thyssen-Bornemisza, inherited both the collection and the villa and a year later opened the gallery to the public. Since then he has not only completed his father's collection but has also added many works of later periods. It is a truly impressive accumulation displayed in a stunning setting.

Two charming polychrome enameled terra-cotta Della Robbia angels in blue tunics holding large candles adorn the entrance to the galleries. Upstairs the visitor gets a dramatic first view through five pink marble doorways to the golden "Votive Painting with the Two Saint Johns and Donor," painted in 1410 by an unknown English artist. Also on exhibit is the superb Cranach "Nymph Reclining by a Spring," painted between 1526 and 1530, and Ghirlandaio's wonderful "Portrait of Giovanna Tornabuoni," with the inscription, "Could you, art, represent also character and virtue, then no finer painting could exist on earth," and the date, 1488, beneath it. We were particularly struck by an early El Greco "Last Supper," painted while the artist was studying in Venice and much under the influence of Tintoretto, and a bucolic depiction of the "Rape of Europa" by Vouet. Two portraits, Holbein's Henry VIII of England, believed to be the only portrait executed entirely by him, and Velazquez' study of Maria Anna of Austria, are first-rate. It is an indescribably rich collection and one that demands to be visited again and again. Suffice it to say that this is possibly the finest private collection in the world and that it in fact surpasses those of many a prestigious museum.

Lugano's wine festival more or less takes over the entire center of the city, and visitors arrive by the busload from far and wide. The streets become jammed with stalls selling anything from flatirons and fox fur pieces to huge round breads, ropes of garlic, and yellow and purple onions. Tents are set up over trestle tables and benches at which one can lunch to the accompaniment of brass bands, mandolins, and accordions. Whole pigs roast on spits, and grilled white bratwurst and risotto and *gnocchi* fill huge vats that are lovingly stirred and tended by visiting chefs. The red and white Merlot of the region, the raison d'être of the festa, flow, and the atmosphere in this beautiful scenic setting is one of great conviviality.

The two-hour-long parade—and what a parade!—takes place on Sunday afternoon alongside the lake. Participating are a dozen different folk groups from the region: flag bearers in bright Renaissance tunics such as one sees at the Palio in Siena, hurling and twirling their banners of scarlet, purple, canary yellow, and black; a group of women from Figino in layered yellow, red, and green skirts and headbands; and pipers in tartan kilts who come not, as one might expect, from Edinburgh but from Lucerne. The floats, at least twenty of them, depict every aspect of winemaking: grapes being harvested, winepresses at work, wine flowing from wooden spigots, and even, to sustain the workers, bread baking in old ovens. Covered with fresh flowers, as are the tractors that pull them, the floats travel down the avenue to the cheers of on-lookers. A small trolley car, a veritable bower of flowers carrying mandolin players, signals an end to the parade. It is a delightful spectacle, and one cannot help but be impressed with the creative effort and planning that have helped make this yearly event such a success. Impressive too is the fact that by nine o'clock the next morning the city of Lugano is tidy and immaculate as though nothing had ever happened.

Villa Ciani in the Parco Civico is Lugano's own museum. This collection includes paintings by Matisse, Pissarro, Utrillo, and Rousseau housed in a classical villa reconstructed in 1839 for the brothers Giacomo and Filippo Ciani. Distinctive and charming aspects of the museum, which was bought by the city in 1912, are the dished ceilings on the first and second floors. One is painted with bright blue peacocks, another with an elaborate seascape, and yet another entirely with swans in round medallions. Outside, in the well cared for and much used gardens of the Parco Civico, benches are set among hydrangeas, wisteria, and flowering annuals, providing a pleasant place to spend an hour or two reading in the sunshine. Or one can simply stroll in the shade of huge old chestnut trees, maples, and beeches. The Villa

Malpensata, on the Riva Antonio Caccia, is also part of the museum, housing exhibits of all sorts that change several times a year.

A short distance from the park, on the Viale Cassarate, lies a new addition to the city's dining scene, AL PORTONE. The chef, Roberto Galizzi, and his wife run an attractive and excellent restaurant. Wooden wine racks, vases of flowers, and platters of fruits and cheeses provide a pleasant welcome at the door, and walls of white stucco set off to good effect the Oriental throw rugs on the floors. The lobster bisque was smooth and delicious, a cream of avocado soup with caviar and a ragout of salmon were memorable, but turbot with duck liver and braised endive was superb. For dessert we were served fresh and light fruit *sorbets* with spirits that enhanced and accentuated their flavors—apple *sorbet* with Calvados and pear *sorbet* with *poire William*. The chef is innovative and obviously has a firm foundation in classic cooking techniques. His daily menus and recipes are tailored to the nature of the produce currently available in the market so that lunch or dinner at Al Portone is always a pleasant surprise.

Lugano, with its sheltered and attractive lakeside situation, is curiously not among the most visited of European cities. To me, this aspect adds enormously to its appeal. The city's ambiance is friendly, slow-paced, and manageable; the hotels and restaurants are good; boat tours on the lake add variety; and the parks and gardens are readily accessible. If a visit to Lugano can be arranged for the early part of October, the wine festival—celebrating traditions rooted in centuries of folklore—is indeed a unique and gala event.

SOUTHERN CLIMES

San Miguel de Allende

*S*AN MIGUEL DE ALLENDE is one of central Mexico's legend-ary "silver cities." About 160 miles north of Mexico City, at an altitude of about 6,500 feet, it enjoys a pleasant spring-like climate year round and a charming colonial atmosphere now strictly protected by historic preservation building codes. Silver was discovered in the north central plateau in 1548 by Spaniards who had, in fact, been searching for gold; by the eighteenth cen-tury towns like Guanajuato, Querétaro, and San Miguel were prospering, boasting handsome town houses and elaborate and costly churches. In 1810 wealthy Mexicans of Spanish extraction, Mestizo (mixed Indian and Spanish ancestry), and Mexican In-dians, all of whom had been denied a say in government by the Spaniards, rose up in what turned out to be the bloodiest of revo-lutions. The fighting lasted for over ten years; independence was finally won in 1822—but not without many lives lost on both sides. The town of San Miguel became San Miguel de Allende in honor of her native son, Ignacio Allende, who had organized an army and is considered to be one of the leaders of Mexico's inde-pendence movement. This revolutionary history is still palpable throughout the town.

Situated on an excellent road from Mexico City, San Miguel

is surrounded by mountains in an arid-brown landscape, punctuated by scrubby trees. The original cobblestones on the streets are rough and unmatched, and both walking and driving on them can be unsettling. The townspeople assert with pride that the cobblestones are authentic and to replace them would sacrifice colonial flavor. The *zócalo*, or *jardín*, in the Plaza Allende is the center of the town's activity and is surrounded by handsome shops, offices, and the Palacio de Gobierno (city hall). Neat, clipped laurel trees, iron benches with elaborate filigree, and a garish bandstand grace the well tended park, where fruit and newspaper vendors sell their wares. At midday many of the town's foreign residents come here to pick up their newspapers and hear local news. La Parroquia de San Miguel Arcangel, the pink parish church, dominates the square. Its pointed Gothic spires rise up, delicate and well proportioned, and the interior sparkles with giltwork and brick. The Archangel stands guard over the central altar in full armor, surrounded by the blue and white tiles that lend the walls of the church its Mexican character. A small chapel has two murals by A. Tommi, a painter who seems to be much influenced by Diego Rivera. The Templo de San Rafael, next door to the Parroquia, features floors of pale blue tile, and a charming statue of Saint Anthony of the Pig presides.

The market of San Miguel is a daily spectacle. On Saturdays and Sundays there are many booths of clothes and household items, and the food and flower markets seem to be virtually inexhaustible. Outdoor stalls along narrow aisles sell dozens upon dozens of varieties of peppers in every shape and color, bunches of glistening scallions, the largest pecans extant, and three-feet-tall piles of avocados. One vendor, wrapped in the ubiquitous rebozo (shawl), was settled among pineapples, papayas, oranges, and limes, looking as though the fruit had been carefully piled around her and she would succeed in extricating herself only when all the produce had been sold. The indoor market is perfumed with stock, freesia, carnations, and roses. In fact, one is reassured, in this flower-loving country, that blossoms still smell as they should and that flowers are happily affordable. Two churches abut the market: Templo de San Francisco—all pink and elaborately carved and mutely inhabited by brown-clad Franciscan statues—and Templo de Nuestra Señora de La Salud, filled with white gladiolas. The churches are places of constant activity. If mass is not in progress, a steady stream of visitors, usually women wrapped in their rebozos, walk from one statue to the other as though they were paying a call. They probably are, for Latins treat their saints with an intimacy reserved for the immediate family, sometimes thanking them for favors received and other times chastising them for requests unanswered. A note was pasted at the feet of Saint Nicholas in the Salud, which read, "Thanks to San Nicolacito for the favor of curing me of an illness which lasted 40 days and 40 nights in the year 1945. I apologize for taking so long to thank you." The date on the note: January 24, 1984.

Shopping is impossible to avoid in Mexico. If you do not go into a shop, shops will come to you. Everything from leather goods, jewelry, and even toothpaste—an item for some reason in short supply in the *farmacia*—is sold on the street. Basket vendors, almost hidden under mountains of their wares in every shape, size, and color, patiently ply their trade day after day in the *zócalo*. There are, however, many shops in San Miguel worth investigating. The Casa Canal at 3 Canal Street has attractive Mexican-made dresses, long and short, embroidered and plain, in a wide choice of stunning colors. Behind the dress shop, in

and around the court of a particularly handsome house, is a treasure trove of furnishings and bric-a-brac, mostly old, but some
contemporary pieces are available too. Across the street at Number 14 is Casa Maxwell, where any souvenir—ceramic, glass,
or locally made clothing—can be found. The Casa Cohen at 25
Calle Reloj is a hardware store but also offers handsome accessories—knockers, bathroom fixtures, accoutrements for the bar,
and number and name plates for one's front door. In a little court
across from the Centro Cultural Ignacio Ramirez, known as the
Bellas Artes, is another attractive shop that sells the work of
local artisans, and the Casa Vidrio (glass house) carries a fine
selection of popular, heavy, brightly colored table glasses. On the
zócalo, El Colibri sells art supplies to the many professional and
amateur painters who populate San Miguel. They also have an
always-welcome stock of books in English. Silver and turquoise
jewelry are not hard to track down here, and Julio, also on the
square, has a particularly comprehensive selection.

Walking along the cobbled residential streets, never seeing
beyond the excessively plain, almost shabby façades, one could
easily deduce a false impression of San Miguel. But behind the
heavy wooden doors courtyards and gardens abound, resplendent with bougainvillea, orange trees, and jacarandas. Many of
these houses are open to the public every Sunday, when tours
are provided to benefit La Biblioteca Publica (the public library).
Tickets are sold on the day of the tour in the library's courtyard. Notices of tour times and places are posted in many of the
hotels. Another fascinating private garden, that of Mr. Stirling
Dickinson, is most generously open daily from 11 A.M. to 3 P.M.
A well-known expert on orchids, Mr. Dickinson has been a resident of San Miguel since 1937 and has, in addition to many other
accomplishments, written several books on Mexico. The name

of his house is Los Pocitos, and it is high on a hill at 38 Santo Domingo, with a splendid garden and greenhouses filled with innumerable varieties of orchids.

San Miguel is known as a cultural center in Mexico, and one of its main drawing cards is the Instituto Allende. Opened as an art school in 1938, it became the Instituto in 1951 and now offers year-round courses for adults in such diverse subjects as drawing, graphics, photography, silverwork, and batik and a complete program in all levels of Spanish. Some courses offer credits transferable to American institutions. The aforementioned Bellas Artes offers instruction in the performing arts and frequent lectures and concerts. Housed in an impressive stucco and brick building with a center court, the school was originally a convent but was formally inaugurated in 1962. An impressive mural painted in 1948 by the Mexican artist Siqueiros depicts the life and work of General Allende.

The CASA DE SIERRA NEVADA is probably the most elegant hotel in San Miguel. It consists of eighteen rooms and suites situated in three old houses on either side of Hospicio Street in the center of town. Luxurious and colonial, the main house of the hotel has a spacious courtyard where bougainvillea, pink impatiens, and a huge cherimoya tree proliferate. Adjacent is the reception, a comfortable bar with a fireplace, and the stuccoed, wooden-ceilinged dining room. The food is excellent and the service in the dining room, exemplary. There are Mexican dishes on the menu, such as *guacamole* and enchiladas, as well as homemade pasta and a good selection of shrimp and meat dishes. It is a popular spot with San Miguel's American colony. Though all the rooms in the hotel are attractively decorated—mostly with local furnishings—the ones on the second floor are particularly choice, complete with terraces and delightful views of the town.

For the athletically inclined, the golf course and tennis courts at the local country club are available for guests of the hotel and La Loma, a beautifully maintained stable just out of town on the road to Dolores Hidalgo, provides horseback riding by the hour with or without private instruction. There are thermal springs to be explored too. The Sierra Nevada will make arrangements for guests who wish to take the waters at the spa, La Gruta. Peter Wirth owns the Sierra Nevada and, as a member of the Swiss family that owns the Hassler in Rome and other hotel properties, has all the experience and credentials required to run a good hotel.

The HACIENDA HOTEL TABOADA, eight kilometers along the road to Dolores Hidalgo, has a fairly elaborate spa, two thermal pools, and a place for lunch. This is a popular spot on weekends for Mexican family outings and at other times for business conventions. The VILLA JACARANDA, a small hotel at 53 Aldama—also in town—has rooms that are small but well furnished and boasts a small pool. The bar and the dining room have recently been renovated; they're bright and pleasant. Set meals, primarily for hotel guests, should be ordered ahead, but also available is a limited á la carte menu, from which I sampled a soup and the apple pie, both good. The hotel is owned by an American couple, Gloria and Don Fenton.

The VILLA SANTA MONICA, a bit beyond the center of town but still within walking distance of it, overlooks Benito Juarez park. Once a private hacienda, it was bought in 1969 by an American, Betty Kempe, and was transformed into a guest-house with eight bedrooms. The rooms are built around a court, complete with fountain, doves, potted plants, and an espaliered yellow-blossomed tree, called *copa de oro* (cup of gold). A parrot, named Far Out presides by the pretty, small-tiled swimming pool. Meals are served in the dining room on chilly nights and at tables in the courtyard when weather permits. I sampled Peggy Zavala's delicious tortilla soup here, a pungent broth with avocado and tortillas, *pollo suiza* (chicken in green sauce), and corn pudding. Here, too, we were given *nopales*, the oval fleshy joints of a cactus that grows abundantly in this part of the country. The sharp thorns are scraped off and the joints are cut into small pieces and boiled till tender. *Nopales* have a distinctive taste and texture and are particularly good in salads. All in all the Santa Monica provided the best food we had. Staying there is like being at a very pleasant house party where the hostess, Natalie Spencer, does everything to ensure her guests' comfort. The kitchen is in the competent hands of Belen Rosas.

Motels in San Miguel are small, and often rooms are reserved from year to year, particularly in the winter months. Many of the foreign colony either own or rent houses and apartments; real estate agents can accommodate visitors with short- or long-term rentals.

Two restaurants in San Miguel are particularly worth visiting. LAS BUGAMBILIAS is the most Mexican. Run by two gracious sisters, the restaurant features truly local specialties. Located at Hidalgo 42 in the enclosed court of a town house, the restaurant sports daisies, calendulas, geraniums, and chrysanthemums in full bloom. As one peruses the menu, *antojitos* ("little temptations" or hors d'oeuvres) are brought to the table—they might be *guacamole* or *picadillo* (spicy beef and vegetables), always served with crispy *tostaditas*. There is tortilla soup and *caldo xochiti*, with a fragrant base of chicken broth, and a large selection of enchiladas, tostadas with chicken, and tacos with hot sauce. *Chiles en nogada* are an intriguing specialty: Large dark green *chiles* are stuffed with a mixture of meat, raisins, and almonds, served with a sauce of cream and walnuts, and decorated with pomegranate seeds. Shrimp is prepared in several different fashions, and chicken and pork dishes afford other interesting choices. The restaurant serves sangria and excellent dark Mexican beer in huge schooners. SEÑOR PLATO, at Jesus 7, is also located in a courtyard with a decidedly Spanish ambiance. A pergola in the center of the room is the bar, and tables are set on a handsome tiled floor. One dines surrounded by banana trees and ferns. *Chiles* stuffed with cheese, burritos, and tortillas with sausage are among the items on the menu. The restaurant also specializes in oysters served in myriad ways and grilled meats and is one of the few places in town that serve prime ribs.

Guanajuato, about an hour and a half drive northwest of San Miguel, is a day trip worth doing. The charming colonial city— one of Mexico's most beautifully preserved—is a difficult place in which to drive due to excessively narrow streets and innumerable small plazas. Guides are available at the bigger hotels on the way into town (Real de Minas for one) and they will either drive your car or escort you in theirs. The tour will include first a stop at the cemetery and the bizarre and lugubrious Mummy Museum. Mexicans are reputed to treat death in a matter-of-fact manner, which perhaps explains why the guides in Guanajuato insist on showing visitors through the grim hall of mummified bodies. It is not an outing for the faint of heart.

Next comes a visit to one of the mines of the region, Mina Valenciana. From 1760 to 1810 this mine produced seventy-five percent of all the silver mined in the world. Reopened in 1970, it is in working order now, and a tour provides a look at mining methods. A shop in the premises sells quartz and ores. The extraordinary church called La Valenciana, or San Cayetano, in all its pink splendor, is on a hill above the town. Constructed by silver baron Don Antonio Obregon y Alcocer to give thanks for his great fortune, it was dedicated in 1765. Inside, the twenty-four-carat giltwork on three elaborate Rococo altars is breathtaking. The pulpit is of cedar and mahogany, inlaid with ivory, and the massive organ was brought from Germany in 1790. This is but one of eighteen churches in the town. The marketplace in Guanajuato is housed in an unusual building that was constructed by the builders of the Eiffel Tower to be used as a trolley car station. It was never put to that use and now, instead, is a clean and airy market with produce on the first floor and ceramics and crafts on the second. At Calle Positos 49 is the birthplace of muralist and painter Diego Rivera. The small house is a museum featuring turn-of-the-century furnishings and the artist's earlier works. The guides enlighten visitors on the bloody history of Guanajuato during the 1810 revolution, while they drive the panoramic road with its view of the valley and the city. The MOTEL GUANAJUATO welcomes the traveler for lunch. The Hacienda de San Gabriel in Maf1, on the way back to San Miguel, is a beautifully restored 1690 hacienda. The dramatic landscaping, the birds, the palms, and the delightful summer houses refresh a flagging spirit.

Dolores Hidalgo, forty kilometers east of San Miguel, is primarily of historical interest, for here the parish priest, Father Hidalgo, gave such an impassioned sermon that it launched the Mexicans into war against the Spanish royalists. This proclamation is known as "El Grito," or the Cry for Freedom. The parish church of Our Lady of Sorrows boasts splendid parquet floors and sophisticated wood carvings. On the road back from Dolores Hidalgo, seven miles from San Miguel, is a small and poor settlement, Atotonilco, which has a well-known monastery. Founded in the eighteenth century, it is now a spiritual center and a famous shrine for penitents. The walls of the church are completely covered with murals, employing every type of Mexican art and depicting figures lurid with details of mortification of the flesh. One wall of the chapel is painted and plastered in an unusual manner to resemble lace. The atmosphere is decidedly eerie.

The great revelation of Mexico is her people. Endowed with a grace and cheerfulness that has little relation to their worldly circumstances, they are a gentle, courteous, kind, and patient people. Though one may see children shabbily dressed and even begging, one seldom sees babies crying, perhaps because they are always held, securely wrapped in mother's or grandmother's rebozo, a garb that reputedly protects the infant from evil winds until he or she has been baptized. In the cities car horns are seldom heard, nor are loud radios, motorcycles, or even raised voices, all of which seems to suggest the innate good manners of Mexicans. A response to a thanks that is frequently heard says it best, *"para servirle"*—in order to serve you.

Oaxaca

*O*AXACA—CAPITAL OF Mexico's southern state of the same name, situated on the huge Oaxaca Valley plateau some 250 miles southwest of Mexico City and ringed by the beautiful mountains of the Sierra Madre del Sur—is an attractive colonial city of 400,000. The town has a palpable Indian presence, and its traditional festivals, dress, and handicrafts have remained remarkably intact in spite of some infringement of modern ways.

There is no better place to sample the spirit of Oaxaca than in the town's handsome *zócalo*, or public square—a space that gives new meaning to the cliché, open-air living room. The northern side of the square is dominated by the cathedral, begun in 1553 and finished in the eighteenth century; and giant laurel trees—their massive trunks painted white—shade the *zócalo*'s benches, paths, and constant stream of strollers. Vendors, often young boys, sell everything from balloons and cotton candy to textiles and handicrafts in stacks taller than they are.

In the center of the *zócalo* a bandstand of white filigree is the scene on alternate evenings of concerts by military and marimba bands, and every Sunday afternoon the concert given by the Banda Sinfónica del Estado from 12:30 to 2 is broadcast on the local radio station. Folding chairs and programs are provided, and visitors and locals alike enjoy themselves immensely. The Sunday concert I attended offered a happy mix of selections— from Smetana's *The Bartered Bride* and a charming waltz, "Morir por to Amor," or "To Die for Your Love," by Belisario de Jésus García to the overture from *My Fair Lady*. Sundown each day sees the lowering of the national flag in a ceremony of great fanfare in which uniformed battalions of schoolchildren take part accompanied by a band.

The *zócalo* is surrounded by restaurants, hotels, some shops, and several cafés, among which El Zaguan, Del Portal, and El Jardín are good spots, day or night, to settle at a table for chocolate, beer, or a bite to eat. The popular *torta*, a large roll filled with ham, cheese, or chicken and generally garnished with slices of avocado and tomato, makes a satisfying lunch or supper. For more serious eating, with fine views from their second-floor windows, Mi Casita and El Asador Vasco overlook the *zócalo*'s passing parade.

MI CASITA, on the northwest corner and open only at midday, serves a fine version of *chiles relleños de picadillo oaxaqueño* (chilies stuffed with chopped meat, almonds, and raisins, then dipped in a batter and deep-fried) and *arroz con menudencias* (rice with chicken livers and gizzards). Mexicans take their *comida*, or main meal, anytime from one until five and then eat lightly at night.

EL ASADOR VASCO, above the café El Jardín on the *zócalo*'s southwest corner, opens for lunch and dinner with a vast menu of both Mexican and Basque dishes. The café's *sopa de ajo tolosana* (garlic soup) is one of the best I have eaten. For main courses, *estofado almendrado con pollo* (chicken with almond sauce) and *camarones gigantes al mojo de ajo* (grilled giant shrimp in garlic sauce) are both excellent. Being inordinately fond of tongue, too seldom encountered on menus, we thoroughly enjoyed a dish of stewed veal tongue. *Flans* are a dime a dozen in most Spanish-speaking lands, but El Asador Vasco's version proved to be something special, richer and thicker than the norm. Strolling musicians in black velvet and knee breeches serenade the diners, and later, in the bar, Martha Vasconcelos, an extraordinarily talented singer, renders some of the hauntingly melodious songs of Oaxaca.

The barely audible crowing of a rooster, an omen full of promise, woke me every morning at the HOTEL PRESIDENTE. This splendid hotel, originally the convent of Santa Catalina, established by nuns of the Dominican order in 1576, is set around handsome, well-tended grassy courtyards. Masses of hibiscus, bougainvillea, palms, and exotic hanging plants provide surprises around each corner. A three-tiered fountain plays in one of the courtyards, and another houses the architecturally intriguing nun's lavabo—a domed structure on a circular row of arches holding up a central pool from which water flows to twelve small and twelve larger washing bowls. Bedrooms, once cells but certainly commodious ones, are high-ceilinged and attractively furnished in local textiles and reproductions of colonial furniture. In some, charming faded wall paintings have been preserved.

Meals are served either in a pleasant loggia surrounding the entrance patio of the hotel or in El Refectorio, the old refectory, closed in at one end by an engaging wall of ceramic water jugs embedded in masonry. Sumptuous breakfast buffets are served on open ranges in the ancient kitchen. Roughhewn earthenware casseroles contain beef stew with onions, black beans, tortillas with cheese, sausage and potatoes, and sweet tamales; or one can choose eggs done in any manner, and, of course, fruits— watermelon, papaya, and pineapple. Cereals, breads, and yogurts

accommodate more conventional appetites. Fragrant hot chocolate—made with either milk or water in Mexico and a fine change
from coffee or tea in the morning—is kept warm on the open fire
in a deep green ceramic pitcher.

El Presidente, as the hotel is known locally, tries to please
everyone when it comes to lunch and dinner selections. The menu
includes daily specials and five *platos oaxaqueños*, so you can order the famous *tamales oaxaqueños* (corn tamales with chicken
wrapped in banana leaves and steamed) or enjoy your first exposure to *enmoladas de pollo* (chicken in *mole* sauce). Known as the
"Land of the Seven *Moles*," Oaxaca specializes in this dark spicy
sauce often blended from a combination of various ingredients
including chocolate, bananas, chilies, cinnamon, and black pepper. The hotel, frequently hosting travelers from every corner of
the world, must necessarily cater to tamer tastes and thus also
offers club sandwiches, cheeseburgers, and chef's salads. Also
available are such "international" selections as fish fillets *meuniére*,
jumbo shrimp with garlic, and beef tenderloin Tetrazzini (a new
one to me). The small bar in the pretty swimming pool area, La
Novicias, serves world-class Margaritas and wonderful peanuts
warmed in oil with garlic—ask for *cacahuates*. On Friday nights,
in the large tunnel-vaulted chapel, the hotel throws a lavish buffet
and also hosts a mini *guelaguetza* (literally "gift"), based on the
well-known Oaxacan dance festival that takes place between the
first two Mondays in July. Dancers in traditional dress perform
the steps of nine different regions, culminating in the *Danza de
las Plumas*, or Feather Dance, in which men in extraordinarily
large and colorful feather headdresses act out Spain's conquest
of Mexico.

Two of Oaxaca's many churches are well worth a visit. La
Soledad, northwest west of the *zócalo* on Calle Independencia,

with its Baroque façade and lustrous golden interior, contains the much revered statue of Oaxaca's patron saint, the *Virgen de la Soledad,* or Virgin of Solitude. Dressed in elaborate gold and white brocade over black fabric, a lace collar, and gold crown, she stands majestically over the high altar. A crystal chandelier hangs from the dome, at each corner of the crossing four angels hold smaller chandeliers, and on either side of the altar two cherubs bear staffs with frosted light globes. As is the custom in Mexican churches, there are masses of flowers everywhere, and on the day of our visit ten huge bunches of white gladioli nearly hid the altar. In the square next to the church, tables with umbrellas are set up near stalls that dispense *refrescos* (fruit juices made with almost any fruit in season), granitas, and flavored sweet ices in such flavors as burnt milk, *guanábana* (the tropical sour-sop fruit), and *cacahuate* (peanut).

North of the Soledad at Alcalá and Adolfo C. Gurrión stands the extraordinary church of Santo Domingo. The austere façade does not prepare the visitor for the interior, where white walls contrast with brilliantly gilded and polychromed stucco sculpture. A dazzlingly burnished altar and the elaborately carved family tree of Don Felix de Guzmán—father of Domingo de Guzmán, better known to us as Saint Dominic, or Santo Domingo, founder of the Dominican order—are among its treasures, as is the gemlike Virgin of the Rosary Chapel. Next door, and in fact attached to Santo Domingo, is the Oaxaca Regional Museum. The building was originally built as a monastery, then served time as a barracks, and now houses a large collection of textiles, costumes, ceramics, and archaeological artifacts. A section exhibiting gold jewelry, stone carvings, and other ornaments discovered in Tomb 7 at the nearby ruins of Monte Albán is particularly fascinating.

A handsome eighteenth-century building with a delightful ochre and brick rear courtyard on Alcalá, a pleasant pedestrian street, houses the Museum of Oaxaca. On display is a permanent exhibit of the work of Miguel Cabrera, a Oaxacan religious painter who spanned the seventeenth and eighteenth centuries, and shows of contemporary artists change monthly. Another important museum, the Museo Rufino Tamayo, at 503 Morelos, between Porfirio Diaz and Tinico y Palacios, presents pre-Hispanic objects acquired by the eponymous painter and his wife, Olga, over a twenty-year period. In the seven galleries—each representative of a different Indian culture—the objects in this splendid and unusual collection are perfectly lit and displayed in glass cases painted in wonderful blues, purples, and pinks. Tamayo, one of Oaxaca's most celebrated native sons, donated and dedicated the museum to his hometown in 1974.

The Museo Casa de Juárez, at García Vigil, 60, celebrates the life of Benito Juárez, Mexico's nineteenth-century president and beloved national hero. Juárez, a Zapotec, came as a boy from the nearby village of Guelatao to work for a well-to-do lay preacher. Mementos of Juárez's life are preserved in this charming small central courthouse.

Shopping in Oaxaca is a popular pastime. Handicrafts, a major product of the region, are colorful and, for the most part, well made and reasonably priced. Literally dozens of stores, and also markets and small stands set up by individual vendors on street corners, offer places to browse and buy. ARIPO, *Artesanías e Industria Populares del Estado de Oaxaca* (handicrafts and popular industries of the State of Oaxaca), has probably the most comprehensive selection, in a pretty patio house at García Vigil, 809. The shop carries the handsome black pottery of the region, a variety of hammocks, and a good selection of table linens, along with dozens of the ubiquitous whimsical painted animals that threaten eventually to overrun the whole town.

On Alcalá, YALALAG, at number 104, is respected and well established. Opened in 1957, this is the only shop that sells the beautiful, embroidered white cotton dresses from San Cristóbal de las Casas in Chiapas, Mexico's southernmost state. Every stitch is done by hand, and exquisite needlework embellishes the fine soft fabric. Yalalag also offers a selection of little wooden boxes with figurines of a mariachi band or of a nativity—perfect remembrances for children's rooms. Or, for typically bloodthirsty grandsons of a certain age, little scenes are available in which skeletons engage in all sorts of everyday activities. This fascination with skeletons is very Mexican—a way of remembering that even life's best moments are temporal. *Huipiles*, the traditional Indian tunics from the Oaxacan coast, come in stunning colors derived from shell dyes, and we only just resisted a particularly elegant raw-silk rebozo, or shawl.

LA MANO MAGICA, on the opposite side of Alcalá, is not only a shop but also a gallery where shows of the work of local artists change periodically. Mary Jane Gagnier de Mendoza, a Canadian, and her Oaxacan husband, Arnulfo—a talented weaver whose works are also shown in the gallery—are the owners. The shop carries ceramic pieces by Josefina Aguilar and Dolores Porras, two well-known local artists, and many other colorful examples of regional crafts. La Mano Magica also provide a small eatery where snacks and light lunches can be enjoyed in a pretty courtyard among papier-mâché beasts.

In the busy downtown area, near the market on the corner of Mina and J. P. García, EL ARTE OAXAQUEÑO—an old shop of good reputation though limited space—stocks a large array of engaging hand-fashioned crafts: tin vegetable ornaments for the Christmas tree; peppers, bananas, and eggplants in smashing colors; and a charming magenta half-moon that would spruce up any powder-room door.

Jewelry in Oaxaca, both gold and silver, is a good buy. Attractive pieces—and prices—can be found at three shops on Alcalá. Across from the church of Santo Domingo, at number 501, JOYAS DE OAXACA sells a variety of silver bracelets and earrings and particularly handsome soapstone necklaces in a wonderful blue hue. Heading south, on the same side of Alcalá, at number 301, ARRIAGA JOYEROS DE OAXACA has a workshop in the back where silverware is fashioned for the table and for the tea tray. We couldn't leave behind a beguiling miniature salt and pepper set of silver inlaid with turquoise that looked as though it belonged in a doll's house. We were also tempted by necklaces of round silver balls with earrings to match and a gorgeous silver bracelet with five stones, including onyx and agate.

Farther along on Alcalá, at ARTESANIAS "EL TEQUIO," we found a great selection of tin frames in various sizes that could make intriguing mirrors and more good-looking bracelets, this time chunky silver with malachite. EL ORO DE MONTE ALBÁN, on Gurrión, the street that runs parallel to the Santo Domingo, sells handmade fourteen- and eighteen-karat reproductions of the extraordinary gold pieces found in the tombs of Monte Albán—which, our interest piqued, we were increasingly looking forward to visiting.

The streets of Oaxaca, which are clean and almost litter free, with only the occasional beggar and no homeless, are rife with tantalizing smells. On dozens of corners, women—often with sleeping babies virtually hidden in their rebozos—peel and cut fragrant mangoes, pineapples, watermelon, and papayas, arranging them with careful artistry in plastic bags to sell to hungry passersby and always offering a squeeze of fresh lime and a dusting of powdered chili to enhance the flavors. Also on offer are little sacks of *cacahuates*, irresistibly salted and often still warm.

HOTEL PRINCIPAL and HOTEL MONTE ALBÁN are two small, simple, well-run, and not-too-costly hotels in central locations. Adequate rooms for rock-bottom prices are available at the Principal, on Avenida Cinco de Mayo, just a block south of El Presidente—but no meals, not even breakfast. Monte Albán, on Alameda de León, right next to the *zócalo*, has a dining room and is slightly pricier. Rooms here are also larger, though a bit dark, and the location is such that street sounds float unhindered into the hotel's front rooms.

A short taxi ride north to the hills above the city brings the visitor to the HOTEL VICTORIA. Really a resort, with tennis court, swimming pool, and fine views of Oaxaca, the hotel offers a very different ambiance from the other hostelries in town. Bedrooms are satisfactory and the dining area—a terrace with a splendid view—pleasant. Avocado filled with shrimp, grilled local sole, and *cazuela de mariscos* (shellfish stew), accompanied by a Baja California Calafia '87, made for an agreeable dinner one evening.

A bit farther from the center of town than the Victoria, at Avenida Cuauhtemoc, 205, the restaurant AQUÍ ES CLEMENTE, or "Here is Clemente," is a simple spot with oilcloth-covered tables outside. Clemente himself, in pristine white, cooks tortillas on a clay griddle over an open fire in the traditional manner and suggests items from his menu. Warm tortillas arrive at the table with sliced avocado, *chicharrón* (crisp-fried pork rind), white cheese, a fiery salsa, and the regional chiles pasillas. These long, thin, dark-brown, and incendiary chilies—a great Oaxacan specialty—are eaten casually by the locals as though they were M&M's. With our northern palates, unattuned to such spiciness, we learned to ask for *salsa mexicana*, a gentler sauce of tomatoes, *cilantro* (coriander), and milder chilies. Pieces of tortilla are eaten with the avocado, pork, and cheese as *botanas* (first courses), along with *memelas* (small thick pizza-like tortillas, about six inches across). These are drizzled with the purest rendered *acieto* or, yes, lard. Arteries notwithstanding, they are delicious. For our main course we ordered chicken in a sauce of black *mole* wrapped in tortillas and a platter of roasted meats— beef, pork, and veal—with potato croquettes. White beans with tomato were also served. Ice-cold local beer was our choice to accompany all of this, but we noticed that many Mexicans seem to enjoy lemonade and other fruit juices with their *comida*.

A block north of El Presidente, a small family restaurant, EL TOPIL, on Plazuela Labastida, provides a *comida corrida*, or set meal, that changes daily and also a menu from which one can choose various light dishes. Soups are excellent, particularly the chicken, and there is a variety of tortillas—tacos and *quesadillas* (tortillas that are filled, folded, and then fried or grilled). Service could not exactly be called speedy, but *la señora* cooks everything to order and that both makes for and makes up for a bit of a wait.

South of El Presidente, just a block away on Murguía, EL SOL Y LA LUNA, which calls itself a restaurant, bar, and gallery, is open every evening save Sunday, and here the visitor can enjoy music with dinner—anything from a full band to a trio playing Latin American music. Tables occupy the open courtyard of an old house, and displays of local art enliven the back room. For a change of pace from Mexican fare we sampled and enjoyed extremely good pizzas and a fine mixed salad that we had been told by a Oaxacan friend was "Okay to eat."

Sorne of Mexico's most varied and interesting markets are in Oaxaca's Central Valley. The Juárez market, on Viente de

Noviembre (Twentieth of November) and Las Casas, is a daily indoor food market offering also some clothes, handicrafts, and household effects. Stalls with dozens of varieties of chilies, dried beans, spices, and herbs both fresh and dried provide a positive feast for the senses—as do the stunning arrays of flowers. A bunch of a dozen carefully arranged and trimmed giant freesia and a dozen cobalt-blue bachelor buttons cost just three dollars and filled my hotel room with a ravishing fragrance for a week. Perfect vegetables and fruit (I sampled the juiciest and sweetest pineapple I have ever tasted), cut while you wait, are just some of the treats to be had.

One block south of the Juárez, the Viente de Noviembre market is comprised entirely of stalls serving cooked food. Signs identify the various *comedores*, where diners sit at the counters or tables of their choice to enjoy their favorite cook's dishes. We had a sense that each stall catered to its own set of loyal regulars. Everything looks and smells delectable; fragrant bubbling *guisados* (stews), slivers of beef grilled directly on hot coals with bunches of scallions, and sacks of warm tortillas—opened for a sale and quickly closed again; so the precious warmth is preserved. I suspect that—if one dares—the best food in Oaxaca, short of in a private house, can be found in these markets.

Oaxaca's main market, or *tianguis*—the word used for cooperatives by the Aztecs—is held on Saturdays on Periferico Sur near the turnoff for Monte Albán—a fifteen-minute taxi ride from the *zócalo*. I was lucky enough to have for my guide Patricia Quintana, the well-known cookbook writer, chef, and originator of the Oaxacan culinary tours entitled "Journey in Taste." The State of Oaxaca, or "Land of the Seven *Moles*," is believed to have the most subtle and complex cuisine in Mexico, inextricably tied in with its past.

As we walked through the large permanent buildings and past outdoor stalls shaded from the noonday sun, Ms. Quintana shared with me some of her knowledge of the local gastronomic traditions. We admired artistically displayed vegetables and symmetrical mounds of chilies in shades of green, red, and deep orange resembling perfect still lifes. Bunches of huge red radishes lay next to bright green scallions, creating an eye-catching twosome. Radishes have a deep cultural significance in this region, and homage is rendered to them in the feast of *La Noche de los Rábanos*, or the Night of the Radishes, part of the Christmas celebrations.

When I remarked that basil always seemed to be displayed on tables apart from those offering other fresh herbs, Ms. Quintana explained that basil is never used in cooking but only as a medicinal tea or to ward off evil spirits. Limes, lemons, guavas, and cantaloupes the size of apples are set off to the fullest advantage next to a stall selling *refrescos*—watermelon, papaya, and pineapple—in stunning colors from huge glass jars. The flowers, carnations in every imaginable shade and milk-white lilies, quite overwhelm. Mexicans love flowers, and even the humblest houses boast lovely bouquets.

Comedores, those makeshift dining rooms, satisfy the appetites of buyers and sellers alike, for on market days everyone is too busy to cook. Bread is first-rate in Oaxaca. At any of the markets one can select from mountainous piles of *bolillos* (small hard breakfast rolls), *teleras* (large rolls used for tortas), and *pan de yema* (yellow egg bread). Saturday's *tianguis* is an adventure, a place to buy everything from live turkeys and wooden tortilla presses to the local munching delicacy, *chalupines* (deep-fried grasshoppers). But a word of warning: It is advisable to leave all valuables in a safe at the hotel as visitors stand out, and this is a land where worldly goods are in short supply. Finally the day dawned for the fulfillment of our main purpose for visiting Oaxaca—to view the pre-Hispanic ruins of the Indian settlements of Monte Albán, Mitla, and Yagul in the Central Valley. All three are within easy reach of the city, and day trips to these noteworthy sites add immeasurably to the visitor's enjoyment of Mexico's southern regions. The best strategy is to hire a cab from the hotel, making certain to settle the fare before departing, and head southeast on the Pan-American Highway toward Mitla—a trip of about twenty-four miles.

En route to Mitla we stopped at Casa Chagoya, a mescal-producing plant whose owners seem happy to escort visitors through the process that transforms the *agave* cactus into this local, fiercer version of Tequila. Samples of fourteen different fruit-flavored varieties of mescal are offered after the tour and are also, of course, for sale, along with the one that has the *gusano*, or worm, in the bottle.

Mitla, proclaim the guidebooks, is second only to Monte Albán among the archaeological wonders of Oaxaca. Elaborate geometric stone carvings—rather than the representations of human figures or myths found elsewhere—and intricate handwork distinguish these ruins. Mitla had been a Zapotec enclave of approximately 70,000 souls as early as A.D. 100, although most of the work started by the Zapotec was heavily reworked by the Mixtec, another local Indian group who later took over the city and were still in residence at the time of the Spanish Conquest. Outside the ruins be prepared for some very persistent vendors pushing dolls, textiles, and other handicrafts.

Heading back toward Oaxaca, the smaller ruins of Yagul can be visited on the way to Teotitlán del Valle, the village well known for its weaving. In the ruins at Yagul—dating from about 400 B.C.

and set on a hill with commanding views—a huge ball court, the largest in the Central Valley, has been carefully excavated.

At Teotitlán del Valle, off the Pan-American Highway, a market in the center of town sells dozens of blankets, rugs, wall hangings, and serapes (blankets used as coats, beds, and rugs) in geometric designs. Cab drivers are familiar with Benito Hernández, a third-generation weaver who still uses high-quality methods and natural dyes in his work. He has some stunning rugs to sell and will tell you, with understandable pride, that his work is displayed in New York City's Museum of Modern Art and The Museum of Fine Art, Boston. For a nice lunch stop visit RESTAURANT TLAMANALLI, on Avenida Juárez, owned by the Mendoza family and run by Abagail Mendoza, sister of Arnulfo who owns La Mano Magica in Oaxaca. Abagail, a talented chef, prepares typical Zapotec food—we sampled an intriguing *higadito*, made with chicken and eggs—in a bright new spot where the family's own artwork is also displayed.

For an enjoyable Thursday excursion (in order also to take in the weekly animal market at Zaachila), the beautiful ruins of the roofless Dominican monastery of Cuilapán lie just nine miles southwest of Oaxaca. Started around 1560 and supervised by the same monks who planned Santo Domingo, but never completed, the monastery has a cloister that exemplifies pure Mexican Renaissance. Openings at the end of windswept corridors reveal glimpses of surrounding hills with wildly blue jacaranda; a small garden is ablaze with red geraniums, roses, and evergreens; and no sound, save that of bird song, disturbs the peace.

From the blissful silence of Cuilapán, a drive of a few miles brings the visitor to the town of Zaachila, the last Zapotec capital in the Oaxaca Valley, where the Thursday morning animal market takes place. In a dusty field just outside of town, sheep, cows, pigs, horses, and oxen patiently stand in massive wooden yokes, waiting to be sold or traded. Nine pink piglets, all tied by the leg and squealing hysterically, were being led calmly around by a small boy.

On the way to Tlacolula, the village of Santa María del Tule and "El Tule" itself—a two-thousand-year-old cypress, purported to have the largest girth of any tree in the world—is well worth a visit. A young boy showed us around, shining the beam of his flashlight to point out pieces of bark that mysteriously resembled such diverse objects as a lion, the three wise men, an anteater, and a full bunch of bananas. Another five miles or so brings the turnoff to the small village of Tlacochahuaya, where the sixteenth-century Dominican church of San Jerónimo is located. The church's stark facade gives way to a colorfully frescoed interior of red, green, and blue Zapotec flower folk-decoration on both walls and ceiling. San Jerónimo is one of the few Mexican churches decorated by the Zapotec, and that fact, together with the lavish use of gilt and some admirable woodwork, makes it a truly unique specimen.

A vast and entertaining Sunday market takes place in Tlacolula, some twenty-one miles southeast of Oaxaca, off the Mitla road. Tlacolula's market is crowded and busy, very like the Saturday Oaxaca affair. Sheets of canvas held up on poles shade vendors and their wares from the sun; piles of deep-purple sweet potatoes and tamarinds and wheelbarrows filled with kernels of white corn and cacao beans line narrow walkways; and the startlingly pungent smell of freshly cut pineapple fills the air. At a small table a man whose wide-brimmed hat casts a dark shadow sells used wedding bands for 1,000 pesos, about 40 cents, apiece. Examples of the high-luster green pottery of the region sit displayed on frayed rugs, and in the main square all manner of clothes are for sale. Both the smell and the look of the cooked food here are tempting: Potato croquettes sizzle in oil next to trays of *memelas* covered with green *salsa* and shredded white cheese.

Monte Albán—a six-mile drive west of Oaxaca and the jewel in Oaxaca's crown of ancient ruins—is an absolute must. Its impressive size (the city once covered twenty-five square miles) and eighteen excavations make it one of the more magnificent archaeological sights in Central America, and its position some 360 feet up on a flattened hilltop overlooking the hills and crater-like valley is truly remarkable. It's hard to imagine the amount of labor and ambition required—with the necessarily limited means at the builders' disposal—to level the mountaintop, to construct the temples and palaces, and to cover the entire exterior with a thick layer of stucco, which was then painted, often in bright red. Development continued here until around A.D. 750, when the Zapotec population numbered over 25,000. Following that date, deserted by the Zapotec, Monte Albán began its decline. From the fifteenth century the Mixtec reused some of the tombs, and, in 1932, a vast archaeological find in what is now known as Tomb 7 was uncovered. Most of the discovered treasures can be seen in Oaxaca's Regional Museum. Wandering through the Gran Plaza, or great plaza, one has a fine vantage point from which to examine the ball court, the main pyramid, and the palace, and also to revel in the serenity of the place. Two handsome laurels of India guard the entrance to the site. Guides—many of whom speak English—are knowledgeable and add much to the tour, a small museum displays some artifacts, and a simple restaurant in the museum complex serves a good toasted *torta*.

On our way back to town we passed a funeral procession. Four men carrying a small casket led a cortege that consisted of a band and several dozen mourners bearing huge bunches of flowers. The group had an innate grace and dignity, reminding me of the words of a native Oaxacan who had said, in describing to me her countrymen, that they are "a poor people with a rich internal life." Mexico is a harsh, beautiful, complicated land. It makes me think of a splendid orange tree I saw on a Oaxacan patio, its branches a mass of thorns but nonetheless heavy with the weight of perfect, ripe oranges.

Nevis

*N*evis, ONE OF THE LEEWARD ISLANDS, is situated approximately fifty miles due west of Antigua. With
neighboring Saint Kitts it comprises an associated state of Great
Britain. This island of fifty square miles is enormously varied in
terrain and has one main road, which circles it, covering a distance of about twenty-three miles. The spectacular views from
this road change with each curve and include, along with vast
sweeps of the Caribbean and Atlantic, glimpses of the islands of
Antigua, Montserrat, Redonda, Saba, Saint Eustatius, and Saint
Kitts, whose nearest point is only two miles away. Nevis is a vol-
canic island, with Mount Nevis rising in the center to a height of
3,232 feet above the sea. The land is rough and rockbound, with
much clearing and cultivation required before the two main crops,
sea island cotton and coconuts, can be harvested. The countryside is pastoral; sheep and cattle graze among the divi-divi trees,
and there is widespread subsistence farming. Nevisians grow or
catch most of what they eat, for the surrounding waters abound
with dolphinfish, kingfish, red snapper, wahoo, and the clawless
lobsters of the Caribbean.

Nevis was discovered by Christopher Columbus in 1493, the
second time he ventured from Europe to explore the New World.

The name, one legend has it, was derived from the Spanish word *nieve* (snow), because Columbus surely first saw the mountains covered with fluffy white clouds, which resembled snow. Another legend holds that early Scottish colonists sick for home named the island after their beloved highland peak, Ben Nevis.

When these adventurers first landed, they found an island wild with acacia and thick underbrush and with none of the coconut palms, mangoes, and breadfruit trees that were later imported and that transformed Nevis into the tropical bower it is today. The island was colonized in 1628, but before that it was known to travelers from Holland, Spain, and France who stopped to bathe in its reputedly therapeutic waters. After that, Nevis became a flourishing sugar producer with as many as eighty working sugar plantations, which operated until the 1940s when the difficulties of transporting sugar from so many separate mills rendered the industry unprofitable. Now many of the plantations stand overgrown, their rusted sugar machinery eerie and ghostlike, reminders of a past life and a treasure trove for those who like to explore far off the beaten paths amid wild thyme and marjoram.

The island's main town, Charlestown, on the southwest coast, is an attractive, sleepy little settlement of low wood-and-stone West Indian houses, where the grocery, hardware, and dry goods stores transport one back a century or so. There are two shops offering island-made clothing: Caribee Clothes, which carries men's shirts, women's skirts and dresses, and children's wear embroidered in Nevis, and Caribelle Batik, which utilizes the native sea island cotton and produces batik and tie-dyed cloth, both in lengths and made up into all sorts of apparel. There are also four or five gift shops, including two craft centers, where baskets, straw hats, flour sack shirts, and local pottery are sold. The Philatelic Bureau, a modern air-conditioned establishment, has a handsome display of stamps designed in Nevis. Since the issue of separate stamps for Nevis and Saint Kitts in June of 1980, the bureau has traded with collectors on a worldwide basis.

On a visit to the Charlestown boatyard one can see the local artisans using adzes and other traditional hand tools to construct sturdy fishing boats from timbers cut on the mountainside. Wandering down the main street, one comes to the site of the house where Alexander Hamilton was born. All that remains is a plaque commemorating the event on January 11, 1757, and two flights of stone steps from which one can see the harbor and the sea beyond. The prosperous parish Church of Saint Paul is across the road.

After a morning of sight-seeing we paid a call to the Rookery Nook, an establishment on the town's main street that dispenses food, drink, but most important, all the island news. Stories are exchanged here over a glass of Carib beer or rum, and a bulletin board displays notices of such events as sailboat charters, weekly flights to Montserrat, and a West Indian lunch at Saint George's church in Gingerland.

The favorite mode of transport on the island, where driving is on the left-hand side of the road, is the Mini-Moke, a cross between a golf cart and a Jeep. These are efficient little vehicles for the bumpy roads and steep drives off the main thoroughfares, but most have seen yeoman's service over long years and mechanical problems are a fact of daily Nevisian life. A motorist with troubles need never fear, however, for one or another of the gracious island folk invariably appears as if by magic armed, as often as not, with a trusty screwdriver to examine the mysterious workings under the hood; a pull here, a push there, and you are once more on your way, with a "good day" and a wave.

From Nevis airport, where six- and eight-seater planes connect the island with the rest of the Caribbean, it is a short drive to the NISBET PLANTATION inn. Nisbet's, now a working coconut plantation in addition to a hotel, was once a thriving sugar estate, owned by one of the island's most distinguished families. It was a Fanny Nisbet, widow, who married Horatio, Lord Nelson in 1787. The plantation was made into a hotel after World War II and is a delightful stopping place.

The stone great house now contains the dining rooms and a charming screened-in veranda that runs along three sides of the building. There are cushioned alcoves, comfortable chintz-covered wicker chairs and sofas, straw rugs on the floors, and innumerable plants in ceramic pots hanging from the ceiling. The bar is a gathering place in the evenings, and the dining room, the handsomest on the island, has large windows that open on a stately grove of coconut palms and a broad grass avenue that leads to the beach. Ceiling fans turn slowly, and at night, with antique tables set with straw mats, blue-and-white old "Willow" china, and flickering candlelight, one can easily imagine living the life of a West Indian planter. Efficient young serving women slip in and out carrying platters of breaded turtle steak, boiled lobster, and broiled dolphinfish, which might be accompanied by a breadfruit pudding or gingered carrots and followed by a coconut soufflé made from the fruit of the trees on the grounds.

The sleeping quarters are ten cottages between the great house and the beach that contain two bedrooms and two baths each and are named for the old plantations of Nevis: Dogwood, Gingerland, Coconut Walk, Spring Hill, and Paradise. They are simply but comfortably furnished and have small porches that are conducive to happy hours of reading or resting. There is one tennis court, a beach with swimming and snorkeling, plenty of chairs, and shade from the palms. (Beware of falling coconuts, signs warn.) Lunch can be taken either at the great house or on the beach, and on Sundays Nisbet's has a barbecue with music by the water. Marianne and Michael Brewer are the managers. They were formerly at Coco Point Lodge in Barbuda and have brought many guests from there to Nisbet's with them.

Continuing south from Nisbet's on the main road one comes to the church of Saint James at Windward. Made of the local gray stone, with a red-shingled roof, it stands on a high point looking toward Saint Kitts. Its little cemetery is a bower of yellow allamanda, and inside is a rare black crucifix. The ruins of two large plantations lie a few miles beyond Saint James: Coconut Walk, with much of the sugaring plant extant and spectacular palms and views to the sea; and New River, where the caretaker gave us a tour of the points of interest, shooing away pigs, sheep, and goats. The pastures on this side of the island are populated by cattle that chomp on the meager grass, ignoring egrets perched on their backs.

A wooden sign in the shape of a sugar mill identifies the entrance to GOLDEN ROCK ESTATE. A steep, narrow drive winds through a grove of breadfruit, orange, mango, and banana trees and terminates at the hotel, twelve hundred feet above the sea. The setting is uniquely beautiful; the main building is stone, and above the door are the initials E. H. and the date 1815, identifying the builder, Edward Huggins. Surrounded by a courtyard of tropical plants, the house, once the plantation kitchen, contains the dining and public rooms. Trees with such names as monkey-no-climb and elephant ear flourish on the grounds, with poinsettia, hibiscus, and petrea, a lilaclike bush with glorious blue blossoms, sharing the limelight. Small wonder that when breakfast is served in the courtyard one shares the meal with hummingbirds, banana quits, and bold Lesser Antilles bullfinches.

The rest of the hotel consists of five cottages, with two bedrooms in each and porches from which the views are both spectacular and varied, and a converted sugar mill, with a huge canopied four-poster on the second floor and two double beds in the downstairs room that make this a delightful place for a family to settle in. There is a pool at Golden Rock and a hard-surface tennis court and everywhere breathtakingly distracting glimpses of the sea and the nearby islands. Pam, a member of the Huggins family, and Frank Barry are the hosts, and nothing is too much trouble for them if it contributes to the comfort and pleasure of their guests. Ralston Hobson, who tends bar, makes the best rum punch on the island and possibly in the entire Caribbean, and Leonard Williams is the talented chef.

Dinners are served, as is the case throughout the island, with a set menu, and Pam seats the tables of six and eight with the expertise of a practiced hostess. The Saturday night buffet is justly famous: Forty or so diners partake of such delicacies as tania fritters, boiled lobster with lemon mayonnaise, fragrant, steaming curry with coconut, raisins, and mango chutney, and corn pudding. After dinner a local band plays in the courtyard to the accompaniment of the cicadas. The Barrys also have a weekly picnic at Pinney's Beach, where lobsters are brought in by fishermen, cooked in a huge pot on the sand, and devoured by the guests with melted butter and quantities of garlic bread. One of the chief pleasures of a stay at Golden Rock, and in fact in Nevis generally, is that all members of the staff are unfailingly cheerful and eager to make visitors to the island feel welcome. They certainly succeed.

Just down the hill from Golden Rock is the little town of Gingerland. There Saint George's Church is set among dwarf banana and breadfruit trees and has a cool and dignified arched interior. Across the road is the parish house, built of the local gray stone, superbly squared and dressed, where on a breezy February afternoon we were fortunate enough to attend a West Indian lunch given by the ladies of the parish. Tables were set out of doors, and, to the sounds of the Franklin Clarke steel band, we feasted on chicken curry, breadfruit salad, pidgeon peas, and a pungent eggplant casserole. Dessert was a first-rate macédoine of papaya, bananas, pineapple, and mangoes accompanied by homemade cakes.

Continuing down the road from the church, one arrives at the windward, or Atlantic, beach, sometimes wild and rough, but on days when the winds have shifted from their prevailing course a peaceful and unpopulated spot to swim and sun. A little farther along the road is CRONEY'S OLD MANOR ESTATE, another former sugar plantation turned hotel. There is a handsome stone court with a sandbox tree and attractive buildings that once were kitchens, slave quarters, and overseers' apartments and an old steam mill used in the sugaring process. At present the hotel has twenty-two beds and the owner has plans for expansion.

On Friday nights a buffet is set up in the court of the old slave kitchen with candle lamps on the tables and a dinner of baked stuffed lobster and fried bananas served under an extravagantly starry sky. A local band plays here, too, and, as always, adds immeasurably to the festivities. A short distance from Gingerland, driving west, is Eva Wilkin's mill studio, and it is well worth a stop. Miss Wilkin, long a resident of Nevis, is the island's most illustrious painter. Her murals of local scenes can be seen at both Golden Rock and Montpelier, and in her converted cane mill many of her paintings, both originals and prints, are on display. Another talented island artist is Dorothy Cleary, who does fine watercolors and pen-and-ink drawings. Her work can be seen and purchased at Golden Rock.

Farther down the road ZETLAND PLANTATION is perched up a drive on the side of a hill. Modern units make up this hotel, with each cottage having a small kitchen for those who wish to do their own housekeeping. There is a pool and tennis court and a splendid vantage point from which to view the island.

The trip from Golden Rock to HOTEL MONTPELIER should take fifteen minutes at the most, but the day we made the journey we met with an unusual delay: a house moving. Twenty or so men were transporting a small green house from one location to another, and for the better part of an hour the little house sat blocking the road while the logistics of the problem were debated. The traffic waited patiently till the house was finally hoisted onto a truck, and as it moved slowly on so did we. Montpelier is at the end of a side road, once rutted and bumpy but now newly repaired. A huge Ficus benjamina, or Jamaican evergreen, dominates the entrance to the court. Two large cannons guard the doorway of the main building where fine stonework has transformed the old boiling house of the estate into a commodious lounge, a bar, and dining areas. Our breakfast one morning—delicious banana fritters, homemade preserves, and dark local honey—was eaten on the west veranda, which offers a panoramic view of Charlestown Harbor. At lunchtime tables are set on the north porch looking out over the gardens and the sugar mill. On one visit we enjoyed a cold cucumber and mint soup, Jamaican eggs (a delectable concoction of spinach, lobster, and egg), and soursop ice cream.

The bar around the pool is decorated with straw rugs and natural wicker furniture with pillows in a stylish print of navy, gold, and white. Cottages are scattered around grounds planted with oleander, hibiscus, poinsettia, and showy double red and white bougainvillea. The rooms are large and comfortable, with old-fashioned spacious bathrooms, fluffy striped towels, and lots of good wooden hangers. Dinner is imaginative and varied, and much use is made of the local produce. James Gaskell, the owner, is an enthusiastic gardener and raises most of the fruits and vegetables on the place organically. His back garden boasts fennel, parsley, basil, thyme, lettuce, onions, peppers, and an orchard that includes orange, lime, avocado, mango, and papaya trees. Elizabeth Hall, a talented chef from London, set up the kitchens before returning to England. Ian McCloud is now the manager, and Gwen Bartlette and Hesketh Wade are in charge of the cooking. Just down the road from the hotel is the site of what was once the plantation's great house, and it is there that Fanny Nisbet and Lord Nelson were married on the eleventh of March in the year 1787.

Back on the main road, a stop at the Morning Star Museum, Robert Abraham's tribute to Lord Nelson, is a high spot on a visit to Nevis. Mr. Abraham has an impressive collection of memorabilia from letters and books to personal effects pertaining to the great naval hero, who, when stationed with the British fleet in Antigua, spent time in Nevis.

A few minutes by Moke from Morning Star is Saint John's Church at Fig Tree Hill. A sign outside, "Welcome the tourist with a clean smile," and a burgeoning date palm greet the visitor to this charming little building. Proudly displayed in the church registry is the record of Lord Nelson's marriage. High on a hill, just before one reaches Charlestown, are the old Bath Hotel and Government House.

The hotel and baths were built in 1778 by John Huggins to accommodate visitors who came to the island to take the waters. Now, though in ruins, the grounds are interesting to amble through. Government House, next door, was built in 1909 to house the governors of Nevis. It is a handsome colonial structure with two overgrown grass tennis courts on the front lawn that conjure up visions of white-clad players happily disporting themselves with racquet and ball.

West of Charlestown, on the leeward shore of the island, is Nevis' best beach, Pinney's; broad, edged with coconut palms, and boasting fine, light sand, it is the archetypal tropical beach. The water is generally clear and calm, the snorkeling good, and the view across a narrow channel to Saint Kitts properly bucolic.

Farther up the coast, on a knoll, is the church of Saint Thomas at Lowlands, which affords another dramatic overview of Saint Kitts. Goats and their kids wander in the fields next to this, the oldest of five Anglican parish churches in Nevis. Many members of the old planters' families from the prosperous sugar days are buried here: The gravestones bear such names as Huggins, Pinney, and Cottle. And slightly off the main road, not far from Tamarind Bay, are the ruins of the Cottle Church. This little chapel was originally known as Saint Mark's and was built by an enlightened planter, Thomas Cottle, so that his slaves could worship together with his family. Because the Anglican church did not countenance sacraments for slaves, the church was never consecrated and fell into disrepair. It is an enchanted spot with fragrant herbs proliferating everywhere and sounds of birdsong and an occasional lost sheep the only disturbances.

CLIFFDWELLERS, at Tamarind Bay, stands on a bluff that commands perhaps the best views of the narrows and Saint Kitts. To sip a drink here and watch the sunset is to experience one of the Caribbean's most spectacular sights. The fourteen rooms in the separate perched cottages are comfortably appointed and also afford splendid vistas. Marcia and David Myers—he is an architect in Boston— own Cliffdwellers, and Harriet Turner is the manager. There is a pleasantly furnished dining room and bar, though any decorations necessarily take a back seat when competing with the scenery. An electric tramway was built to negotiate the climb to the cluster of cottages that make up the hotel. Unfortunately, due to power problems, it was not operating during our visit, but the owners were confident that it would be fully operative for the winter '81–'82 season. In the meantime one would certainly get plenty of exercise walking between the tennis court and pool at sea level and the other facilities of the hotel. It is also possible to drive up, but the road is steep and tricky. Cliff-dwellers has a weekly Sunday buffet lunch by the pool with island music. The day we were there we lunched on icy, well-seasoned gazpacho, a tomato, cheese, olive, and anchovy quiche, *moussaka*, and a particularly good breadfruit salad. Dessert was coconut pie.

Nevis is an Arcadian island made special primarily by its people—citizens with grace, pride, and a gentleness of manner and demeanor. It is not, however, an island for everyone. There is no nightlife, no gambling casino, no discotheque, and no television. The "action" is definitely missing. There is also no golf course, little to buy, and telephone communications with the outside world are iffy, to say the least. The beaches are good, but there are finer ones on other Caribbean islands. Nevis appeals to those who respond to the natural beauty of flora and fauna and are satisfied to create their own diversions. It is a place where the slow pace is associated with a time long gone, a spirit alien to today's world. Mr. Powell, the owner of the garage that rents most of the island's Mini-Mokes, put it succinctly one hot March afternoon when he said, "What you want to hurry for? It only going to make you tired."

Cartagena

*T*HE IDEAL WAY TO ENTER the city of Cartagena de Indias would be in a full-rigged Spanish galleon, on a cloudless day, with a sky to match the incomparable blue of the Caribbean. The Spaniards, one Pedro de Heredia to be exact, approached the northern coast of Colombia just this way in 1533 and dubbed the city Cartagena "of the Indies" to distinguish it from the Cartagena that is a seaport in southeastern Spain. The city's life and fabric are dominated by the sea. The beaches are the center of activity, and the *brisa* that comes off the water after midday offers blessed relief from the torrid Colombian sun. Palms bend away from the breeze, and houses are constructed for maximum exposure to it. Apart from the sea, the contrasts and contradictions of the city create the most lasting impressions. Cartagena on the one hand meticulously restores and maintains her antiquity and on the other allows high-rise building to thrive. The Cartageneros seem equally comfortable with both realities.

Bocagrande is the newer part of the city: a thin spit of land with the Caribbean on one side and the *bahía* (bay) on the other. Neatly trimmed white-trunked *mangli* trees line the avenues, and coconut and date palms shade the houses of this residential district. The smart shops are in Bocagrande; boutiques with designer resort clothes intermingle with stores displaying local leather goods and jewelers selling the world-famous Colombian emeralds. These gems are available in every size and quality from branches of such well-known international establishments as H. Stern as well as innumerable smaller shops.

Here, too, are the hotels of Cartagena. Since the opening some thirty years ago of the venerable Caribe there has been a building boom, and modern apartments and hotels now line the wide, mile-long beach. The latest addition is the 298-room CARTAGENA HILTON, a first-rate hotel located at the very end of Bocagrande, with a splendid view of the city skyline from the front rooms and the sea from the back. Decorated with an emphasis on things Colombian, the public rooms and the bedrooms surpass in style and comfort other accommodations in the city. From the stylish brown-and-white tiled lobby, with wicker sofas cushioned in bright red, and mobiles swinging from the ceiling, to the upstairs corridors carpeted in lush green and yellow, all is a model of sumptuous good taste. The bedrooms are not large but are furnished with every possible amenity. Service is excellent; one gets the feeling that the management and staff cannot do enough for the guests. There is an elegant dining room, EL TINAJERO DE DOÑA ROSA, modeled after a seventeenth-century colonial mansion of Cartagena, and a very pleasant coffee shop, LAS CHIVAS. The name of the latter actually means the goats, but it is also the term Cartageneros affectionately apply to the colorful city buses. Here, in the representation of a marketplace, one can order anything from a complete meal to sandwiches and milk shakes and enjoy them in an airy, open setting with splendid views of the sea. The beach at the Hilton is sheltered and quiet, the water calm and clean. There is a pool, of course, tennis courts, and all manner of activities for those who wish to be entertained. In fact, it would be difficult to think of anything that has not been provided for the guests' enjoyment and well-being.

Among the other hotels, LA CAPILLA DEL MAR and LAS VELAS are well thought of. Though many of their accommodations are apartments, some of the rooms on the higher floors are just bedrooms and are quite attractive. All have easy access to the beach.

We dined our first night at one of Colombia's best known restaurants, LA CAPILLA DEL MAR (not connected with the hotel), located in a bayside house in Bocagrande. The restaurant consists of two large, airy rooms and a porch that runs the length of the house with deep, arched windows that look out on the bay. The tables are set with immaculate white napery and small fresh flower arrangements, and the general atmosphere is one of a serious and well established eating place. On the walls are paintings by pupils of the late owner, Pierre Daguet, who was not only a restaurateur but an artist and teacher as well. We began dinner with a delicious pâté (Mademoiselle Michelle Daguet, Pierre's sister, is the chef and, even after many years in Colombia, remains thoroughly French) and an hors d'oeuvre selection that included *seviche, mortadella*, shrimp, lobster, spicy salami, and the tiny local clams, *chipi-chipi*. Our main courses were *pargo* (red snapper) Marguery and *mariscos mixtos*, a combination of lobster, shrimp, and flaky fish napped with a rich white sauce advertised as a "creation of the house." With these we were served a tart beet and lettuce salad. The breads at La Capilla del Mar are made there and arrive warm in a small basket at the start of the meal. Moist corn sticks are among the offerings and hark back to the years

Mlle. Daguet spent in Texas. They are an inspired complement to the seafood dishes. We ended our dinner with coconut ice cream served with grated fresh coconut, *crème Chantilly*, and a splash of rum and flan, a dessert found on almost all Colombian menus but particularly good here. A dry white Chilean Santa Emiliana was a fine accompaniment to our meal. French and Italian wines are prohibitively expensive in Colombia, but the Argentinian and Chilean wines are more than adequate. Instead of coffee we had *aqua aromática* or *agüita*, as herbed tea is called, a pleasant ending to dinner.

The following night we visited PACO'S SEAFOOD, a highly recommended restaurant in the Pierino Gallo, the casino complex at the very tip of Bocagrande. The creation of Paco de Onis, a young American of Spanish descent, it is an informal spot, with rough-hewn tables and chairs, hanging plants, and a lobster trap on the ceiling of the main room. Swinging saloon doors lead into a bar with deep, cushioned banquettes and swivel barstools sitting at attention before a handsome handmade bar. There are hurricane lamps on the tables, a map of the world on one wall, and a wooden ceiling rack from which dozens of gleaming glasses are suspended. We had a first-rate *seviche* and a spicy and robust fish chowder conceived by Paco's sister, Sita, and for the main course, *langostinos "sifu,"* the restaurant's name for anything deep-fried. Because there is no word in Spanish for that method of cooking, Paco dubbed it *"sifu,"* an imitation of the Colombian's pronunciation of seafood. The crustaceans were served in a large wooden vessel with tomato sauce, homemade mayonnaise, and melted butter for dipping and perfect coleslaw and fried potatoes. Accompanied by the local beer, the meal was simple and satisfying. Paco and Jody Hagberg are warm hosts, and it is easy to see why their restaurant is patronized by a large, convivial group of young regulars. They are also open for lunch and have good shrimp and lobster salads.

The clock archway is the main entrance to the old walled town of Cartagena, an easy taxi ride from any of the hotels in Bocagrande. Construction of the original walls was begun in 1586, but the walls were replaced several times after being destroyed by pounding storms from the sea and the cannonballs of pirates. What remains intact today dates from 1796 and is rather a fortification than a wall, with ramps leading to sentry posts and a series of loopholes for cannon. One truly enters another world walking through the clock archway. The streets are narrow and rimmed by plain stone houses with wooden balconies and heavy wooden doors. Most of the houses have lush central courtyards where guava and mango trees thrive, but, like the famed Barrio de Santa Cruz in Seville, the façades give no hint of the wonders within. To walk along streets with names such as Calle de las Damas, Calle de la Inquisición, and Calle del Candilejo is to be transported back two centuries.

The Plaza Bolívar is the main square of the old town. An equestrian statue of the liberator stands in the center, and fountains mark each corner. Tall palm and almond trees shade the park, and there are benches where one can enjoy the passing sights. The Palace of the Inquisition, a balconied colonial building dating from 1776, displays, in contrast to a charming inner court where a tamarind tree and plantains flourish, all the grim instruments of torture used in this violent age. The cathedral across the square is majestic though simple, with Roman-style arches. The high altar is carved wood with a gold leaf finish. The plaza, surrounded by buildings that have been restored to their original state, is thoroughly delightful.

One of the most recently restored structures houses

MARCEL'S RESTAURANT. Marcel Venckeleer, a Belgian, has lived in Cartagena for eighteen years and is a chef in the grand tradition. He has cooked for the king and queen of Spain, Prince Charles, and other visiting royalty. The restaurant's dining room is white-walled with a dark wood-beamed ceiling and a black wrought-iron chandelier. Banquettes in a black-and-white print and a handsome black, white, and brown wall hanging complete the décor. There is a small court with a fountain that is some-times used for dining and a pleasant little bar. The menu changes almost daily according to the produce available in the markets, and the day we were there we were thoroughly pampered with papaya with local cured ham, delectable *fondants* (croquettes) of shrimp, a veal chop cooked with Sherry, and *pargo a la costeña*, Marcel's version of the plentiful red snapper. The meal was ac-companied by a chilled Argentinian Rincón Famoso and ended with a perfect apple tart with *crème Chantilly*. No royalty could have been better fed.

The church and monastery of San Pedro Claver is one of the most interesting sights in old Cartagena. It was originally built by the Jesuits but was later named for the Spaniard Pedro Claver, a champion of the poor who took the first steps to free the slaves and was subsequently canonized. He lived and died in the convent next to the church. Today the complex is an oasis of peace and beauty. The court, with an old cistern and fountain, is verdant with date palms, mango trees, and earthenware pots of tropical plants. The four storeys of galleries afford views of the garden and the sepia-toned dome of the church. San Pedro Claver is used now by Cartageneros for religious retreats. The church was restored in 1888 and the present dome added in 1921 by the French architect Gaston de Lelarge.

A visit also should be paid to the church of Santo Domingo,

the oldest religious building in Cartagena, dating from the end of the sixteenth century. In the northern part of the walled town, between the forts of Santa Clara and Santa Catalina, are the Bóvedas (vaults), which were used as military barracks and later as dungeons. Today they house a series of small shops that sell Colombian handicrafts: baskets, woolen *ruanas* (ponchos), straw mats, and primitive wall hangings made in the mountain towns, where the craft has been passed from generation to generation.

There are many houses that nave been, or are in the process of being, restored and are open to the public. One of the most charming of these is the house of the Marquis de Valdehoyos, where the Colombian National Tourist Corporation is located. Another elegant restoration houses the restaurant BODEGÓN DE LA CANDELARIA. The building is actually lived in, but the restaurant leases the first-floor courtyard and a room on the second floor that is used for lunch. Tables are set in the court, where one dines on such delicacies as avocado stuffed with tiny shrimp, veal tenderloin with lobster, and *pargo en papillote* (red snapper baked in paper). A trio of musicians adds to the atmosphere. A guide will escort dinner guests up the marble stairs on a tour of the living quarters, providing a fascinating glimpse of life in colonial Cartagena.

The *castillo* of San Felipe, outside the walls but still within the city limits of Cartagena, provides an interesting excursion. It is a dramatic example of the elaborate fortifications built by the Spaniards in the New World and affords a remarkable view of the harbor and surrounding terrain. A tour of the parade grounds, magazines, kitchens, and ramparts is an integral part of a visit to this city. La Popa and Candelaria Convent, which can be reached by a steep and winding road, command the most spectacular view of the city. The Convent of Our Lady of Candelaria was founded by Augustinian friars as a cloister at the beginning of the seventeenth century and subsequently became the site of many bloody battles, changing its function to the billeting of soldiers. It was abandoned for many years and then restored by Augustinians in 1964.

If one feels inclined to explore the waters and harbor of Cartagena, an excursion boat, the *Alcatraz*, leaves from the pier near the clock archway every morning at about nine-thirty for the hour-and-a-half trip to Bocachica. Here, at the mouth of the harbor, one can see the forts of San Fernando and San José, dating from 1753. A market is set up out of doors, and booths sell everything from sets of china to canned goods. There is a beach, bathhouses to rent, and a simple eatery, where, if one is daring (the hygiene appeared questionable), one can order fried local fish, rice, and a salad. We settled for a cold beer and peanuts. The *Alcatraz* returns to Cartagena at about three in the afternoon.

Manga, an island in the bay, became the residential part of the city when the old families moved out of the walled sector. It has a number of intriguing houses of whimsically eccentric design: a combination of Moorish, beaux arts revival, Victorian gingerbread, and pure architectural flights of fancy. Most of these buildings have been designated national landmarks and will therefore be preserved in their original state.

On the island of Manga, too, in the old fort of San Sebastian del Pastelillo, is the CLUE DE PESCA, a yacht club and restaurant. We lunched there on our last day in Cartagena, and it was a fitting end to a delightful sojourn. Lunch was served in a tiled courtyard in the shade of a hundred-year-old banyan tree. We watched fishing and pleasure boats glide by as we selected from the menu. One of the Club de Pesca's specialties is *paella con mariscos*, the seafood and rice dish so popular in both Spain and

Colombia. A note indicated that its preparation required ninety minutes, so we lunched instead—and very well—on an excellent melon with Spanish ham and the catch of the day, *sierra* (Spanish mackerel), perfectly grilled whole and served with coconut rice, *patacones* (fried slices of plantain), sliced tomato, and juicy wedges of the local lemons. For dessert we found the kitchen's coconut and pineapple pies first-rate.

Sipping into our *tinto* (demitasse) in this charming setting, it was easy to picture old Cartagena de Indias, her waters alive with caravels and galleons under full sail and her lush and unexplored lands populated by dashing conquistadores. Even with the concessions that have been made to today's world, Cartagena manages to retain much of the color of her past.

Caracas

CARACAS, VENEZUELA'S capital and chief city, lies just south of the Caribbean in a long, beautiful valley sheltered from the sea by the green height of Mount Avila.

Named after the Indian tribe that originally lived there, Caracas enjoys "such a heavenly climate," a writer once rhapsodized, "it seems that springtime chose it for its permanent abode."

One of the pleasantest parts of this city can be found at its heart, in the Plaza Bolívar, which dates back to colonial times. Dominated by an equestrian statue of Venezuela's liberator, Simon Bolívar, the tree-shaded plaza is planted with poinsettias and lush ferns. Children alternately feed and chase pigeons, which take flight over the heads of formally dressed elderly gentlemen who watch from folding chairs. Surrounding the plaza are the handsome Casa Amarilla (Yellow House, quarters for the foreign ministry), Congreso Nacional (National Congress), and Concejo Municipal (City Hall), which lend a charming Old World flavor to the scene. At the northeastern end of the plaza stands La Torre, the bell tower of the nearby Catedral de Caracas, a nineteenth-century cathedral built on the site of the city's original sixteenth-century chapel. A block away on a cobbled street is Bolívar's birthplace, Casa Natal del Libertador. The golden domes, tiled courtyards, fountains, filigreed balconies, and abundance of flowering plants in the plaza evoke the age when Caracas was acclaimed as "the beautiful city of red roofs."

Sadly, Caracas has changed .since then. In the past thirty years it has grown dramatically from 400,000 to 4,000,000 souls, all living in a narrow stretch of land. To accommodate this burgeoning population, much of the colonial city has been torn down and replaced by modern apartments and office buildings. In fact, the Plaza Bolívar is considered to be the last remaining fragment of the colonial town. Traffic jams have become commonplace; the Autopista Francisco Fajardo, which runs from one end of Caracas to the other, is usually clogged with cars, though *caraqueños* accept the delays cheerfully—or at least philosophically.

To compound the problem of making one's way around Caracas, addresses can be perplexing, for they are often listed by corners, which have names, instead of by streets, confusing taxi drivers as much as their passengers. But the drivers are polite and good-natured and charge reasonable fares, as do the cars that can be hired by the day at any of the big hotels (you will need one or the other to get around Caracas), so it is neither a hardship nor a great extravagance to wander a bit or even to get a little lost.

Caracas has been blessed with significant immigrations from Europe at various times, making Spanish, Italian, and German communities a very real part of the city's fabric. Seven blocks east of the Plaza Bolívar is one of the most atmospheric districts, the Spanish enclave of La Candelaria, a rewarding place in which to roam about and stumble upon one of the simple, modestly priced, and truly delicious restaurants. In the bustling LA TERTULIA, between the corners of Alcabala and Urapal, a mural of a small port and colorful tiles of fish provide a backdrop to the lively patrons, who help themselves from plates put in the middle of the tables. For our *tapas* (hors d'oeuvres, on which one can also lunch) we ate fried squid, succulent mushrooms bathed in oil and garlic, lovely steamed fresh shrimp garnished with lime slices, and fried whole green peppers. These were followed by entrées of squid in their ink and *chuletas* (pork chops) cooked to a tender turn in an assertively seasoned gravy. Good bread and very cold Polar, the local beer, made ideal foils for the spicy fare.

Several blocks to the southeast of La Candelaria is a city within a city, the Parque Central. Begun in 1966 and finished four years ago, this ambitious urban renewal effort was designed to restore space to the center of Caracas "for living, breathing and enjoyment." That effort met with success; the park's grounds have been attractively landscaped, encouraging people to take full advantage of the fine weather, and the Caracas Hilton International, vast apartment blocks, and office towers stand cheek by jowl with Caracas's main cultural institutions.

The Museo de Arte Contemporáneo (Museum of Contemporary Art) houses an impressive collection, including paintings and sculptures by such artists as Henry Moore, George Segal, Calder, Dubuffet, and Matisse. Prints and reproductions of those works can be purchased in the museum shop, along with lusterware vases and pitchers, unusual crystal plates in pale pastels, and stylish polished wood-and-silver boxes and jam jars. At the nearby Museo de los Niños, a children's science museum, youngsters can participate in exhibits and demonstrations of physics, biology, communications, and ecology.

Across Paseo Colón is the equivalent of New York City's Lincoln Center, the Complejo Cultural Teresa Carreño, named for the world-renowned Venezuelan pianist, conductor, and composer who gave Caracas its first musical credentials. Here, in a large hall or a small, intimate one, the Venezuelan Symphony Orchestra, the Operatic Chorus, the National Youth Orchestra, and a ballet company appear in a full schedule of performances. Visiting companies can also be seen at the complex, adding to the varied and generous cultural life of the city.

The Galería de Arte Nacional (National Art Gallery) and the Museo de Bellas Artes (Museum of Fine Arts), located in adjoining buildings near the Teresa Carreño complex, specialize, respectively, in the work of Venezuelan artists—Arturo Michelena, Cristóbal Rojas, Antonio Lazo, and Armando Reverón—and the international plastic arts, including an impressive collection of Chinese porcelain. The Museo de Bellas Artes is an agreeable place in which to pass some time, no less because its courtyards are filled with greenery and sparkle with lily ponds.

The CARACAS HILTON INTERNATIONAL, convenient to all of the Parque Central area, satisfies one's expectations of a convention hotel, being big, busy, and so sealed that the balmy Caracas climate might as well not exist. But the spacious rooms are innocuously decorated and perfectly comfortable, and room service is efficient, particularly for those staying on the executive floors at the top of the building, where guests are treated to a complimentary Continental breakfast served in the sunny twenty-second–floor lounge. Naturally, the Hilton offers every imaginable service. It also houses some enticing shops, among them H. Stern, the well-known Brazilian jewelry concern whose specialty is handworked eighteen- and twenty-four-karat gold pieces. (Other H. Stern shops are located in the Hotel Tamanaco Inter•Continental and at the airport.)

After touring a museum or two, weary sightseers may feel it's time for a little nourishment of the flesh, having seen to the demands of the spirit. They should head to VISCONTI, a stunning Art Deco restaurant next door to the Museo de Arte Contemporáneo. Stylishly done up in pinks, grays, and blacks, with Venezuelan goblets, cutlery, and china on the tables, Visconti is a real gem. We lunched there quite well on figs and prosciutto, a *"Carpaccio"* of salmon trout, and two pastas: duck *raviolini* with mushrooms and lobster ravioli in a rich seafood sauce.

North of the Parque Central on Avenida Panteón in San Bernardino, one of the foothill areas named after bygone sugarcane, coffee, or cacao plantations, is the Museo de Arte Colonial, Quinta de Anauco. The splendid eighteenth-century *quinta*, or country residence, was built by Spanish loyalists who fled the revolution in 1821. It was later owned by General Francisco Rodríguez del Toro, one of the heroes of the Venezuelan war of independence. Bolívar visited him frequently here; the Liberator loved the estate and mentioned it often in his letters. In 1861 it was bought by Don Domingo Eraso, whose grandchildren donated it to their country in 1958 with the provision that it henceforth house the Museo de Arte Colonial.

Since then, the *quinta* has been painstakingly restored. Influenced by Andalusian and thus Moorish architecture, the walled main house encloses a central patio, and its red-tiled roof and floors contrast with the white-stuccoed walls. Fine local period furniture, paintings, and religious artifacts fill the large rooms, the walls of which are painted below the chair rails and at the tops in charming flowered patterns. One splendid bedchamber was used in colonial times for such important events as births, deaths, and birthday celebrations, when presents were laid out on the ceremonial bed.

Wide loggias afford views of the gardens, where orchids, violets, pomegranates, hot peppers, orange vines called *tango*, and even specimens of coffee and cacao proliferate. The bathroom, one of twenty-four outbuildings on the expansive grounds, contains a wonderful, deep stone tub through which runs water fresh from a mountain spring. Kitchens, storerooms, and stables, equipped with period tools and carriages, provide glimpses into life on a colonial estate. Nowadays concerts are occasionally held at the *quinta*; in this setting, they must be truly magical events.

Before leaving, stop at the Tienda Anauco (Anauco Shop) to examine the one-of-a-kind brass jewelry, ceramics, and well-made toys and mementos, all of which are crafted by hand in Venezuela.

Not far from the museum in San Bernardino, set in a garden at the dead end of the quiet Avenida Jorge Washington, lies the small and delightful HOTEL AVILA. Built by Nelson Rockefeller in 1942, the hotel is pervaded by a charm out of the past. The simply decorated rooms are comfortable, if not spacious, though larger suites are available; all are incredibly well priced. Breezes waft through the public areas, and guests dine alfresco on a terrace hung with baskets of ferns beside the oval pool. (There is also a tennis court.) When you open your window at night, the song of the cicadas will lull you to sleep. Because the Hotel Avila is a fifteen-minute ride from central Caracas, it can sometimes be a problem getting taxis there, but with what you save on your room you can hire a car and driver by the day.

When you have an opportunity, walk the pleasant pedestrian boulevard, Avenida Abraham Lincoln, through Sabana Grande, a shopping and business center in west-central Caracas. Proceed as far as the Chacaíto metro stop, where a dramatic aluminum and polished chrome Jesús Soto sculpture shines in the sun, board a train, and ride for a stop or two and then back. Caracas's metro is something to see, a sort of urban miracle. Inaugurated in 1983, it was constructed over a period of years at great inconvenience and expense to the city. Perhaps that explains why residents treat it with the utmost respect and affection. Platforms are immaculate; Caracas is generally a clean city, but as one approaches a metro station not even a gum wrapper can be seen. In the pristine cars the passengers sit, nicely dressed, hands folded, expressions almost beatific, looking as though they're attending mass instead of riding mass transit. A native *caraqueño*, a grown man, told us that he was close to tears when he first rode the metro.

Because Venezuelans—nay, all Latin Americans—are passionate shoppers, they are also inordinately proud of their malls. Centro Comercial Chacaíto was Caracas's first. Two shops worth visiting there are Raymar, which sells pretty table mats and napkins, fabrics by the yard, and bed linens; and Heidi, a purveyor of children's clothes, which seems particularly well stocked with baby apparel and smocked dresses.

If it's lunchtime, CITY ROCK CAFÉ, next door to Raymar, is a good bet. A favorite of Caracas's younger set, it resembles the trendy Hard Rock Cafe. The chef there whips up crisp, fresh *nachos* and ribs doused in a delectable barbecue sauce, the secret ingredient of which is watermelon. Venezuelan chocolate is among the finest in the world, making chocolate desserts almost always first-rate; the café's chocolate brownie topped with ice cream and chocolate sauce proves richer than the object of one's most avaricious dream.

One stop east of Chacaíto on the metro line is the neighborhood of Chacao, where every Thursday morning a market is held at the intersection of Calle Mata de Coco and Calle Cecilio Acosta. Huge, thin yucca pancakes, the size of wheels, are sold here, along with large avocados, papayas, bananas, and plantains; bags of dried yellow and white corn; and bin upon bin of different varieties of onion and garlic. Unlike North Americans, *caraqueños* needn't abstain from using tomatoes for months on end or make do with hard, tasteless specimens, for glorious fresh tomatoes form part of the market's bounty year round.

La Castellaña, just north of Chacao, has three noteworthy eateries as diverse as could be. PRIMI, a stylish and justly popular addition to Caracas's culinary scene, was opened on the Avenida Principal de La Castellana a year ago by Jean-Paul Coupal, an energetic and knowledgeable restaurateur.

Upon entering his high-tech, spacious dining room, one encounters a table bearing a cornucopia of colorful local produce: a long-grain rice from the Guárico state; *ají dulce*, tiny, highly perfumed sweet red, yellow, and green peppers from the island of Margarita; intensely flavored tomatoes, also from Margarita; and okra, sage, and rosemary, which are new to Venezuelan agriculture. Royal blue sweetwater prawns and the freshest lobsters might also have been purchased at the day's market. Coupal, who has French and Californian roots, takes advantage of his countless sources to acquire the best available produce for Primi. In the dining room, black steel girders support a vast glass roof. At night it reflects the tables below, but in daylight it permits views of sky and cloud through a curtain of running water—a natural air conditioner. Black and white napery dresses the tables, and black plates set off the food. Large, colorful canvases by Venezuelan artists hang on the walls in an ever-changing exhibit. Stacked in cases built into one wall is part of the restaurant's cellar, dozens of choices in both French and Italian reds and whites and a fine selection of Chilean wines, particularly attractive in Caracas because of the exorbitant taxes on European imports.

Born and trained in Normandy, the *chef de cuisine*, Jean-Luc Lemonnier, has traveled in French Guiana and Martinique, where he learned to combine French methods with Caribbean ingredients. Exemplary items on his menu, which is the same at lunch and dinner, were a chicken salad with mixed greens in a balsamic vinegar dressing and zucchini blossoms stuffed with locally made buffalo mozzarella. Lemonnier also prepares an intriguing *linguine* of cacao with Venezuelan white shrimp and saffron sauce and a risotto with *porcini* mushrooms and truffled olive oil. Fillets of red snapper with a Dijon-mustard sauce and grilled blue prawns were two fine selections from the list of daily specials. Giving prominence to local fruit and Venezuela's world-renowned cacao, desserts included a flaky mango tart, a guava tart with an unusual mint sauce, and a rich chocolate *sablé* with a crust of chopped Venezuelan macadamia nuts. Primi's cuisine is fittingly described by a phrase printed on the menu: "*Cocina Creativa—Ingredientes Nobles.*"

EL CARRIZO, on Avenida Blandín, exemplifies the Caracan steak house, with its rustic, dark wood interior and rush ceilings overhead. Start with *guacamole* and sangria while you await thick steaks, sausages, or chicken, which—if they are grilled—will be given a final searing on the hibachi at your table. The beef is good, not as tender as our American prime, but leaner and more flavorful. For dessert we ate a coconut custard layered with cake called *bien me sabe*, meaning "it tastes good to me," which it did.

La Sifrina, also located on Avenida Blandín, is one of Caracas's most popular *areperas*, establishments that prepare *arepas*, white-cornmeal griddle cakes. The city's answer to fast food, *areperas* are a ubiquitous kind of Caracan institution, open twenty-four hours a day and crowded morning, noon, and late into the night with people eating *arepas* filled with avocado, chicken, pork, white cheese—or almost anything else you can imagine— and served with *guasacaca*, a spicy avocado sauce. *Areperas* also sell *cachapas*, yellow-cornmeal pancakes eaten with a variety of garnishes. *Batidos*—fruit shakes made of pineapple, soursop, tamarind, or guava—make the perfect accompaniment for these snacks.

Bordering La Castellaña to the north and east are Altamira and Los Palos Grandes, two attractive residential areas that climb into the foothills. Apartment balconies positively burst with flowering green plants, creating the illusion that vines cover the façades. ALTAMIRA SUITES, an apartment hotel at Primera Avenida and Calle 1 in Los Palos Grandes, provides a reasonably priced alternative to big commercial hotels, but you must stay there at least a week. The nicely appointed suites are equipped with kitchenettes, though there is a pretty dining room that reportedly serves good food. In addition to a pool, the hotel has a new rooftop health club, which affords spectacular views of Caracas and the mountains.

Not far from the hotel is the chocolate-maker La Praline, at a typically convoluted address: Segunda Avenida between Transversal 1 and Avenida Francisco de Miranda, Edificio Artelito. Owned by Ludo and Lisette Gillis, who studied the precise art of chocolate-making in Belgium, the company has for four years supplied hotels, airlines, and individuals with its dozens of varieties of delectable wares. Packaged in attractive blue boxes, the bonbons taste as good as Europe's finest.

You will find the most interesting and well-made handicrafts in the city nearby at Galería Yakera, on Avenida Andrés Bello between transversals 1 and 2. The objects sold there are the work of Warao Indians, who live in the Orinoco delta. Their beautiful, delicate baskets, woven of soft dyed and undyed palm, come in unusual shapes, and their expertly handmade hammocks and carved wooden animals occupy a class by themselves.

Altamira, the residential area beside Los Palos Grandes, boasts several good restaurants of its own. VIA APPIA, a star Italian establishment on Avenida Luis Roche, would shine in any city. Simple but chic, it is decorated with cartoons of celebrities, and—in the best Italian tradition—nothing else is allowed to interfere with the enjoyment of food. Starters of *Carpaccio*, paper-thin with a bit of creamy mayonnaise and shards of Parmesan, and *vitello tonnato* (veal with tuna sauce) were flawless. *Raviolini* filled with grouper and napped in a squid and shrimp sauce were impeccable, as was a saffron risotto. We ran out of superlatives lunching at Via Appia, but we knew how to describe our ethereally light *porcini gnocchi*: They were the best we had ever tasted. With our meal we drank a Vernaccia di San Gimignano, but beware: Because imported wines command such very high prices, a lunch for three can cost less than the wine that accompanies it. For dessert we enjoyed an ice cream called *zuccotto* with bits of *biscotti* and candied fruit mixed in, served with a delicious chocolate sauce.

High in the foothills of Altamira, at the north end of Avenida San Juan Bosco, is TARZILANDIA. Sitting outside beneath slanted roofs, diners are surrounded by cages of parrots and colorful birds, clumps of bamboo, and flourishing plants, which create a distinctly jungle-like atmosphere. Meat and chicken sizzle on a large grill nearby. Tarzilandia's house specialty, grilled steak presented with fruit sauces, sounds bizarre, but both steak with bananas and with mango were, in fact, most pleasing.

South of Altamira on the opposite side of the valley lies the slightly old-fashioned, partly residential neighborhood of Las Mercedes, where one can walk from one notable shop to the next, enjoying the excellent weather, the flowering shrubs, and the exotic trees. Fürst, an elegant jewelry store on Calle California at Avenida Jalisco, crafts all its goods, from gold copies of pre-Columbian figurines and necklaces of pearl, crystal, and emerald to bracelets that clink with gold coins. For men it creates stunning blazer buttons and unique studs that clip onto cuff buttons to masquerade as cuff links. (Fürst's other shop is in Rome on the Via Veneto.)

Next door, Galería Sagitario displays handsome prints of flowers, fruits, and birds. Mostly of Italian origin, the prints have been framed in Venezuela with local materials, an illustration of the fact that, since the dramatic devaluation of the bolivar in 1983, Venezuelans have begun to make almost everything. They are accomplished craftsmen with fine taste, due at least in part to their European heritage.

For children's clothes, visit the delightful Mariquita Perez, on Avenida Principal de Valle Arriba. Hand-done smocking embellishes the girls' frocks, and hand-stitched embroidery decorates the sweaters for babies and older boys and girls. The store also sells charming beach hats for wee ones, guaranteed to appeal to grandmothers. The most chic of boutiques, Gloria Tagliaferro, can be found on Avenida Orinoco. The store's belts, blouses, and original hand-knit sweaters merit consideration. Given a week's time, the seamstresses there will whip up almost anything you might wish to wear.

LA CASA BRIOCHE, on Principio Calle Madrid in Las Mercedes, is a pleasant pastry shop and coffee bar. A fragrant *tinto* (small black coffee) and a slice of pizza, a sandwich, a croissant with ham, or a tempting pastry will stave off hunger pangs until the next meal. Thus refreshed, embark on the delightful pastime of gallery-hopping in Las Mercedes.

Sotavento, a gallery on Calle Jalisco in the Edificio San Carlos, actively promotes the work of postmodern Venezuelan artists. Recently the gallery installed intriguing wire mobiles and other constructions by Gego, a German-born woman who came to Caracas in 1939. (The shop at the Museo de Arte Contemporáneo duplicates one of her creations on its eye-catching black-and-white boxes and shopping bags.) In Sotavento's pretty garden stand several larger sculptures, casting shadows in the sunlight.

Two noteworthy galleries on Avenida Orinoco are the respected Galería Siete Siete (Seven Seven) and the Galería Freites. Last year the former showed the colorful canvases of Maria Elena Lavié, a still-life painter who has exhibited widely in Venezuela. On the roster of well-known painters at Galería Freites is Picasso's contemporary and countryman Julio Gonzalez.

Two years ago the private club MAJESTY, on Calle Madrid in Las Mercedes, opened to the public, a boon to those who love fine food. The Majesty's namesake, the Belle Epoch Caracas Majestic, was felled by the wrecker's ball in 1949; today in the Majesty's bar a gilded mirror and some paneling saved from the destruction conjure memories of the past. On the walls in the elegant main dining room hang enlarged photographs of the Majestic, giving diners something to contemplate as they relish their starters of *mille feuilles* with lightly poached oysters in a saffron sauce or warm shrimp, scallop, and squid with ginger, served on lamb's-lettuce and *radicchio*. Among the entrées are loin of lamb with *flageolets*, snook on red cabbage, and grilled shrimp with a mango curry sauce. Pierre Blanchard, another talented young chef from Normandy, produces these splendid dishes, as well as making his own goat cheeses, one of which is rolled in coconut. He also transforms the local chocolate into a sublime dessert, a torte dusted wih edible gold leaf.

For people-watching in Las Mercedes, go to PIAZZA, on

Avenida Principal, a late-night spot that hits its trendiest stride after a ballet or concert. Here Caracas's beautifully dressed beautiful people congregate to eat pasta and be seen in a contemporary setting in which subdued lighting and shades of gray create a neutral background. Rigatoni with tomato, basil, and mozzarella tasted quite good, and the *gnocchi* were light and satisfying. A bottle of Barolo seemed just the right accompaniment, though it was as costly as dinner.

On a hill overlooking Las Mercedes stands Caracas's venerable HOTEL TAMANACO, a bustling commercial hostelry owned by the Inter•Continental chain. A large outdoor pool dominates the landscaped lawn, where one can recline on a comfortable chaise longue to read or enjoy the sun. Service throughout the hotel is courteous and attentive, but some bedrooms are small, and their décor is dull. At TERRAZA CACIQUE, the hotel's outdoor dining area, steaks and seafood are grilled over wood fires seven nights a week, while music from the lively bar accompanies the song of cicadas. It's an agreeable setting in which to relax and sip the delicious local rum, Pampero (which is now available in the United States).

Located near the Tamanaco, the HOTEL EUROBUILD-ING, the newest hotel in Caracas, is owned by a Spanish company that has lavished money on Italian marble, glass-bubble elevators, and attractive modern furnishings. Bedrooms are not large but contain every comfort, including small safes in the closets. CASSANDRA, the hotel's ornate gold and black dining room, features Spanish dishes well suited to a leisurely lunch or dinner. An informal cafeteria, two bars, and two swimming pools rank among the other amenities. Here, too, service is first-rate.

Shopping malls tend to be one man's meat and another man's poison, but in Caracas they are an indisputable part of life. The huge Centro Ciudad Comercial Tamanaco (Commercial Center of Tamanaco City, or C.C.C.T.) encompasses literally hundreds of shops. Vogue, a stylish men's store, stocks stunning shirts of silk and cotton in luscious colors and leather belts in shades sure to dandify the most conservative wardrobe. The store also sells natty, well-cut jackets and trousers of linen and gabardine.

Directly across from Vogue in the C.C.C.T. is Mayela's, a women's boutique to which one can turn for party dresses, pants, and blouses of the *dernier cri*. Among the store's fashionable merchandise, the pretty silk evening bags, elegant shoes, and an almost perfect copy of Hermès's Kelly bag deserve attention. Here and elsewhere you will notice that Venezuelans are masterful duplicators of goods; every detail, even down to the labels, looks somehow more like the genuine article than the genuine article itself.

Scattered about the C.C.C.T. are other shops of interest. Charles Jourdan-Gucci is actually nothing of the sort, though it does sell good-looking, Venezuelan-made shoes. (Some even bear the stamp "Gucci by Pucci.") At Pecari you will find quality luggage in leather and combinations of leather and vinyl; the wallets and change purses there make attractive peace offerings for disgruntled family members and friends who were left at home. Another children's clothing store, Juvenet's, is rife with temptations, among them more hand-smocked dresses for girls of all sizes. From the Krön shop—which has nothing to do with the U.S. company Krön Chocolatier—you can take away delectable chocolates, some in the shape of trucks and cars that would please any child—and the prices will please the purchaser.

In the southeastern hills above the city is an area called El Hatillo, meaning "the small bundle," here colonial-style buildings line a central tree-shaded plaza. Try to visit two handicraft shops there: Hannsi, at 12 Calle Bolívar, with a vast stock of straw mats, hammocks, espadrilles, sandals, and T-shirts; and, just down the street at number 15, El Rincón del Hatillo. Though smaller than Hannsi, this shop possesses a nice collection of pottery, brasses, and charming ceramic houses and street scenes.

About thirty kilometers northeast of Caracas, just outside the village of San Antonio, is Arte Murano ICET, a rewarding destination for an afternoon's drive. Founded in 1958, the glass factory manufactures and the showroom sells glass almost identical to that made in Murano. In fact, artisans are brought from Italy each year to train Venezuelan workmen in glassblowing and design. You can watch them work before visiting the shop, where delicately crafted glass animals, fish, and birds, including a particularly fetching rooster, shine in the light. You may find that you can't live without one of the heavy colored-glass bowls or something from the huge inventory for the table: goblets, wineglasses in all shapes and sizes, and plates. The artisans even make Venetian-looking chandeliers, another example of the Venezuelans' great gift for reproducing quality items.

After leaving Arte Murano, head back to Caracas and all its treasures, great and small. Dine at one of the city's sophisticated restaurants—among the best in Latin America—and spend the evening attending a concert or ballet with the enthusiastic *caraqueños*, whose mixed European heritage adds such flair to their culture. *Caraqueños* are enormously proud of their city; after a pleasurable stay there, you will understand why.

NEW ENGLAND

GOURMET | JUNE 1981

Coastal Maine

ORTSMOUTH, NEW HAMPSHIRE, and Kittery, Maine, are separated by the Piscataqua River. People who live in Maine say that when they cross the bridge that spans the river the air immediately has a different smell; it is a heady combination of pine and salt spray that follows one along the coast. This coast, from Kittery to Eastport, is about 225 miles as the seabirds fly, but it is in fact 2,500 miles of craggy, jagged points and innumerable deepwater harbors, a haven and heaven for sailors. To travel Maine's coast by car, even if not all twenty-five hundred miles of it, is to experience scenery of dramatic variation and contrast.

Our first stop in Maine this time was Ogunquit, and because it was after two and past our usual lunch hour we headed straight for The Whistling Oyster, a restaurant located at Perkins Cove that has been serving local delicacies in an attractive setting since 1907. The dining room is paneled in dark wood, there is a large fireplace in the corner, and the tables were set with brown place mats and yellow daisies. As the pleasure boats sailed in and out of the little cove, we lunched on a creamy and fragrant seafood bisque, which arrived with freshly baked rolls. Swordfish followed with crisp *al dente* zucchini, and for dessert there was a house special, Grand Marnier soufflé served in a scooped-out orange. Thus fortified, we walked around the town, a mecca of innumerable shops with an excellent summer theater that opens each year at the end of June.

The Black Point Inn in Prouts Neck was our first night's destination. It is a summer hotel in the old tradition: a large, shingled building with white trim and adjoining guest houses set in a well-kept lawn overlooking the wide, heart-shaped sandy beach, a rarity on the Maine Coast. Prouts Neck has been an active resort since the 1800s, and until 1950 there were as many as seven inns, all housing summer visitors. Now the B.P.I., as it is called, and the white clapboard Atlantic House, a landmark building, are the only two left in a thriving community of summer residents. The rooms at the B.P.I. are comfortable and simple; the food is plain and abundant. Generations of New England families have vacationed there, and, because most of them were raised to take cold baths every morning and to believe that life afforded one certain joys through discipline, they did not surround themselves with unnecessary trappings of luxury at their summer resorts. Everyone breakfasts early and heartily in the dining room, and the only lolling about that seems to be tolerated is in a rocker on the wide porch that looks out toward the sea. There is also a saltwater swimming pool at the inn, and guests may use the tennis courts and golf course of the Prouts Neck Country Club next door.

Winslow Homer, who summered in Maine as a boy, spent most of his last twenty-five years in Prouts Neck. His studio, housed in a tiny green cottage near the B.P.I., is open to visitors. He is buried behind the house in a plot overlooking the seacoast that he loved so well and immortalized.

The city of Portland, about ten miles up the coast, has experienced a renaissance in the past few years, and a visit to the

refurbished harbor area, the Old Port Exchange, is well worthwhile. Most of the early buildings were twice destroyed: once by
the British bombardment during the Revolutionary War and then
again by the great fire of July 4, 1866. They were rebuilt in brick
and stone, many with cast-iron façades. Today they house shops
and businesses as well as a wide choice of restaurants. Among
the eating spots is F. Parker Reidy's, a pub-restaurant in the old
Portland Savings Bank, where one can lunch while contemplat-
ing erstwhile bank vaults.

The Portland Museum of Art, on High Street, contains a
collection of nineteenth- and twentieth-century Maine paintings
and sculpture and has just acquired seventeen Winslow Homers
as a gift from Charles S. Payson. The Payson family, Portland
natives, has also given the city a gallery of art on Stevens Avenue, in memory of Joan Whitney Payson. The collection includes
Impressionist and Post-Impressionist paintings and nineteenth-
and twentieth-century American works. These are but two of the
several museums and innumerable galleries in Portland. There is
also the fifty-six-year-old Portland Symphony Orchestra, which
performs from October to May in the City Hall auditorium, making a significant contribution to the burgeoning cultural scene.

Continuing up the coast about thirty miles one comes upon
the city of Bath, a handsome old settlement on the Kennebec
River. The historic area dates mainly from the nineteenth century,
when, after the ravages of the French and Indian Wars, Bath became one of the most important shipbuilding centers. Many fine
examples of the architecture of the day remain, affording one an
intriguing walking tour along Washington and Middle streets.
The Maine Maritime Museum, housed in four locations around
the city, is a treasure trove for those interested in sea lore. There
is also the Wife of Bath, an excellent restaurant in a new complex

of buildings on the river. There one can lunch or dine on a pleasingly coarse pâté followed by broiled East Coast salmon napped with *mousseline* sauce and accompanied by potatoes au gratin and end the meal with strawberries served with *crème anglaise*.

One of the great joys of motoring on Maine's coast is to leave the larger routes for the points and spits of land that jut into the various bays. On one such detour we left Route 1 at Damariscotta and headed south on Route 129 to Christmas Cove, for no better reason than that the name intrigued us. All along the two-laned road were fields of blue and pink lupine in wild profusion. Bleached-out barns stood deep in buttercups, purple clover, and daisies, fluffy white clouds dappled a perfectly blue sky, and every once in a while we had a quick glimpse of the sea and an offshore island. Neat white houses, with an occasional sign announcing antiques for sale, displayed borders of orange lilies and scarlet poppies, and here and there a quiet old cemetery was framed with bridal wreath. Lobster pots were piled high in tiny South Bristol, a serious fishing village a mile or two from our destination. Christmas Cove was not a disappointment; it is a charming town on a point of land in Muscongus Bay, with comfortable houses that surely contain a host of happy summer memories.

The drive was so pleasant that we were glad to retrace our steps to Route 1 on our way to lunch at Le Garage, nearby in Wiscasset. There, in a spacious restaurant on the water, we sampled the fish chowder and an attractive lobster and crab salad.

We were headed for the East Wind Inn in Tenants Harbor, once again off the beaten path and once again a delightful drive on Route 131, which goes south from Route 1 at Thomaston. Tim Watts is the proprietor of this small inn, which is situated right on the harbor of a busy fishing village and stays open all year. The front porch with its white rockers and hanging geraniums is a perfect vantage point from which to see the lobster boats returning from their day's work. As a matter of fact, the inn is positioned in such a way that all of the bedrooms, neatly spartan but quite comfortable, have a splendid view of the water and the pine trees that line the shore. The dining room with scenic blue and white wallpaper, patriotic red American eagle curtains, and red hurricane lamps on the tables also looks out on the harbor.

We ordered the baked stuffed lobster, and, as we sipped a glass of wine and waited for the chef's fish chowder, we saw a young boy running up the hill from the dock, gingerly holding our two lobsters, as alive as could be. The chef, John Thomas, prepared them for us with a stuffing of crabmeat, scallops, shrimp, and lightly sherried cracker crumbs. Strawberry shortcake ended a thoroughly satisfactory dinner.

Dawn comes early on Maine's coast, and by four-fifteen the sky is a luminescent gold, the gulls are gliding and calling, and the lobstermen are readying for the day's excursion. It was an intoxicating sight from the window of the little bedroom in the East Wind Inn. Breakfast later that morning, as is the case all over Maine, was hearty, with a myriad of choices ranging from homemade blueberry muffins and pancakes to eggs with ham, sausage, or bacon. The inn also serves simple lunches of chowder, sandwiches, and salads. We headed off after breakfast, leaving behind a lovely inn in a setting of extraordinary beauty.

Heading northeast again toward Camden on Route 1, we detoured slightly to lunch at the Sail Loft in Rockport. The restaurant had been highly recommended, and we were not disappointed. It has a particularly pleasant situation on the picturesque harbor. We feasted on native mussels steamed in white wine and heard tales of one of the town's celebrities, the honorary harbormaster, Andre the seal. Andre has gained a wide following, who come to see him perform his tricks at the public landing on summer afternoons. In the winter he used to be kept in the Boston Aquarium, but he always managed to swim back, without direction, to his Maine home. According to natives Andre is smarter than ninety percent of all humans. In Rockport you will also find the Gallery of Maine Coast Artists, which has an interesting collection of local painters, on Russell Avenue, just a few blocks from the harbor.

Camden is a delightful town on Penobscot Bay. On its main street are a wide variety of shops and galleries, and its harbor is a favorite gathering place for yachtsmen. The Maine Windjammer fleet of schooners sets out from there to cruise the coast, and the harbor is always a busy and active spot. The town also boasts a repertory company that performs every summer in the Bok amphitheater overlooking the village and harbor, and there is the weekly Bay Chamber Concerts series in the Opera House in nearby Rockport. There is also a plethora of eating spots where one can indulge in delicious seafood fresh from the icy Maine waters and observe nautical comings and goings: The Waterfront, Peter Ott's Tavern, and the Eating Gallery are but a few. The unique feature of these waterfront eateries is that their clientele arrives almost as frequently by boat as by car.

The Whitehall Inn on High Street is a venerable Victorian landmark whose tradition of hospitality started eighty years ago when a sea captain's widow took in guests. There are forty-four bedrooms, most with bath, a spacious dining room, and good, simple New England food. Off the large main sitting room is a cozy parlor called the Edna St. Vincent Millay room, where the poet, who lived in Rockland and attended Camden High School, read her poems one night before an audience that included a New York publisher. There are scrapbooks, pictures, and other mementos, and the innkeepers proudly proclaim that it is here that she was "discovered." Camden cherishes the memory of Miss Millay and has erected a memorial to her at the top of Mt. Battie in Camden Hills State Park, where she often came to walk. A bronze plaque contains the first lines of her poem "Renascence."

On Belmont Avenue, a short distance from Camden's Main Street, a Victorian house has been transformed into a first-class restaurant by a young couple from Philadelphia. Kerlin and David Grant opened Aubergine in May of 1979. David graduated from the Restaurant School of Philadelphia, had a six-week apprenticeship in the Armagnac district of France, and worked in a Philadelphia restaurant before he came to Maine. He is a talented and energetic chef with innovative ideas. Kerlin's hand is apparent in the white chairs, blue tablecloths, flower arrangements, and charming Laura Ashley wallpaper of griffins and birds in the bar. Light suppers there may include soup, *salade niçoise* with smoked trout, and cheese and fruit with a glass of Champagne or one of the daily wine specials for those who do not wish a complete dinner.

The adjoining dining room has yellow walls with gray trim and handsome gray table linen with an aubergine stripe. The pretty china is an old flowered set that the Grants inherited with the house, which had, in fact, been Camden's first inn. In the summer the porch is used as an overflow dining room with lush purple fuchsia decorating it. Kerlin is both a horticulturist by training and a calligrapher, as one can see by the stylish menus that change monthly.

Dinner when we visited consisted of a mouth-watering avocado *mousseline* with fresh tomato sauce, ramekins of mussels with leek, and perfectly executed medallions of lobster with mussels. The combination of tastes and textures was outstanding, and a dish of pasta with saffron and crab was equally successful. Dessert was a sinfully rich peach *génoise* with peach buttercream and a blackberry charlotte. The carafe of house white was fine, but the Grants pride themselves on their knowledge of wine and have an extensive list. Aubergine also has seven rooms with baths, and a continental breakfast is served. It is open from May 1 to November 1 except on Mondays.

A few miles north of Camden, on Route 1, the ferries leave the slip in Lincolnville every hour for the thirty-minute sail to Islesboro in Penobscot Bay. The Islesboro Inn will, if forewarned, meet the ferry and transport guests to lunch in their dining room. The setting is delightful, and the inn is a pleasant place to spend the day for a taste of sea air. Twenty miles or so north on Route 1 is Searsport and the Penobscot Marine Museum. The museum, opened in 1936, is actually a village consisting of seven buildings that house memorabilia of the sea and one of the most comprehensive collections of marine paintings in Maine. There are numerous articles of porcelain, ivory, and embroidery brought back by ship captains from the Orient and fascinating model exhibits of nineteenth-century sailing vessels.

Traveling due east toward Northeast Harbor on Mt. Desert Island, we were not able to resist some tantalizing turns off the main road—the first to Castine at the end of a narrow peninsula that juts into Penobscot Bay. There the Maine Maritime Academy is located, and the town, which exudes history, puts up about one hundred markers each year to instruct visitors on the events that took place during the French and Indian Wars and the Revolution. The main street is lined with stately old houses leading steeply down to the sheltered deep harbor. Our next turn off the main route was a loop on winding two-lane roads to Blue Hill, Sedgwick, Brooklin, North Brooklin, and back to Blue Hill.

The lupine was abundant again, the towns are tiny and charming, and, when one least expects it, the road affords a spectacular view of Mt. Desert, the smaller islands, and the sea. Firepond on Main Street in Blue Hill, an old mill and blacksmith's shop converted to a restaurant, serves good light lunches and dinners in a tranquil setting.

Some of the most dramatic Maine scenery is on Mt. Desert Island, where a truly rockbound coast is lined with fragrant pines and pounded by the relentless icy surf. Samuel de Champlain discovered the island in 1604, but the first permanent settlement was in 1762, when Abraham Somes brought his family from Massachusetts. By 1880 there were thirty hotels in Bar Harbor, which had become a fashionable summer colony. In 1947 a devastating fire burned down most of the resort, but unfortunately it was rebuilt with motels and a distinctly honky-tonk ambiance— not so the thriving vacation communities of Northeast Harbor, Southwest Harbor, and Seal Harbor.

We headed for the Asticou Inn in Northeast Harbor, a huge old shingled building that looks out on the harbor over sloping green lawns, a pool, and a tennis court. The inn is attractively furnished in bright colors, with comfortable chairs, a porch with a splendid view, and a sunny dining room with yellow wallpaper and brass chandeliers. The bedrooms are cheerful and comfortable, particularly the ones that overlook the water. Dinner was a good clam chowder and scallops with cauliflower and zucchini, both dishes simple but well cooked. At the time of our visit three handsome new cottages had just been added to the establishment.

The gardens in Northeast Harbor are well worth a visit. Across the street from the inn are the Asticou Azalea Gardens with shaded paths, little ponds, and running brooks, and up the road about a mile is the entrance to the Thuya Gardens, a positive bower of annuals and perennials intermingled with towering pines. At the entrance are wooden doors with carved panels that celebrate some of the inhabitants of the gardens: bees, rabbits, and woodpeckers. In Seal Harbor the Rockefeller gardens are open to the public on Wednesdays from the middle of July until the end of August. It is worth the effort to arrange a trip to coincide with their opening day, for they are truly spectacular.

The Claremont Inn in Southwest Harbor is another wonderful old summer hotel, painted cream with green shutters. A long porch faces the water and fronts a croquet lawn. The rooms and baths are bright, and there are nine cottages where families come year after year to spend part or all of the summer. When we were there Chef Billie McIntire's dining room, with a perfect view of the sea, had flowers on all the tables as well as in hanging baskets. It is easy to understand why these marvelous inns have a devoted roster of guests who have been vacationing literally from generation to generation.

While on Mt. Desert visit Finest Kind in Hulls Cove, a new restaurant in an old house, run by Eleanor and George Tilghman. A dish of mussels called "Up the River Mussels" was fresh and pungent, and the swordfish was well prepared. And for steamed clams and lobster in a no-frills setting, we liked Abel's Lobster Pound in Somes Sound on Route 198. It is surrounded by what is advertised as America's only natural fjord.

Our last stop was a French restaurant and inn called Le Domaine in Hancock, just north of Mt. Desert Island on Route 1. This charming oasis was started in 1946 by Marianne Purslow-Dumas. This talented, energetic French lady was the mother of Nicole Purslow, the present owner, who earned her diploma from the Cordon Bleu School of Cookery in Paris and assisted her mother in the restaurant before she took over. It is difficult to imagine how Le Domaine could be in better hands. Nicole is a conscientious and gifted chef, and her restaurant would shine anywhere.

From the outside the simple red house on Route 1 is unprepossessing, but inside the atmosphere is that of a French country inn. The dining room has a massive fireplace at one end, red and white cloths on the tables, maps of the French *départements*, and pictures of old crests and costumes of France. There were flowers everywhere: clover and daisies on the tables and a huge vase of Queen Anne's lace. Dinner was an occasion to celebrate. There was a delicious *brandade de morue*, cod pounded with a wooden mallet and made into a smooth purée by the slow addition of warm olive oil; and *soupe de poissons*, a combination of several varieties of native fish and shellfish accompanied by a garlicky *rouille*. For the main course that night Nicole had a perfectly poached salmon with sauce *rémoulade* and a delectable veal dish with cream and mushrooms. The rabbit with prunes, a great specialty of Le Domaine, was also on the menu; the problem was in choosing from an embarrassment of riches. For dessert a frozen raspberry mousse with meringues and the special chestnut coupe were offered, both sublimely concocted temptations. It was hard to believe that we were "Down East" and not in some wayside inn in the Périgord or Burgundy.

We stayed the night in a small bedroom upstairs that encouraged one to linger; the bed was comfortable, the carpet thick and soft, and there were lots of fluffy yellow towels. On our bedside tables were the latest *Réalitiés*, and our window looked out on the kitchen garden where lettuce, cabbage, chives, and rhubarb were flourishing. Someone had put columbines in a bowl on the dresser. The next morning we breakfasted on freshly squeezed orange juice, raspberries with cream, and warm bread with the inn's own honey and cherry preserves—not to mention real French coffee in the pot. Marjorie Pierce, Nicole's able assistant, took care of the guests at both dinner and breakfast as though her only wish was their comfort. We left Le Domaine feeling thoroughly pampered, with promises to return someday. As the French say, it was *vaut le voyage.*

We drove down the coast, headed home, leaving this country of harsh weather, cold water, and short, short summers—but summers of incomparable natural beauty. From the plaque on Mt. Battie I had copied the first lines of "Renascence," and, as I read it again now, it seems somehow to capture perfectly the beauty of coastal Maine:

> All I could see from where I stood
> Was three long mountains and a wood;
> I turned and looked another way,
> And saw three islands in a bay.
> So with my eyes I traced the line
> Of the horizon, thin and fine,
> Straight around till I was come
> Back to where I'd started from;
> And all I saw from where I stood
> Was three long mountains and a wood.

Three New Hampshire Inns

*T*O THOSE WHO were brought up on the European grand
tour or motor trips through Tuscan hill towns or
Provence, there is a tendency to ignore one's own "backyard." For
example, there are innumerable excursions that can be taken in
New England to inns no more than twenty or thirty miles apart,
where beautiful scenery, a plethora of activities, and fine dining
await. A recent visit to three inns in the southwestern corner
of New Hampshire, known as the Monadnock region, was just
such a trip. Though we motored there from New York City on
less than a full tank of gasoline, we could have also flown via Air
New England to Keene, New Hampshire, and there rented a car.
A drive, starting from and returning to Keene that includes a sojourn at each of the three inns, totals no more than one hundred
miles, even with some serendipitous detours, which in this part of
the world tend to occur.

The area is dominated by Mount Monadnock, one of the most
climbed mountains in the world, with an elevation of 3,166 feet.
The two neighboring counties are Cheshire and Hillsborough,
and they both abound in picturesque towns: Nelson, with its lush
green common and Colonial church; Harrisville, called "America's most painted mill town," with old brick factories on the

pond; Dublin, at the base of Mount Monadnock, New England's highest town with an altitude of 1,493 feet; Hancock, a fine example of the architectural splendor of the late eighteenth and early nineteenth centuries; and Peterborough, where the tourist association of the region will supply the visitor with all pertinent facts. There are three active ski areas in the vicinity—Crotched Mountain and Bobcat, near Bennington, and Temple Mountain, near Peterborough. And, of course, all of this territory is paradise for the cross-country skier. The summer visitor will find a plentiful supply of golf courses in Jaffrey, Keene, Peterborough, Sullivan, and Walpole. There are tennis courts, too, in many of these "clubs," most of which welcome visitors.

This is not a part of the world for just the sports-minded, however. There is an active music program called Monadnock Music Summer Concert Series that gives performances from mid-July to the end of August in churches and meetinghouses throughout the region, and from Nelson, New Hampshire, the Apple Hill Chamber Players, a chamber group, plays locally and is well-known nationally. There are also two excellent summer theaters: the Peterborough Players, one of the first groups in New England, and the Keene Summer Theatre at Keene State College. It is a part of the world where people are interested in the arts, and the MacDowell Colony, outside Dublin in Peterborough, is probably the oldest and most prestigious of the artist colonies. Founded by the family of composer Edward MacDowell, the colony thrives today granting writers, painters, sculptors, and musicians a secluded place to work for a month or more while they are free from the cares of day-to-day existence.

Route 123 originates in Walpole, a classically handsome village on the lush eastern bank of the Connecticut River that wends its way through well tended meadows and towns consisting of no more than a post office and eight or ten houses. Just before the town of Stoddard, on the crest of one of the higher hills, is the Pitcher Mountain Farm, where shaggy Scotch Highlander cattle graze on the rocky slopes.

The Pitcher Mountain Inn is on that same road, and it and perhaps a dozen other buildings are, in fact, the village of Stoddard Center. The inn, a neat, buff-colored house with a bright red front door, was built in 1830, when the region was a thriving glass center that produced the famous amber glass for which the town was named. Allowed to fall into disrepair with much of the rest of Stoddard, the inn was bought and completely restored by a Boston architect in 1930. Then, in the spring of 1978, Bill and Dawn Matthews—onetime owners of a small restaurant in Stoddard who were on the lookout for something larger—bought the establishment. They did all the refurbishing themselves, mainly cosmetic work, and added a larger stove and walk-in refrigerators to an almost professionally equipped kitchen.

The house is much grander than one would expect from the entrance. There is a small front parlor on the left and an even smaller bar on the right. A long, narrow hallway leads to the dining room, which is a delight with dark wood paneling and the back and side walls all windows (the dining room was extended to include the porch). The room can seat thirty-five people at tables covered with crisp green and white napery. Flowers in charming pewter containers adorn each table. Outside is a wonderful horseshoe stone wall that borders the lawn, with clumps of lemony day lilies blooming in profusion with pansies, huge jack-in-the-pulpits, and marigolds the color of fresh butter. Herbs that are used in the kitchen proliferate at the foot of the wall, and beyond, the kitchen garden thrives. Several varieties of sedum and thyme carpet rocks with their blossoms. Everything that grows is used in the inn: The purple flowers of chives float in bowls of soup, and day lilies decorate plates of pâté. They are there to be eaten and are, in fact, delicious.

Bill and Dawn Matthews are a remarkable pair. They both were born and grew up on Maryland's Eastern Shore. Bill has always had a passion for food and its preparation and is uncompromising in his search for fresh supplies for the inn, not an easy task in this rural part of the world. With the exception of Portuguese rolls from a baker in Nashua, all the baking is done at the inn. Both Matthews are self-taught cooks. Dawn has become accomplished in pastrymaking. Bill believes that the less ingredients are tampered with, the better. Dawn serves as host and maitre d'hôtel, and both the Matthews obviously have a talent for not only keeping their guests happy but also creating what seems a particularly harmonious combination of staff. Along with the Matthews and their three young children, everyone eats together in the evening. Because Bill Matthews is also a musician, as are some others on the staff, there are frequent impromptu concerts. The Sunday afternoon that we were there the sounds of a Chopin nocturne floated out the open windows across the garden.

The inn is primarily a place to dine, although there are three simple, comfortable bedrooms for those wishing to stay the night. When one sits down in the dining room, the first thing to appear is a dish of *crudités* with homemade curry mayonnaise. There are six starters to choose from besides onion soup and a soup du jour. We opted for the pâté, which was perfect—velvety in texture, well seasoned, and attractively presented on a bed of crisp lettuce. With excellent homemade bread it makes for a satisfying first course. The soup of the day was cold cucumber, and it, too, was first-rate. There are eight main courses of fish, fowl, and meat, regulars on the menu, and then there are the specials of the day, which when we were there included lobster Pernod, swordfish with hollandaise, and *calamari* (squid) salad. We chose scallops *provençale* from the menu, which were lightly cooked and fragrant with tomatoes, garlic, herbs, and white wine and were served on croutons. Another entrée, suprémes of chicken Normandy, boned chicken breasts with apples, Gruyére, white wine, and Cognac, proved an intriguing combination of flavors. Our final sampling, lamb brochette, delicately marinated chunks of meat broiled on a skewer to just the right degree of doneness, was served with a moist and flavorful rice Soubise. The vegetable that night was broccoli, bright green and *al dente*. A tray was brought to the table so one could choose from Dawn's delicious pastries—a Grand Marnier or a chocolate cheesecake and a mocha rum cake. We sampled both cheesecakes as well as a refreshing boysenberry parfait. Throughout we drank a carafe of the house white wine, which was dry and well chilled. All in all, a thoroughly pleasing dinner in an exceptional setting.

We wound out of Stoddard on Route 123, heading southeast past Highland Lake and Island Pond, clear and reflective among the pine trees, to Hancock, a typically beautiful New England town with a wide, tree-shaded main street, neatly painted old houses proudly featuring their dates on the front, and a meeting-house that boasts a Paul Revere bell. From Hancock it is just a few miles on Route 137 to Bennington, once called Hancock Factory and part of Hancock town. Our second stopping place, David's, is on the main square there and is a blue clapboard building with cream-colored trim and shutters, a coral-colored door, and pots of red geraniums in bloom. The house was built in 1788 and has been restored to its post-Colonial design: The granite steps and some of the plastering are original. Inside is a delightful dining room with dark beams against light walls, charming stencils, wide floorboards, and a handsome banjo clock that strikes, with perfect resonance if not accuracy, at twenty past the hour. On the day that I visited, the dozen tables were set with white cloths, red and blue napkins, and bunches of daisies, and a huge spray of mock orange adorned the piano in the corner. A relish tray was brought in with creamy cottage cheese, a delicious rhubarb and strawberry conserve, and what I soon learned was Hazel's famous five-bean salad. I sampled these with a perfect yeast roll and honey buns while waiting for my salmon pie, the special on the lunch menu. I was told later by David himself that the relish tray is the responsibility of Hazel, a lady who comes in every morning to do just that and who changes the offerings—sometimes watermelon pickle, pickled pumpkin, apple butter, or cranberry orange relish—according to what produce is available. In summer, when melons are in season, they will be included in the selection, and because customers clamor for it Hazel's bean salad is offered year round. The salmon pie was served with carrots, green beans, a delectable little potato rosette I had not intended to eat but finished, and a garnish of sliced orange. The pie was sublime—a light salmon filling, a perfect crust, and a rich egg sauce. Other choices that day were lobster salad, Welsh rabbit, and roast tenderloin of beef hash, all served with vegetables and delicious home-baked rolls. David later told me with understandable pride that no prepared foods are used and that all the cooking is done with butter. For dessert I succumbed to his meringue with ice cream and strawberry sauce. I also glanced at the dinner menu, which featured panfried New Hampshire trout, David's country chicken pie, and Maine lobster pie with crumb crust. For dessert there would be apricot rum cake in addition to German brownies and the meringues. David's mother is responsible for much of the baking and is a key member of the kitchen staff.

The David in question is David Glynn, a dedicated and knowledgeable innkeeper and chef. His French grandmother ran a boardinghouse in the very building where his inn is today, and David thinks that he acquired his innate skills from her. After high school in Bennington, David decided to go to the Fannie Farmer Boston Cooking School for further training. All of his cooking is typical of the best regional fare of New England, where, because of the many dairy farms, cream and butter are used liberally.

After graduating from cooking school David managed for fifteen years an inn in Antrim, a small town just north of Bennington, and after that experience was able to start his own place. He is attentive to every detail, and, as is the case with so many of today's young chefs, nothing was too much trouble if it improved the quality of the food. Upstairs at David's there are two small, immaculate bedrooms, furnished in charming period pieces, with baths. It is comforting to know there is a pleasant place to spend the night after the indulgences of one of David's dinners.

From Bennington, Route 202 leads south to Peterborough and from there to the charming town of Jaffrey Center. The common of the town is dominated by the Old Meeting House, a handsome steepled building that was erected the day of the Battle of Bunker Hill in 1775. The black-faced clock with gold hands is testimony to the passage of the hours, but to stand on the green surrounded by shaded white houses that date from the late 1700s is to feel oneself transported back to a more peaceful time. There is a long shed behind the meetinghouse that was used for the horses and the carriages of the congregation, and this, thanks to the efforts and generosity of some citizens of Jaffrey Center, was brought back to its authentic state in 1954. There is also a little red schoolhouse in perfect repair. In the cemetery just off the common, down a gentle slope and under a spruce that has left a soft, brown blanket of its fallen needles, Willa Cather is buried. The gravestone reads:

WILLA CATHER
Dec. 7th 1876–April 24, 1947

The truth and charity of her great
spirit will live on in the work
which is her enduring gift to
her country and all its people.

"... this is happiness
to be dissolved into something
complete and great"
—from *My Antonia*

The day I was there, there was a small pot of pink geraniums on the grave. A stone rests at the foot of the plot, which states: Edith Lewis 1882–1972. She, I discovered, was the author's lifetime companion and housekeeper. Willa Cather, whose writings deal mainly with America's West, summered at the Shattuck Inn on Mountain Road in Jaffrey Center and also spent some time at the MacDowell Colony. There is a story told that one of her friends, who had a farm up the hill from the town, used to pitch a tent in her most remote mowing so that Willa Cather could have the necessary tranquillity and solitude to write. Willa Cather must indeed have had a very special feeling for this corner of the world to ask that it be her final resting place. We drove to see the Shattuck, a typical New Hampshire summer hotel of years gone by, which now houses something called the Charismatic Center.

The main road goes straight through the middle of Jaffrey

Center, and The Monadnock Inn is on the right-hand side of the road if one comes from the Old Meeting House. It is a large white clapboard building with dark green shutters, four huge maples that shade its entrance, and an American flag blowing in front of a spacious screened porch that is bordered by window boxes with red and white impatiens. As one enters, there is a pleasant, small bar on the left and a cozy sitting room with a fireplace on the right. The dining room is really three rooms with the porch used for dining in the summer. Upstairs are fourteen bedrooms, eight of them with private bath, not luxurious but all restful.

Sally Roberts is the owner and official greeter and, on the day I was there, the bartender as well. She came from New England originally, spent a good part of her life teaching school in New Jersey, and arrived in Jaffrey in February of 1977 to run The Monadnock Inn. She has two daughters and a son of college age who all help out, at least during the summer months. The rest of the staff consists of enthusiastic and capable young women who live in the community and who, sporting yellow Monadnock Inn T-shirts and denim skirts, do first-rate work as waitresses. Tom Ponticelli is the chef.

We lunched on the porch with an enjoyable view of the passing parade on the tree-shaded main thoroughfare. The soup of the day was a smooth and well-seasoned cream of vegetable; my husband had the *quiche lorraine*, which he found excellent, and I had broiled scrod served with carrots and mushrooms and sautéed cabbage. For dessert we had the chef's chocolate mousse, one of the best I have ever eaten, and rhubarb crêpes, both served with sweetened whipped cream.

The dinner menu is interesting and varied. There are five starters, among them very good cauliflower fritters *rémoulade*. Main courses include steak *au poivre vert* (with green peppercorns) and stuffed loin of pork Vouvray, a great favorite with the regular patrons. There is always a fresh fish, and one of the specialties that evening was *paupiettes* of sole. Desserts range from various crêpes to cheesecake and that delectable chocolate mousse. Again, all of the baking is done on the premises.

Though there are bound to be some limitations of choice when a restaurant is far from the larger purveyors of comestibles, there is the challenge to these three inns to use what is in season and to exercise creativity and innovation with those goods. It would be difficult to eat better at reasonable cost and in more pleasant surroundings than in these delightful inns in the Monadnock region.

Vermont's Shelburne House and Farms

*I*N 1880 WILLIAM SEWARD WEBB, doctor turned businessman, boarded a train in New York City headed for Burlington, Vermont. His mission: to scout out the Rutland Railroad as a possible acquisition for his boss, railroad magnate William Henry Vanderbilt. Webb's report on the advisability of a take-over was not favorable, but his enthusiasm for the area that he had visited knew no bounds.

Webb would soon forge even closer ties with Vanderbilt, as he was engaged to marry Vanderbilt's daughter, Lila. He lost little time in escorting his fiancée to Burlington, and she, too, was smitten with the lush Lake Champlain countryside. For a socially prominent young Victorian couple, a move to remote northern Vermont was considered a curious choice, a far cry from Newport or Saratoga Springs. But choose it they did, and following their marriage in 1881 the couple rented in Vermont in order to supervise the construction of their first house. Known as Oakledge, the relatively modest dwelling overlooked the lake from the site of a former apple orchard.

In 1885 William Vanderbilt died, and his daughter inherited the princely sum of ten million dollars. Webb started to acquire additional lakefront properties, eventually buying up thirty small farms. In 1887 ground was broken on Saxton's Point, about three miles south of Oakledge, for the construction of a shingled "cottage," as the Victorians modestly called their summer mansions. By 1899 the redesign and expansion of the cottage to the sixty-room Shelburne House that stands today was complete. Guests have been received at the house since 1987, when it became an inn.

The planning and building of the agricultural estate, Shelburne Farms, was not simply for the purpose of providing a luxurious residence and entertainment facility for a social and wealthy family. Dr. Webb, far ahead of his time, wanted not only a retreat that would evoke memories of a pre-industrial era, but he envisioned, too, a working farm that would achieve new goals in animal breeding and experimental agriculture. *The House at Shelburne Farms*, a historical account by Joe Sherman, available at Shelburne House, tells the tale of the Webb family's dream and puts it thus: "Central to the vision from its inception was this farm of the new age, vast in dimension, functioning outside typical economic restraints, embracing both the pastoral landscape of yesterday and the scientific farm of tomorrow. A not-so-distant visual past surrounded and defined a desirable agricultural future. This concept of an experimental farm in an inspired landscape distinguished Shelburne Farms from all the others."

The spirit carries over today for, when it became clear in 1972 that the place could no longer be maintained as a private estate, Derick Webb, grandson of William Seward Webb, and his children formed the nonprofit company Shelburne Farms Resources. The mission of this corporation was to "maintain and adapt its historic buildings and landscape for teaching and demonstrating the stewardship of natural agricultural resources." In 1976 Derick Webb deeded Shelburne House to the corporation, but it was not until 1983 that the directors voted to pursue the necessary alterations that would transform the house into an inn. With Derick's son Marshall as forester and woodlot manager for Shelburne Farms Resources, his other son Alec as general manager, and Marilyn, Alec's wife, as president, the company began two years of extensive renovation and restoration in 1985, and the inn opened in 1987.

From the main gate of the farms to the entrance of Shelburne House is a distance of nearly two miles. The splendid park through which one drives was designed by Frederick Law Olmsted, who had become well known for his work on Central Park in New York. His models for Shelburne Farms, with its one thousand acres of open meadows, vast stands of trees, and lake vistas, were surely the great English parks. Past the gigantic Farm Barn, constructed of limestone quarried in the area and shingles, the road meanders through fields where Brown Swiss cows graze, creating a perfect replica of a Constable landscape.

After passing the massive brick Coach Barn, the road leads to Shelburne House, set on well tended lawns overlooking Lake Champlain. One would feel far more at home in a four-in-hand driving under the porte cochere of this extraordinary brick-over-wood Queen Anne-style mansion. The first impression is one of great size—the house's guest rooms alone number twenty-four—it seems to go on and on. Chimneys, dormers, and numerous roof angles give character to the massive structure. The charming conical-roofed porches on either end of the house serve as pleasant places to doze, read, or enjoy views of the lake and Coach Barn.

The entrance hall, paneled in golden quartered oak with a beamed ceiling and furnished in the Victorian manner, is welcoming. Fires illuminate the two hearths when even the slightest chill wind blows up from the lake, and flower-filled vases add a burst of color. Harold Macmillan, the former British Prime Minister, when told that the Astors' great house Cliveden had been made a hotel, remarked, "It always was." One cannot help but find this remark applicable to Shelburne House where literally hundreds of guests—most rich, many famous—walked through the front door to enjoy the hospitality provided by a staff of thirty.

The Webb presence in the house is palpable. To the left of the hall one enters the pale green library stocked with bound volumes of Balzac, Thackeray, Dumas, and George Meredith, in addition to Lila Webb's collection of gardening books. Her desk stands near a window that looks out on her beloved garden. The pink and white tearoom, where the tea ritual continues to be observed every afternoon, is situated to the right of the hall. Family portraits—of Lila Webb, her father, her father-in-law, and her only daughter, Frederica Webb Pulitzer—adorn the walls.

Upstairs warm shades of deep red enliven the hall. Fabric wall covering and a carpet in burgundy at the head of the stairs lead to long corridors with charming red and white flowered paper. This, along with many of the bedroom papers, was reproduced by the Old Deerfield Fabric Company from originals used by Lila Webb. After careful research of old photographs and household records, the current generation of Webbs have restored Shelburne House, as if by magic, to its heyday with much of the original family furniture.

Each guest room has a unique identity. The Rose Room features moiré wallpaper with a border of roses, cabbage-rose chintz curtains, a canopied double bed, and views of the lake. A handsome sleigh bed, mauve velvet on chair seats, a decorative mirror with golden garlands and caryatids, and beige wallpaper with gold medallions set an elegant tone in the Empire Room. Dr.

Webb's Room, at the head of the stairs, expresses an airy feeling with three large windows set high above the lawn, gardens, and lake. Green patterned William Morris wallpaper and a similarly shaded floral carpet, needlepoint valances, an ornate rosewood bed, and a velvet chaise make up the furnishings here.

Accommodations on the third floor, once the children's rooms, offer somewhat simpler but still wonderfully comfortable lodging. Beguiling hummingbird paper, four-poster twin beds, and a bathroom with splendid views highlight the Pink Room. Bathrooms throughout the house are commodious with the over-size tubs and washbasins of a more gracious age. Lila Webb had a penchant for white bathrooms, and her preference was considered of sufficient interest to the public that an article entitled "Lila Webb's White Bathrooms" once appeared in the *New York Herald Tribune*. In the White Room, white wicker and striped pink and white wallpaper create a bright atmosphere.

Downstairs, at the north end of the house, one finds the dining room, known as the Marble Room. Burgundy silk damask covers the walls and the seats of handsome Queen Anne and Chippendale chairs. Black and white marble floors, decorative relief plasterwork on the ceiling, and French doors opening onto the terrace with views of the lawns and lake make dining here a pleasure. In the evening white Villeroy & Boch china and white napery tied with a red satin ribbon add a touch of the elegance of the Gilded Age. In the kitchen, where eighty-five years ago Lila Webb's cook reigned supreme, David Taylor directs operations as *chef de cuisine*. Marnie Wolcott, manager of the inn, and Marilyn Webb lured him to Vermont from his native Scotland, where he had been head chef on the luxury train *The Royal Scotsman*.

On the first night of our visit we started dinner with a fine smooth, flavorful cream of vegetable soup and a delicate sweetbread and *shiitake* mushroom *vol-au-vent*. Rack of lamb with rosemary sauce and squab roasted with Port were accompanied by perfectly cooked broccoli, tiny zucchini, and summer squash. Dessert was blueberry *crème brûlée* and a three-berry tart containing raspberries, strawberries, and blueberries. Shelburne House has a good wine list from which we chose a renowned red Hermitage. The menu generally consists of five main courses and changes every day, so a stay of a few days will furnish plenty of gastronomic variety.

Lasagne in ramekins and zucchini and carrot timbales began our dinner the next night, followed by roasted local quail and sliced leg of veal with white wine and lemon sauce. All was attractively presented and nicely seasoned. For our last evening David Taylor produced the Scottish specialty Cullen skink, smoked fish chowder, aromatic and flavorful. Chicken suprêmes, stuffed with spinach and *foie gras* and napped with a saffron and nutmeg sauce, tasted every bit as good as they sounded. We celebrated with a gala dessert of mixed-berry crêpes and Champagne sabayon. Our wine of the evening, Mount Eden Vineyards Chardonnay, was the proverbial icing on the cake.

Breakfasts are cause for celebration too. Colorful chintz cloths adorn the tables, and one can help oneself from the buffet table laden with a luscious assortment of fruits, yogurts, cereals, sliced ham, croissants, and, each day, a different muffin, possibly grape, cranberry, or apple. Generous pots of jams and butter accompany these delicacies. Then guests can order a "cooked" breakfast: perhaps eggs with cob-smoked bacon or herb sausages or the hard-to-resist daily special. We sampled the special breakfast on two mornings and can wholeheartedly recommend the Cheddar and three-pepper omelet—the yellow, green, and red bell peppers teaming perfectly with the sharp cheese—and the eggs Shelburne, eggs Benedict made with *pancetta* (cured pork belly) instead of ham or Canadian bacon and a basil hollandaise. Continental breakfast, prompt and hot, is also served in guest rooms upon request.

The inn does not serve a midday meal as such but will pack a first-rate box lunch to be consumed in some pretty picnic spot on the grounds or to be taken on the road. Delicious prosciutto, roast beef, and salami were ready for us the morning we left, with little yellow tomatoes, lettuce, fine French bread, grapes, and ice-cold mineral water.

David Taylor apprenticed in Italy before his stint on *The Royal Scotsman*, and there, I am certain, he became accustomed to locally grown and produced comestibles. Fortunately he has this fresh abundance at Shelburne House, one of the main reasons that one eats so well. David Miskell, who modestly calls himself a market gardener, is, in fact, a talented horticulturist. He has acquired a considerable knowledge of European growing methods and plants and puts these to use in the estate's Market Garden. We enjoyed walking among the rows of lettuces and sweet red bell peppers and in the greenhouses where tiny yellow tomatoes, sweet beyond belief, were flourishing. Miskell supplies the inn's needs first and then sells the remaining produce to restaurants and shops in the Burlington area. The same arrangement applies to O Bread, the bakery housed in the Farm Barn. The resident bakers turn out fine French, raisin, and sesame wheat bread for the inn and market the rest. Cob-smoked hams and bacon and herbed sausages come from a local farm and are packed in Hinesburg, Vermont. And lastly, the inn serves and cooks with Shelburne Farms Cheddar, one of the best I have tasted, made in the Dairy Barn from milk of the Brown Swiss herd.

At the Visitor Center, near the entrance gate, one can view

an entertaining slide presentation on the background and goals of the farms. Tours of the estate leave every hour from the center. In a small hay wagon, with a guide, visitors have the opportunity to see, at close hand, the extraordinarily beautiful nineteenth-century barns.

The Farm Barn, with its huge impressive courtyard, was designed by Robert Robertson, who did the drawings for all the main structures on the estate. Its mix of building materials—red rock limestone, cedar shingles, green pine boards, and copper roof—produces a uniquely varied effect. O Bread, a boat builder, and a cabinetmaker are all housed here, as are storage rooms for maintenance equipment and cold rooms, kept at forty-two degrees, for aging the farm's cheeses. A slate roof, cluster chimneys, and diversified window shapes are the striking features of the brick Coach Barn, where, in former days, coaches were lifted on a platform elevator and stored on the second floor. The Stewardship Institute Teacher Workshop, the division of Shelburne Farms devoted to promoting education in agriculture and natural resources, has offices and classrooms here. Groups of schoolchildren from all over New England come to Shelburne Farms, a National Historic Site with one thousand acres of forest and farmland.

The tour also includes a visit to the Dairy Barn for a look at cheesemaking. Bill Clapp is the talented, hardworking, and charming gentleman in charge of the production of Shelburne Farmhouse Cheddar. By tradition in England, the term "Farmhouse" can only be applied to cheese that has been made from the milk of a single herd on the property, and such is the case at Shelburne Farms.

A two-mile walking trail also starts at the Visitor Center and winds through fields of oats, alfalfa, and blue-flowering wild chicory to a halfway point, the highest part of the estate, Lone Tree Hill. From here one has a spectacular view of Shelburne House, Lake Champlain, and New York's Adirondacks to the west and Mount Mansfield and Camel's Hump, the two highest peaks of the Green Mountain range, to the east. A small granite bench bears the inscription: "In memory of Vanderbilt Webb 1891- 1956 and Aileen O. Webb 1892-1979, grandparents of the Webbs who care for Shelburne Farms today." The shop in the Visitor Center stocks a tempting array of gifts and comestibles. Cow lovers will have difficulty choosing from among a selection that includes sweat shirts and T-shirts in all sizes and colors with a handsome bovine emblazoned on them, cow coffee mugs, and cow tote bags. A good assortment of books on Vermont and locally crafted pottery stock the shelves too. Shelburne Farms Cheddar and honey, cob-smoked meats, and maple syrup make perfect presents. The shop publishes a mail-order catalogue and will ship anywhere. Tours of the farms are not given in the winter, but the Visitor Center and Farm Store are open year round.

No excursion to this part of Vermont would be complete without spending at the very least a day in the Shelburne Museum, a mere three miles from the inn. Founded in 1947 by Electra Havemeyer Webb and her husband, Watson, son of William Seward and Lila Webb, the museum is a treasure trove of Americana and folk art. According to a presentation given at the museum, Electra Webb found her inspiration in the beauty of the American spirit that she saw expressed in everyday things. This extraordinary collection has continued to thrive through private funding and public donations since Electra Webb's death in 1960. Winslow Homer, Ammi Phillips, George Henry Durrie, Edward Lamson Henry, and Erastus Salisbury Field are among the American painters exhibited in the museum who capture the essence of

New England. A plethora of weather vanes, cigar-store Indians, toys, and examples of nineteenth-century wood carvings are also displayed along with Chinese export porcelain and probably the largest quilt collection extant.

Among the museum's highlights are the *S.S. Ticonderoga*, landlocked and here to be visited. The last of the passenger and freight side-wheel steamers intact, the *Ticonderoga* was built in Shelburne Harbor in 1906. And in the Circus Parade Building is a charming 525-foot-long, hand-carved scale model of a circus parade. In the Electra Havemeyer Webb Memorial Building, constructed in 1967, one can go back in time by visiting rooms re-created from the New York apartment of the museum's co-founders, complete with furniture, Old Master and Impressionist paintings, and Degas bronzes. The aforementioned treasures are but an infinitesimal part of the vast collection.

Shelburne Museum and Shelburne Farms are incomparable American landmarks. The Webb family has made a generous and unique contribution. The museum provides a glimpse of our heritage, and to visit the inn makes for a rare experience—to be a guest at a great family house, beautifully restored and preserved. Both the museum and the house are open from June till mid-October.

Old Deerfield

*T*RAVELING NORTH ON I-91 from Hartford, one notes that the scenery begins to change perceptibly at Northampton and Hatfield. The median is suddenly awash with Queen Anne's lace and black-eyed Susans. There are broad, green fields and stands of oak and willow on either side of the highway. Evergreen tree farms begin to replace factories, and on Route 5—the Deerfield turnoff—strawberries and seedlings are the most important business.

Deerfield's quiet Main Street runs north and south, parallel to Route 5 for one measured mile. About halfway down the street is Deerfield Academy, the boys' boarding school, numbering today about 550 students and founded in 1799 as a small co-ed day school. In front of the school's main administration building stands a monument to the town's Civil War dead, and next to that the First Church of Deerfield carries a tall steeple on which perches a handsome gilt cockerel. The old houses of the village coexist well with the Academy. Though the past is celebrated here, the present is much in evidence. Two other schools, Bement and Eaglebrook, are as integral a part of the town as the Academy.

Deerfield lies in the Connecticut Valley, sandwiched in lush farmland between the Deerfield and Connecticut rivers. According to one local resident, the valley's abundance is second only to that of the Nile Valley. The area has fortunately remained agricultural: Because both rivers tend to flood in the springtime the crops are plentiful, the cattle's grazing fields are verdant, and development would be costly and impractical. Greenfield, the pleasantly bustling county seat a few miles north, is the area's commercial center. Dairy farmers share the historic main street with museums, and herds of Holstein graze in the fields that surround the town. If the wind is blowing in the right direction the smell of silage permeates the air. It is beautiful, unspoiled farmland.

The valley and hills to the east were called Pocumtuck ("clear open stream") after the tribe of Indians that lived there in the seventeenth century. This tribe was virtually wiped out by the Mohawk Indians of the Hudson Valley around 1650, and so it came about that eight thousand acres of land here were purchased by the town of Dedham, Massachusetts. Streets and lots were laid out, the settlement was called Deerfield, and the first Deerfield native was born to the Hinsdale family in 1673.

But the town was to suffer a series of calamities. The first took place soon after the founding when a group of Indians fell upon some unwary citizens, killing dozens of them in an encounter known as the Bloody Brook Massacre. Deerfield was abandoned, and Indians took over the land. In 1682 some daring settlers returned and this time, building more permanent houses, re-established the village. On February 29, 1704, Deerfield was attacked for a second time by a marauding band of Indians and French, who entered the town before daybreak, looted, burned, and either tomahawked or captured half the population. Two years later many of the former inhabitants returned to rebuild. In 1733 the governor of the Province of Massachusetts Bay met with leaders of the Indian tribes in Deerfield and a peace—of sorts—was made. In 1746 there was a final Indian raid that ended, once and for all, Deerfield's history of bloodshed.

During the pre-Revolutionary period the town was an important storage place for ammunition and supplies for the English troops. The residents of the village began to prosper, building fine houses filled with furnishings befitting their new affluence. When the conflicts over independence began, however, the town experienced the same bitter differences of opinion that split so many Colonial settlements—differences that were resolved when the war actually came and the men of Deerfield united to fight at Bunker Hill and Saratoga. Once it was all over they went gratefully back to farming. Indeed, the pastoral beauty of Deerfield today belies her bloody past.

Mr. and Mrs. Henry N. Flynt became interested in preserving the historic character of Deerfield in the 1940s. Mr. Flynt was born in nearby Munson, Massachusetts, and their son was a student at the Academy. They were, too, longtime friends of Frank Boyden, the legendary headmaster of the school from 1902 to 1968, who was keenly interested in the maintenance and restoration of the village. The Flynts' early efforts sought to improve the school, and in 1945 they renovated the Deerfield Inn and gradually acquired some of the old village houses, which they restored as apartments for faculty members. In 1952 the Flynts established the Heritage Foundation to subsidize these improvements, and in 1971 its name was changed to Historic Deerfield. Mr. Flynt died in 1970, but Mrs. Flynt and the trustees carry on the work today.

The starting point for a tour of the twelve fully restored and furnished houses is the Hall Tavern and Information Center. Here an orientation slide show relates tales of the town and its historic characters. Thus prepared, one can tour any or all of the houses with guides, in groups of six visitors, or arrange in advance for private tours. The Allen House, where the Flynt family lived until quite recently, is the only house where a visit must be prearranged. For those who aspire to in-depth knowledge of the collection, forums are given in the fall and spring on such topics as Oriental influences on early America, flowers and the decorative arts, or Queen Anne and Chippendale furniture at Historic Deerfield. The Hall Tavern, a seven-room museum, features a fine collection of New England country furniture and a stunning stenciled ballroom. Across the street the museum shop carries a good selection of literature about the village, along with such locally made items as potpourri, maple syrup, candles, and pottery.

The Frary House and Barnard Tavern was the first building in Deerfield to be restored. In 1890 Alice Baker, Springfield-born and Deerfield-raised, bought the house to "bring it back to life." Her quest to know Deerfield's history took her to Canada to track down some of the descendents of the survivors of the 1704 massacre. In restoring the house to its authentic décor, she collected furnishings, and the south parlor, or pewter room, has an impressive pewter collection and an intriguing wooden box commemorating the Bloody Brook Massacre. In the south bedchamber a fine example of embroidery preserves the work done by those Deerfield women of the early 1900s who called themselves the Blue and White Society. The bed cover and canopy are blue and white linen embroidered with the society's logo, a blue *D* in a spinning wheel. When Alice Baker's refurbishing was completed she gave a ball upstairs in the tavern ballroom, where guests were invited to wear full Colonial regalia.

Memorabilia from a lawyer and a doctor can be found in the Wells-Thorn and the Dwight-Barnard houses. Wells-Thorn, resplendent in a coat of robin's-egg-blue paint, displays furnishings and architecture from the earliest Colonial times to the elegant Federal period. Mr. Strong, one of the house's inhabitants, practiced law in the north chamber on the second floor (with a separate entrance for his clients). In the south chamber a small turn chair (so called because the spindles are turned toward the sitter) echoes the past with this blood-chilling inscription:

Eunice Allen
Born June 6, 1733
Tomahawked August 25, 1746
Died August 16, 1818

The much-photographed Dwight-Barnard House has gray, blue, and red trim, a gambrel roof, and an interesting broken-scroll pedimented doorway. There is a charming low wooden fence with turned finials. This Springfield merchant's house was bought and moved to Deerfield by the Flynts, and here the visitor can see how one doctor practiced his profession. Dr. Thomas Williams and his son, William Stoddard Williams, were the community's doctors for almost a century, and their office in the front of the house is filled with such paraphernalia as apothecary jars, medicine bottles, and scales. An elaborate Boston Bombay secretary in the south parlor and a fine mahogany turreted tea table are just a sampling of the Dwight-Barnard's treasures.

The Allen House, dating back to about 1720 and restored by the Flynts in 1944 for their own use, is an unpainted, center-chimney Colonial saltbox. It is filled with an overwhelming array of high-quality American pieces. Whenever possible the antiques used have been locally owned or made, resulting in the most comprehensive collection of Connecticut Valley furniture and pewter to be found anywhere. When local pieces were not available, the Flynts found Colonial articles elsewhere, creating a sort of antiquarian's dream world. It is easy to see why Old Deerfield has been called a major museum for the study of American culture and one of the most notable reclamations in this country. To take advantage of the town's heritage, allow at least a half-day to note the Copley portraits, tall chests, Queen Anne chairs, and gateleg tables in the Allen House.

The Ashley House and the Sheldon-Hawks House are next door to each other at the head of Main Street. They were built in 1730 and 1743, respectively, and were restored from 1946 to 1956. In the Ashley House there is an exceptional New London cherry chest and a portrait of John Williams, one of Deerfield's first ministers. In the south chamber a Colonial equivalent of a Murphy bed pulls up to the wall when not in use. The doorway of the Sheldon-Hawks House is the logo for Historic Deerfield, and the house has the distinction of having two kitchens back to back. In the first kitchen there is a contrivance called a blanket crane, where blankets were hung to dry before the fire, and a collection of ninety brass candlesticks. And on display in the south parlor is a uniquely nineteenth-century bone china asparagus partitioner, made to fit in a serving platter so that each dinner guest would have precisely the right share of asparagus, not one stalk more or less.

The only two brick houses on the street were both contracted by one Asa Stebbins, Franklin County's richest landowner. He had the first one built for himself from 1799 to 1810 and the second, the Wright House across from the Ashley House, in 1824 for his son. The Asa Stebbins House is an interesting example of the Federal style and a sharp contrast to the Colonial houses in the village. In the Federal period, rooms began to be used specifically as dining rooms and parlors; closets and mantles, too, began to make an appearance. Swirls, swags, and scrolls, fashionable at the time, adorn fabrics and wallpaper, and the commodious entrance hall, unknown till then, is covered with a charming scenic paper depicting Captain Cook's voyages. In the north parlor a sewing table and a writing desk attest to the more leisurely pursuits enjoyed in nineteenth-century America. The Wright House, where Asa Junior lived, has on loan the impressive Cluett collection of Chippendale and Federal furniture, as well as an extensive collection of Chinese porcelain belonging to Historic Deerfield. The north bedroom windows afford a dramatic vista of the lush green farmland of the valley.

The museum's various collections are spread among different barns and buildings. The silver shop, next to the Allen House, is in a farmhouse that features a workroom in the kitchen and an exhibition room containing outstanding examples of American and English silver that include the work of such well-known smiths as Revere and Coney and of two local craftsmen, Isaac Parker and John Russell. The Helen Geier Flynt Fabric Hall has an interesting display of textiles (brocade or loom silk, painted silk, crewel, quilts, and costumes of the period), and in the loft are dolls and children's clothes. The Wilson Printing Office has a working wooden press and a cabinetmaker's shop. Two cavernous barns off Main Street house the carriage collection as well as a collection of architectural fragments that can be seen by making arrangements in the Hall Tavern.

The Memorial Hall Museum on Memorial Street, east of Main Street, is not part of Old Deerfield as such, but a visit there certainly adds much to the general knowledge of the town and its history. George Sheldon, the Deerfield historian, played a vital part in preserving the village's past. Sheldon was one of the founders of the Trustees of Reservations in Massachusetts, after which England's National Trust was patterned, and in 1870 he organized the Pocumtuck Valley Memorial Association. In 1880 the museum, which features collections of Indian artifacts, military memorabilia, quilts, early furniture, and portraits, was opened to the public by the association; the first permanent period room, dating from 1880, is also on display. The most popular exhibit in the museum is the Indian House Door, which came from the 1698 Ensign Sheldon homestead and shows the damage done by Indian attacks during the 1704 massacre. The house itself is long since gone but has been replicated on Deerfield's Main Street and is called the Indian House Memorial. It is open to the public, and behind it is the Bloody Brook Tavern, which sells Deerfield pottery. Quilting classes using frames that are over two hundred years old are given here.

Visitors to Deerfield are thrice blessed: The historic restoration constitutes a first-rate museum; the village and surrounding countryside are quintessentially New England; and the Deerfield Inn is a fine stopping place. The neat white building, with its twelve new bedrooms in the back barn, stands in the center of town. After suffering a fire of major proportions in 1979, the inn has now been completely and most successfully renovated. The lobby, with its comfortable chairs, blue-flowered chintz sofas, and some fine American antiques, is most welcoming. The yellow Beehive Parlor was so named for the wallpaper, a copy of an early-nineteenth-century paper acquired by the Flynts. This room boasts two Windsor rockers, a tall clock, and some early portraits. The bar next door sports stenciled paper, old tables of varying shapes and sizes, and Windsor chairs. The bedrooms are all furnished with the guests' well-being in mind. The fabrics and furniture are in keeping with the Colonial period, but the bathrooms are the epitome of modern comfort. Rooms are named after such famous local characters as Horatio Alger, Consider Dickinson, and Captivity Jennings.

The dining room is inviting. The tables, chairs, chandeliers, and sconces are reproductions or adaptations—but good ones. Our first lunch consisted of an intriguing cold cherry-raspberry soup, biscuits that literally melted in the mouth, and poached salmon with hollandaise. There was also a pasta of the day, tomato fettuccine with *pesto*, and a good choice of salads and sandwiches. A quicker and lighter lunch, and breakfast too, are served downstairs, and on a fine day one can eat at umbrella-shaded tables outdoors.

Dinner is an elegant occasion, and the valley-born chef Christopher Opalenick, does himself proud with a menu featuring smoked salmon trout, a fine *pâté maison*, soups of the day such as creamed broccoli or cheddar, and tempting entrées including veal medallions *grand-mère*, napped with a cream sauce, and filet mignon with béarnaise sauce. Accompanying many summer meals is some of the sweetest corn I have ever tasted. Paul J. Burns, the efficient and genial manager of the inn, says that the local vegetables used in the dining room are growing while the guests sleep. The wine list at the inn is a good one; half bottles of Châteauneuf-du-Pape and Mâcon Blanc were fine accompaniments to dinner. And the desserts! As is the case in much of New England, the choices are numerous and succulent: chocolate pecan pie, brandied raisin custard bread pudding, and Indian pudding. The Inn has recently opened a bakery, and its freshly baked pies, cakes, and other desserts can be bought to take home. The Inn will also pack picnics, and, in fact, the staff goes out of its way to pamper guests. Would that there were more Deerfield Inns along our highways and byways.

Martha's Vineyard Off Season

Y DICTIONARY DEFINES *dolce far niente* as "it is sweet doing nothing" or "pleasant idleness," and the island of Martha's Vineyard, after the summer crowds have left, is a splendid place to indulge this pursuit. From the moment the whistle of our ferry, the *Uncatena*, gave its first blast we had the sense of a real voyage, a departure; a feeling that this would be a great getaway and change of pace from normal, everyday activities and cares. During the off-season (post-Labor Day through mid-June) ferries leave Woods Hole, Massachusetts, on the southernmost tip of Cape Cod, every hour for the forty-five-minute crossing to Vineyard Haven. Gulls swoop and dive alongside, hoping to be fed, and, if the day is fine, puffy white clouds cast shadows on the water.

The first Englishmen set foot on Martha's Vineyard in 1602, and the captain of their ship, the *Concord*, one Bartholomew Gosnold, is said to have named the island for the many grapevines he saw and for his infant daughter. According to island historians the first official settlement took place in 1642, when Thomas Mayhew Jr., whose father had bought the island the previous year from two English noblemen, was given authority to inhabit and plant the islands of Martha's Vineyard, Nantucket, and the Elizabeths. The Indian population declined greatly over the following century as white settlers flourished, farming the land and taking to the sea for their livelihood. In the early eighteenth century sheep farming (until all the island's animals were requisitioned and removed by the British during the Revolutionary War) and the whaling industry played important roles in the economy of the island. Masters of whaling vessels would sail home from voyages of three or four years, the holds of their ships filled with vast and valuable cargoes.

Visiting Martha's Vineyard when it is not overrun with summer folk has much to recommend it. The weather remains balmy long after summer is just a memory, and dahlias and roses flourish through October in the neat gardens of Edgartown. Mile after mile of beautiful beach is deserted, encouraging long walks and rock and shell collecting. Country roads, of which there are many, are blessedly free of traffic so that explorations can be made on foot, by bicycle, or by car to one's heart's content.

But if a little *far niente* goes a long way, there is also much to do. The Island Theater Workshop, founded in 1968, performs in Vineyard Haven, and music in an atmospheric setting is provided by the Abendmusik Choir concerts in the Federated Church of Edgartown. The chorus has thirty-two members, all local folk, and the church boasts a fine organ, which has been completely rebuilt to the specifications of Cavaille-Coll, the renowned nineteenth-century French organ builder. Also there is a good selection of movies shown at the Edgartown town hall.

Edgartown, Vineyard Haven, and Oak Bluffs are the largest communities, and, during the quieter months, they are where most of the island's activities take place. A good spot to begin a tour of Edgartown is the Dukes County Historical Society Museum on School and Cooke streets. Island memorabilia, scrimshaw, tools from the whaling trade, and over a hundred miniature pictures of whaling captains are nicely displayed. On the museum's grounds an enormous Fresnel lens from the old Gay Head Light is exhibited, along with an 1854 fire engine and various boats. Two particularly arresting headstones are on view in the carriage shed, lovingly inscribed by poet Nancy Luce, a resident of West Tisbury a century ago, for two of her pet laying hens. Her verses are included in a biography by Walter Teller entitled *Consider Poor I,* which can be obtained at the Historical Society. Also available is a pamphlet entitled *Walking Tour of Historic Edgartown,* providing a brief history of the island and descriptions of many of the houses. Winter hours at the museum are 1 to 4 P.M. on Thursdays and Fridays and 10 A.M. to 4 P.M. Saturdays.

A stroll through the quiet back streets of Edgartown is a very pleasant way to spend a morning. Cooke, School, Davis, and Summer streets all display fine examples of New England architecture, and an infinite variety of gates and fences enclose well tended gardens. In contrast to the quaint and comparatively small houses of the back streets, the great mansions of the whaling captains on North Water Street, with their stately columns and porticoes, seem very formal and grand. These command fine views of the harbor, the Edgartown lighthouse, and Chappaquiddick Island. Picturesque touches are added by red brick sidewalks and neat foundation planting.

The island's venerable *Vineyard Gazette* has its offices and press on South Summer Street, and one should be sure to read the weekly newspaper for a better enjoyment and understanding of the island. The *Gazette,* published on Fridays, is sold on Main Street at the newspaper store and the pharmacy. Getting to know Edgartown must include acquainting oneself with the local shops. A good number of these are open after the summer season has ended and remain so through the island's old-fashioned pre-Christmas weekend celebration around the middle of December.

If you are after clothes, the largest shop—it is, in fact, a small department store—is The Fligors at 27 North Water Street. The store carries a good selection for men, women, and children, including Diane Freis and the Geiger line of elegant sportswear, and also toys, china, and other gift items. Wilson House, just down the street at number 17, features leather jackets, bags, and belts, and scarves, hats, and sweaters made of toasty Icelandic and Irish wool. Sundog, at 41 Main Street, has a handsome array of men's attire—corduroys, scarves in eye-catching colors, suede jackets, and rugged outdoor wear. Farther up Main Street is Claudia, an excellent jewelry store, and, at number 37, Sassafras offers women's clothes, lingerie, and particularly attractive accessories, such as pretty velvet scarves in rich paisley prints and elegant patterned stockings.

If you can't live without more items for the house, a number of shops will indulge your cravings. Cork Corner, at 15 Winter Street, has, as its name suggests, place mats, trays, and trivets, all made of light, durable cork, and a marvelous assortment of handmade Amish and Mennonite quilts from Lancaster County, Pennsylvania. Walk a block north on Winter Street to The Vermont Shop for unusual items for the kitchen: tabletop butter keepers and vegetable steamers of sturdy Vermont stoneware and made-in-Vermont comestibles. Their Good Stuff mustard is a unique sweet-and-sour sauce made with dill that has no additives, preservatives, or salt. Vermont peach, apple, rum walnut, and strawberry Amaretto conserves are also delectable and different. A new line of cakes, including chocolate rum and lemon butter, from An Honest Loaf Baking Company was highly praised by both the storekeeper and a passing customer. A Gift of

Love on North Water Street has beautiful area rugs, hand-painted gift items, and large screens that can be ordered with almost any scene or design of your choice.

We're always on the lookout for a good bookstore, and Edgartown does not disappoint. Unicorn Tales Bookshop at Summer and Main has a full stock of current titles, and in addition they specialize in books on philosophy, backlist fiction classics, and women's literature.

After all this strenuous shopping, thoughts of lunch start to surface, for which, in Edgartown, three good options exist. SAVOIR FARE, on Post Office Square, is a small spot with a seating capacity of only about twenty-five, also selling goodies to go. Wonderful aromas are the first good sign as one enters the single room where everything takes place. Here the cooking is done behind a counter displaying breads and cakes, next to a large refrigerated case for salads. Specials of the day might include oyster Brie soup, individual chicken potpie in a Cheddar crust, venison pastry puffs, or crab and Saga blue quiche. Some of the cold dishes (a small helping of each makes a fine lunch) are *tortellini primavera*, Oriental beef with snow peas and sesame oil, and marinated plump mussels. Charlotte and Scott Caskey, the owners, clearly know their way around a kitchen. On fine days Savoir Fare can accommodate another forty on an outside deck, but the owners hope to either enlarge the current space or find a new location, which would provide more tables for the enthusiastic crowds. As we were leaving, we couldn't resist taking with us a small bag of their delicious chocolate chunk cookies.

For a completely different lunch experience try THE WHARF PUB on Lower Main Street. Pewter tankards hang over the long wooden bar where many locals congregate. Old photographs of the Vineyard are an integral part of the surroundings, as are the brass ceiling lamps. The food is good, hearty pub fare: Much-ordered specials are the chowders, hamburgers in hefty rolls, lobster and chef's salads, and pastrami sandwiches. The pub also serves variously stuffed potato skins, which are toasted to a turn for a filling lunch.

ZACHARIAH'S, the dining room in THE KELLEY HOUSE HOTEL on Kelley Street near the harbor, is our third Edgartown possibility for the midday meal. Sunshine pours into the large, cheerful room decorated in a pretty peach and green wallpaper. Crisp white curtains, little vases of flowers on each table, and wooden furniture create an old-fashioned summer hotel atmosphere. Choices for lunch are not particularly fancy, but they are good and served promptly. Scallop stew, broiled Atlantic scrod, and steak sandwiches are on the menu, and, for lighter selections, club sandwiches and omelets. The Kelley House, with its pleasantly unpretentious décor and fine location, is open all year.

When it comes time to make reservations for a visit to the Vineyard, book well ahead if your plans include a stay at THE CHARLOTTE INN on South Summer Street, for this is a veritable jewel, one of a kind. The owners, Paula and Gerret Conover, have, over aperiod of eighteen years, done an extraordinary job of refurbishing and furnishing what is now a compound of several buildings. The largest of these is the inn's main house, where an airy enclosed porch serves as the dining room. Along with the seven bedrooms that are also housed here are the Edgartown Gallery and the Gallery Shop. A variety of watercolors, oils, and prints by local artists are on view at the gallery, and the shop offers antiques and attractive gifts. Behind the main building are the three rooms and large garage that make up the Carriage House, which is currently being renovated to provide yet more space. Next door is the inn's latest acquisition, the Summer House, and across the street, oldest of all the buildings, the Garden House.

In all, The Charlotte Inn has twenty-four rooms; some are suites, some have working fireplaces, many have private terraces, and all are furnished in impeccable taste, mostly with English antiques collected by the owners in the antiques shops of New England and abroad. Charming touches are everywhere: A comfortable wing chair, reading lamp, end table complete with current magazines, and cut-glass decanter filled with Sherry are arranged invitingly in a nook in an upstairs hall. This kind of attention to detail is just as apparent in the bedrooms, several of which sport handsome brass beds, others four-posters with eyelet bedspreads, masses of pillows, and soft, warm blankets. An ornate set of silver hand mirror, buttonhook, and nail buffer and old photographs in silver frames are other details that add to the elegant yet homelike atmosphere. Attached to each differently decorated bedroom is a spacious bathroom that boasts a huge tub, electric towel rack, and every imaginable comfort.

The inn's grounds and gardens are also rife with pleasing aspects—flower pots amply filled with yellow chrysanthemums, perfectly trimmed diminutive box hedges, fountains, and neatly cobbled walks.

Breakfast for guests is served in the enclosed porch in the main house amid white furniture, much greenery, and a working fountain. A Continental breakfast of fresh orange juice; homemade apple-spice, bran, or pumpkin muffins; and coffee or tea comes with the price of lodging. For those with a morning appetite there are full breakfasts of French toast, omelets, or eggs any style. Breakfast, unhappily, is not served in the bedrooms, the only nicety that we can think of that The Charlotte Inn does not observe.

In the evenings, an elegant restaurant, L'ETOILE, takes

over the premises. Michael Brisson, who acquired much of his expertise at L'Espalier in Boston, is the chef and co-owner with his wife, Joan Parzanese. Dinner begins with such exotic dishes as *mille-feuilles* of smoked salmon mousse or grilled marinated shrimp on a panfried pasta cake with shrimp Champagne sauce. Main courses might be roast loin of veal with Stilton ravioli and wild mushroom sauce or rack of lamb with Cabernet rosemary sauce and butternut squash flans. The wine list is excellent: Jordan Cabernet Sauvignon '82 was our choice, and it was just right. Hazelnut chocolate mousse cake with coffee sauce and a walnut torte put the finishing touches on a memorable meal. L'Etoile's off-season opening hours vary, but usually include Thursday, Friday, and Saturday nights.

The Charlotte Inn is reminiscent of those wonderful English country-house-turned-hotels where no detail that might add to the well-being of guests is overlooked. Would that there were dozens more Charlotte Inns!

WARRINER'S, on Post Office Square off Main Street, is open for dinner every day but Wednesday. The softly lit, handsome paneled room—furnished with flower prints, Queen Anne chairs, bookcases filled with books, and a profusion of flowers— gives the impression of being in a private house. Our *prix fixe* dinner one evening started most satisfactorily with duck pâté accompanied by beach-plum chutney, sautéed cloves of elephant garlic, and goat cheese. The main courses included fricassee of rabbit and a standout chicken breast with sun-dried tomatoes and Romano, both served with corn fritters, miniature beets, beans, squash, and carrots. Lemon curd in a meringue shell and a deliciously decadent chocolate cake were our two dessert choices. The wine list is good, and Warriner's also offers wines by the glass; not just white and red but also Champagnes and Ports.

Under the same roof an offseason favorite called SAM'S—named for the owner of both establishments, Sam Warriner—provides lighter, simpler food in a less formal setting.

An excursion around the rest of the island is always an appealing activity on the Vineyard, particularly off season when beaches that were not only crowded during the summer months are now gloriously deserted. One of the finest of these is South Beach; miles and miles of fine white sand along the Atlantic coast, an appropriately pounding surf, and gulls and terns mingling overhead with the crows that inhabit the adjoining moors.

A drive to Gay Head at the westernmost tip reveals the island's extraordinarily varied terrain, formed as the result of three separate glacial actions. The fields, farmlands, hedgerows, and clusters of trees in the center of the island are reminiscent of the south of England and stand in sharp contrast to the beaches and the dramatic multicolored clay of Gay Head cliffs. The little fishing village of Menemsha is northeast of the Gay Head Light. It is quietly stunning in every season, and in the autumn and winter, when it is all but deserted, it has a ghostlike fascination.

Another delightful jaunt is the ferry ride from Edgartown to Chappaquiddick Island. The *On Time* ferry—so named because it goes only when there are passengers—departs from Town Dock at the foot of Daggett Avenue, and the crossing takes approximately one and a half minutes. The little boat holds just three cars at a fare of $1.75, and asks $1 for bicycles, 35¢ for passengers on foot, and 75¢ each for horses and cattle. Only private houses dot "Chappy," as the island is known to the locals, but a beautiful Japanese garden, My Toi, is open to the public, as are some of the splendid beaches. These are accessible on foot from the road and on a fine day make ideal places to picnic.

In West Tisbury, about four miles out of Vineyard Haven,

the LAMBERT'S COVE COUNTRY INN on Lambert's Cove Road offers a taste of seclusion and quiet. Originally a farmhouse, the inn, part of which dates back to 1790, is set in an apple orchard at the end of a long, bumpy dirt road. A stand of pines, old vine-covered stone walls, a vegetable garden, and a tennis court add to the inn's charm.

The interior is comfortable; nothing splashy, but with the look of some of grandmother's nice old things. The seven bedrooms of the main house are all different, named rather than numbered, some with individual decks, and all put together with a special touch. Orchard and Blossom overlook the apple trees, Rafter boasts the hand-hewn beams of the original farmhouse, white wicker furniture gives Wicker its name, and Sweet Pea is for the spring flowers that grow around the tennis court.

Continental breakfast, also included in the price of a night's stay, is served in the breakfast room. First-rate croissants and homemade nut muffins were brought warm to our table accompanied by a beach plum conserve also made at the inn. The dining room, like the rest of the house, does not suffer from delusions of grandeur but is made comfortable and welcoming by a crackling fire in the grate. The new chef in charge for a well attended Friday night dinner served mushrooms sautéed with Madeira, a bay scallop stew, rosemary *focaccia* (Italian flatbread), *coq au vin*, and flounder on a bed of spinach. Panfried new potatoes with rosemary accompanied the main courses, and a nice old-fashioned chocolate layer cake and an apple tart followed for dessert. Like all the towns on the island except for Edgartown and Oak Bluffs, West Tisbury is a so-called "dry" town, but the staff is happy to chill, open, and serve any beverage guests bring with them.

Lambert's Cove Inn is a homey, informal place where one has the sense of being a welcome houseguest, where, indeed, guests and help become part of an extended family. The day of our departure, as we paused to say our good-byes, some of the young staff and the innkeeper, Marie Burnett, were conducting a serious discussion on the front porch. The dilemma was as follows: Should the swallows' nests of last spring be razed so that the porch could be painted or should they be left undisturbed on the chance that they might be reinhabited? It did not take long to decide: The porch could wait.

Our ferry was to leave the island from Vineyard Haven, and so we took the opportunity for a walk around town and lunch before embarking. The Bunch Of Grapes, at 68 Main Street, is another excellent bookstore—one of the country's finest—offering a comprehensive selection of books on Cape Cod, the Islands, and almost every other topic. No one seems to mind prolonged browsing, presumably because it is likely that browsers will eventually become buyers. On the other side of Main Street is The Vineyard Gourmet, selling an interesting variety of cheeses and meats and a line of flavored vinegars made by the local Chicama Vineyards—raspberry, wine, and dill are available, along with a spicy orange mustard also made locally.

For a quick lunch in a real Vineyard institution stop at THE BLACK DOG TAVERN down by the harbor. A large bulletin board displaying all sorts of cards and notices attests to the fact that this is the meeting place for *le tout* Martha's Vineyard. Three meals a day are served here, 364 days a year: The restaurant, not unreasonably, is closed on Christmas Day. Quahog chowder, chili, hamburgers, and *nachos* are the specialties for lunch, but at dinner things get fancier with choices such as steamed mussels with cream, sautéed West Tisbury oysters in garlic, and fillet of flounder with sage. The Black Dog Bakery around the corner provides the desserts. Chocolate pie, peach cobbler, and cheesecake can be purchased here along with some of the best croissants and sourdough rye bread that we have tasted in a while. A visit to The Black Dog, just a stone's throw from the ferry, seems a fitting way to end a stay on Martha's Vineyard. A longtime local resident, when we inquired about The Black Dog, paused for a moment and then said, "Well, it was the first place I went for a meal when I came to the Vineyard, and it will probably be the last place I'll go when I leave. "

Christmas in Nantucket

*E*BENEZER SCROOGE would never have been able to remain true
to his nasty character during a Christmas season in Nantucket. Even the most committed Christmasphobe's prejudices
will be whittled away by the special flair and style with which
this unique island off the coast of Massachusetts celebrates the
yuletide. There's not a sign of red-nosed reindeer or Styrofoam
Santas. Instead, evergreens laden with traditional trimmings,
wreaths made from greens picked on the moors, and dozens of
tiny blinking lights set the tone. The chimes of the First Con-
gregational Church on Centre Street peal carols at noon and six,
and in the same stunning building with fascinating trompe l'oeil
the Community Chorus and Theatre Workshop present a traditional Christmas choral program and nativity pageant with a real
baby. Perhaps quintessential Nantucket is the agile dory emblazoned with a lighted tree that floats happily every Christmas in
the catboat basin parallel to Easy Street. On the island you will
find in the best sense Christmas past.

Celebrations officially begin at noon on the first Saturday of
December, at which time lower Main Street is closed to vehicular traffic. A town crier in Colonial dress rings his bell and kicks
off the festivities, "Hear ye, hear ye, let the Christmas shopper's

stroll begin!" The stroll originated in 1977 with the purpose of encouraging islanders to shop at home instead of in the malls on the Cape. It has since become an event for off-islanders who reserve rooms in hotels and guesthouses from year to year and arrive, like a flock of elegant birds, to stroll, shop, and enjoy the weekend's special activities: They include a Friday afternoon house tour of five or six handsome whaling captain's mansions, on view for the benefit of the Friends of Nantucket Public Schools; and a Saturday morning auction of antiques, books, and assorted treasures that is held in the American Legion Hall. At twelve o'clock the fun really begins, with most shops throughout town decorated for the event and serving hot soup, punch, eggnog, and holiday treats. The Nantucket Town Brass Quartet performs at varying locations, and carolers, cloggers, jugglers, and magicians are all part of the happenings. At dusk the Christmas tree lights on lower Main are turned on, and the street, free of cars and gleaming with its Christmas décor, is a splendid sight. The cobblestones and period architecture seem to belong to this time of year. In the evening the Methodist Church on Centre Street holds an ecumenical service, and, on Orange Street, the Unitarian Church Choir performs a program of Early American Christmas music. Church suppers and community carol singing are part of the day's events, too.

The Sunday of stroll weekend, ferries returning to Hyannis are filled to overflowing, while Nantucket, in all its Christmas finery, almost visibly breathes a sigh of relief. Now is the perfect time to walk on an uncrowded Main Street and examine the trees that have been festooned by the children of the island. "Strawberries" made of walnut shells and painted scallop shells hang on the Brownies' tree; wooden sleds constructed from tongue depressors are the motif for the Boy Scouts'. Christmas cards adorning the Wee Whalers' (nursery school) tree stop halfway up, perhaps a sign that spirits flagged but more likely an indication of the height of the microdecorators. The Quaise Day Care Center tree stars lighthouses, and the M.S.P.C.A. tree offers edible ornaments of puppy biscuits. Prizes are awarded for the prettiest and most original trees. Shopwindows, too, are judged for originality of decoration. They run the gamut from old-fashioned night-before-Christmas scenes to surreal arrangements of beach grass, bayberries, and holly.

The CORNER HOUSE, 49 Centre Street, is one of dozens of bed-and-breakfast inns on the island that provide pleasant home-like accommodations. Sandy and John Knox-Johnston do much to ensure that their guests feel as welcome as an old friend. In the heart of Nantucket's Old Historic District and a short walk from the center of town, its location is prime. The main building, dating back to 1790, exudes a special ambiance owing to its original wide pine floorboards, paneling, chair rails, and fireplaces; and a fine collection of ship models contributes to the atmosphere of this seaport house as well. Bedrooms, all with private bath, are comfortable and cozy but might not suit those who require modern touches at their fingertips, such as a bedside telephone and television. However, a television is situated in the front parlor, where the Knox-Johnstons trim a Christmas tree in time for the stroll. Continental breakfast juice, homemade muffins, cocoa, coffee, and teas—is served in the downstairs sitting room. Tea and mulled cider and homemade fruit breads and cookies are served there in the afternoon.

Most of the guesthouses are festively decorated and plan a special event for the holidays. At Martin's Guest House, a shingled, dormered dwelling at 61 Centre Street, Anne Foye gives a Christmas party complete with wassail bowl, which has evolved into a charming tradition. Richard Carey, director of Nantucket's Actors Theater, joins in by reading Dylan Thomas' "A Child's Christmas in Wales" to the delight of guests and friends.

Another charming place to stay is THE FOUR CHIMNEYS, an elegant mansion at 38 Orange Street. It is furnished with handsome four-posters and serves breakfast in the bedrooms, a touch that might appeal to the sybaritic. If a traditional hotel is more up your alley, both the JARED COFFIN HOUSE with 58 rooms and HARBOR HOUSE with 112 offer comfortable lodgings in pleasant surroundings. Though there are often last-minute cancellations, rooms are reserved months in advance. The Nantucket Information Bureau, 25 Federal Street, has established a clearinghouse for accommodations on the island and will provide information on the availability of rooms on a daily basis. The telephone number is (617) 228-0925.

Nantucket restaurants are one of the island's main attractions and, I'll wager, have much to do with the influx of stroll visitors, many of whose dinner reservations have been made by guesthouse and inn owners weeks before they arrive "on island. " 21 FEDERAL is a case in point. In a stylish setting of whitewashed walls hung with handsome brass sconces one dines on sophisticated fare. A salad of grilled fennel, eggplant, and peppers with mozzarella and a tomato vinaigrette was a light but satisfying way to start a meal. Portuguese seafood stew with *romesco* (almond, hot pepper, and garlic) sauce took the chill out of the evening air. Bob Kinkead, executive chef, admires the local foods and features them on the menu and list of changing specials. Nothing is better than the breast of Nantucket duck with sautéed apples and roasted shallots, which was accompanied by duck sausage when I had it. And grilled Nantucket bay scallops with lobster and seafood strudel is a pleasure both to behold and to consume. Desserts alone, in the capable hands of *chef de cuisine* Ris LaCoste, are well worth the visit. Her bread pudding, served warm with a crusty caramelized top, buttered pecans, and bourbon custard sauce, is not only appropriate to the season but one of my all-time favorites. A trio of chocolate desserts consists of white chocolate ice cream and slices of luscious chocolate spongecake and chocolate pecan lace tart. While we enjoyed our meal, carolers in Colonial costume arrived to serenade diners, creating, in combination with masses of potted crimson poinsettias, an almost perfect Christmas scene. 21 Federal serves lighter fare for lunch and has a charming take-out shop, 21 FEDERAL SPECIALTIES, located at 2 East Chestnut Street.

Robert Kuratek is in charge at THE BOARDING HOUSE, 12 Federal Street, another first-class eatery, and visually appealing, too. Walls are a flattering shade of pink as is the table linen; the main dining room is dominated by a mural of giant asparagus bunches on the beach. At dinner, a starter of Nantucket oysters and bacon with a balsamic vinegar *beurre blanc* was close to perfect, as was the venison sausage served with sliced Granny Smith apples and cranberries. Codfish cakes, not usually associated with elegant dining, were served with *rémoulade* sauce and an accompaniment of snow peas and Brussels sprouts. For dessert, cranberry, quince, and apple cider *sorbets* and cinnamon ice cream were exemplary; and a delectable hazelnut concoction laced with raspberry sauce, called French icebox cake, was truly special. At lunch The Boarding House serves such tempting and imaginative items as "baby" pizza and roasted garlic with marinated goat cheese.

Shopping is, like it or not, a crucial component of Christmas; therefore, to be able to do it in as pleasing a setting as Nantucket town is a great drawing card. Here one need not cope with unruly crowds, uninformed sales help, or traffic jams. Within an area of but a few blocks, the whims of the most demanding can be satisfied. Start with a visit to the KENNETH TAYLOR GALLERY, headquarters for the Artists Association of Nantucket, on Straight Wharf. The charming flower paintings of Ellen Selden, a well-known local artist, are among the many appealing works from which to choose. Up a few doors toward Main Street is the FOUR WINDS CRAFT GUILD, featuring a stunning display of extraordinary lightship baskets, long a Nantucket specialty. Decorated with ivory and whalebone and meticulously crafted, this is a Christmas present for even the most difficult to please on one's list. Four Winds also has a quality assortment of scrimshaw for collectors. Two shops at the foot of Main Street, THE LION'S PAW and EVEN KEEL, are worth calling on. The Lion's Paw carries a delightful selection of beautiful linens, trays, pottery, and various other household goods. Next door, Even Keel boasts great skirts, trousers, sweaters, and jackets for women, all in knockout colors and styles. They also have an especially good collection of shoes and handbags. Continuing up Main Street is NANTUCKET LOOMS, an intriguing stop. Weaving is actually in progress on the premises, to which the clatter of a loom attests, and beautiful fabric is transformed into stoles, throws, and jackets lined with lovely prints.

By this time you may be ready for some sort of sustenance, and, if so, SWEET INSPIRATIONS, 40 Main Street, is the place to go. Not only can a Christmas craving for hot chocolate with whipped cream be indulged, but you can buy some of the best butter-crunch extant or delight in a pistachio ice-cream cone. The buttercrunch is packaged attractively in several different sizes, and it, too, would make a fine gift.

THE MAIN STREET GALLERY, on the same side of the street as Sweet Inspirations, tempts gift-givers with a superior assemblage of paintings and sculpture. I found a series of watercolors depicting the twelve days of Christmas by Jan Brett particularly eye-catching and colorful. I never tire of browsing in bookstores, and MITCHELL'S BOOK CORNER, 54 Main Street, is no exception. It offers a special section of books on the history of the island and the whaling industry in addition to a fine selection of best sellers and most current titles in both hardcover and paperback. There is plenty more to see on both sides of Main Street, and eventually almost everyone ends up at The Hub for a newspaper, magazine, or just a chat. If weather permits, Bartlett's Farm Truck will be parked outside dispensing perfect little yellow onions, potatoes, Brussels sprouts still on the stem, shiny eggplants, and a variety of squash.

At 5 Centre Street, just off Main, you'll have another chance to placate your sweet tooth. NANTUCKET FINE CHOCO-LATES, succinctly named, carries just that, including a luscious assortment of bonbons. Naturally they are suitable for consumption on the spot or, for the more selfless, to buy as gifts. Just a few doors away at number 19 is PETTICOAT ROW, carrying household items such as top-of-the-line bed and bath linens, Quimper faience, Vietri pottery, soaps, and herbs from Provence. I fell for a particularly beguiling pillow resembling a King Charles spaniel that I felt sure was just right for a certain someone who *thought* he wanted a dog but really didn't. And just across Centre Street at number 40 is the SAILOR'S VALENTINE GALLERY, representing a large stable of artists and definitely worth a stop.

CRAFTMASTERS OF NANTUCKET, 7 India Street, is a tiny shop with, among other things, a huge inventory of hats, all hanging from the ceiling. Dozens of shapes and sizes are available, but there was one stylish, nay rakish, model in suede with a band of colorful feathers that particularly appealed. Either male or female would cut a wide swath turned out in such a hat. The shop also stocks leather goods, bags, knapsacks, and belts. On nearby Broad Street, next to Nantucket's Whaling Museum, is the MUSEUM SHOP, stocking fine furniture reproductions and boxes in which to store pipes, knives, and sewing supplies. Chowders and wonderful beach plum jams and jellies are also available here. If marine antiques are your thing, or someone's on your list, NINA HELLMAN at 22 Broad will surely come up with something that pleases. She has fine scrimshaw, a good choice of quilts, and sets of rare nautical prints, which would be elegant on almost any wall.

Just a few doors from Nina Hellman's, at number 24, is LE LANGUEDOC, owned by brothers Neil and Eddie Grennan and partner Alan Cunha. Four dining rooms, located on the second floor of what was once a house, are elegantly decorated in deep reds and gray, with Christmas greens and holly berries adding seasonal warmth and spirit. The food is equally elegant and suited to the surroundings. From a changing menu we found a ramekin of sweetbreads and smoked pheasant with puff pastry to be a flawless starter, as was American sturgeon caviar served with scallion and chive *blini*. Soups were particularly imaginative: Butternut squash purée with crumbled bacon was a winner one cold day; and salmon, scallop, and leek bisque was nearly as good. Medallions of New Zealand venison with cranberry fritters and sweet potato and butternut squash purée seemed just right for the time of year, hearty and satisfying. One can also dine downstairs in the bar before a cheery open fire on somewhat simpler, lighter fare. A delicious *quesadilla* with green chilies, *guacamole*, and Monterey Jack was perfect, and so was my companion's smoked chicken and red onion sandwich on French bread. Desserts of eggnog crème brûlée, cranberry nut tartlets, and steamed ginger pudding with cinnamon crème anglaise were every bit as good as they sounded. The atmosphere at Le Languedoc is club-like, the sort of place where one is made to feel like a regular after one visit and the sort of place where one would indeed like to be a regular.

Another don't miss choice in the embarrassment of Nantucket restaurant riches is THE CLUB CAR at 1 Main Street. One enters through the bar, an old railroad car turned diner, which opens into a large pleasant room. Red banquettes and tables set well apart with extremely comfortable cane-backed chairs produce a genteel, traditional sort of ambiance in which, it is clear, dining is serious business. Chef/co-owner Michael Shannon (his partner is Joseph Pantorno) has been trained in the old French school with classic techniques. Calves' brains with balsamic vinegar and capers and New York State *foie gras* napped with a dense *demiglace* for openers clearly were executed by an experienced cook. For main courses, sweetbreads, crisp and brown on the outside and tender within, were enhanced by *shiitake* mushrooms and a Madeira sauce. They were also superb with Grand Marnier and ginger. Loin of veal is given a different presentation each night. If it is served *périgourdine*, with truffles and foie gras, you'll be in luck. Flourless chocolate cake with creme anglaise and maple creme brulee put the perfect finishing touch on another splendid meal.

Three excellent lunch choices are within an easy walk from anywhere in town. ATLANTIC CAFE, obviously the "in" local meeting place, on South Water Street is a lively spot with ship models hanging from the rafters. The bar is always busy and cheerful, and so, for that matter, is the dining area. You can be assured of good chowder, hamburgers, crab cakes, and a creditable version of Buffalo chicken wings. THE BROTHERHOOD, 23

Broad Street, is a Nantucket institution, so popular that it's not unusual to see a queue of hungry patrons on the sidewalk—it's worth the wait. You'll be greeted by a low, beam ceiling; stucco and brick walls; and roughhewn tables. Generous sandwiches, char-broiled hamburgers, and dozens of exotic mixed drinks with such names as Nuts to Chicago, Scarlett O'Hara, and Goombay Smash are among the consumable attractions. And finally, just opened in August, is the delightfully funky MELO'S at 6 Oak Street. The small space has been transformed with Art Deco decoupage and Andy Warholish murals by New York City designers Lisa Frank and Maureen Fullam. We have heard from impeccable sources that Melo's serves state-of-the-art crab cakes, barbecued baby-back ribs, and chicken potpie. Melo's is open for breakfast, lunch, and dinner seven days a week year round.

Our last night on the island we walked up a deserted Main Street toward the Corner House, taking in the sparkling Christmas lights, shopwindow decorations, and children's trees, which appeared to great advantage against the backdrop of the night. As we turned on Centre Street and the lights of town faded, the stars above shone with a magnified luminescence. A deep quiet was pervasive, the sort that makes one feel indeed thirty miles at sea, and it was at that moment we decided Nantucket was a perfect place to enjoy Christmas past, present, and future.

Newport

A VISIT TO NEWPORT instructs and delights. Situated at the southernmost point of Aquidneck Island in Rhode Island Sound, the city was founded by a group of religious dissidents from the Massachusetts Bay Colony. In search of the personal freedom they had been denied in a Puritan community, the settlers established Newport to provide a climate congenial to groups that included Jews, Baptists, and Quakers. Fortunately, the city has a penchant for preservation, and, as a result of the efforts of The Preservation Society of Newport County and Doris Duke's Newport Restoration Foundation, the history of the Rhode Island Colony can be viewed here today. Dozens of buildings from the seventeenth, eighteenth, nineteenth, and early twentieth centuries have been restored and refurbished, and many are open to the public; others, known simply as the Doris Duke houses, are rented as private residences.

The old Point area is the ideal start for a tour of the city. Washington Street, running from Long Wharf to Battery Park, is lined with old gas lamps and Colonial houses that boast handsome doorways and fences. Hunter House, one of the finest, is open to the public thanks to the Preservation Society. The house—built in 1748 by Jonathan Nichols, Jr., a prosperous ship owner and trader—was sold upon his death to the son of the governor of Rhode Island and was later confiscated by the new state government. During the Revolution it was used as a residence for Admiral de Ternay, commander of the French naval forces. The house remained naval headquarters for the French until 1781, and in commemoration the tricolor flies there today. In 1805, when Newport's economy was suffering from the effects of the war, William Hunter bought the then seriously deteriorating property for $5,000. The Hunter family sold the house, and in 1917 it was given to St. Joseph's Church to be turned into a convent.

Now faithfully restored inside and out, Hunter House is a treasure trove of carved paneling, faux-marble pilasters and baseboards, and expertly reproduced paint colors. It contains some extraordinarily fine examples of furniture made by the legendary Rhode Island cabinetmakers, Townsend and Goddard. Unusual purple delft tiles, Chinese Export Porcelain, and a rare collection of paintings are some of the choice items. A particularly charming rendering of two dogs is said to be Gilbert Stuart's earliest known work, painted when the artist was thirteen. Atop the handsome front doorway is a polychromed pineapple, a memento of Newport's great trade with the West Indies. The pineapple, the symbol of Colonial hospitality, is widely used decoratively throughout Newport and is the logo of the Preservation Society.

Trinity Church, on Queen Anne Square, is another memorable example of Colonial architecture. Organized as a parish in 1698, the congregation petitioned the Royal Governor of Massachusetts to send them a priest from the Church of England. Reverend James Honyman arrived in 1704 and spent his whole ministry, till his death in 1750, in Newport. The present church, built in 1726, was hailed then as "the most beautiful timber structure in America." That description is not far off the mark today.

Perfectly maintained and graced with an admirable clock tower, the church is truly stunning.

In pew eighty-one, small engraved plaques are reminders of some famous visitors. George Washington knelt there in 1781 and 1790, Queen Elizabeth II on July 7, 1976, Prince Andrew in July, 1983, and Bishop Tutu with his wife, Leah, prayed there on November 2, 1984.

Further testimony to the religious tolerance that existed in Rhode Island and specifically in Newport is Touro Synagogue, the oldest standing temple in the United States. The Jewish community probably settled here as early as 1658, the families coming from Portugal and Spain. In 1759 ground was broken for the synagogue on Touro Street, and construction was completed four years later. Designed by English-born Peter Harrison, who came to Newport in 1740, the building has a classically simple Georgian exterior with a columned portico over the entrance. In contrast, the interior is delicate and ornate with five massive candelabra. The Torah, containing the scrolls and the law and housed in the Holy Ark, is situated at the east end of the room. Above the Ark is a rendering of the Ten Commandments in Hebrew, painted by Newport artist Benjamin Howland.

Occupying two houses on the corner of Thames and Mary streets is The Inntowne. Within walking distance of many Newport sights, this bed and breakfast offers twenty-six rooms, each decorated differently and all attractive. Cheerful chintz with matching wallpapers, modern bathrooms, telephones in the rooms, and individually controlled thermostats for heat and air conditioning all add up to solid comfort with a nice Colonial flavor. Breakfast, consisting of coffee and tea, fresh orange juice, and homemade muffins or scones, is served in a pleasant room adjoining the "lobby," where afternoon tea is also set out each day.

Two other pleasant places to stay in the same part of town are the Admiral Farragut and Admiral Benbows inns. Admiral Farragut Inn, at 31 Clark Street, is a charming Colonial house dating from 1702, which, it is said, housed two of General Rochambeau's aides-de-camp. Today there are ten well-appointed rooms, some with four-poster beds and stenciled armoires. Breakfast is served in the old keeping room. Under the same management is the Admiral Benbow Inn, at 93 Pelham Street, with fifteen rooms. Built in 1855 by a sea captain, Augustus Littlefield, the inn has large rooms nicely furnished with antiques. A complimentary breakfast is served in the common room.

The White Horse Tavern, located on the corner of Marlborough and Farewell streets, dates from 1673 and is the oldest operating tavern in the country. We settled into the attractive, low-ceilinged, stuccoed room for a lunch of duck salad with spinach and sun-dried tomatoes, basil and tomato fettuccine, and a flavorful sautéed trout *meunière*. An extensive French and California wine list includes several good choices by the glass, and an outrageously rich fudge-nut brownie pie was a standout among the desserts. Dinner on a return visit proved to be just as delicious. We began with veal- and cheese-filled ravioli with a soy and ginger sauce and bright, shiny *gravlaks*. Among main-course offerings were grilled tuna garnished with salmon mousse and a pleasant *saltimbocca alla romana*. A light Beaujolais went down well with both fish and veal.

La Petite Auberge, at 19 Charles Street, another well-established eatery in this same part of town, is made up of several small rooms with a distinctly Provençal flavor. One evening quail stuffed with goose liver and glazed with Madeira was an elegant starter, as were *escargots* and a worthy rendition of oysters Rockefeller. Grilled swordfish with béarnaise sauce, plump and garlicky frogs' legs, and chicken with morels and cream were excellent main dishes. Crêpes Suzette, prepared with the proper flourish, took us back in time. La Petite Auberge has a good list of French wines to complement the Gallic fare.

One could spend literally days visiting the mansions of Newport. Kingscote, a relatively modest dwelling on Bellevue Avenue, really set the town's building mania into motion. Merchants from the South had traditionally spent summers in Newport to escape the heat, and in 1839 one of them, George Noble Jones of Savannah, chose an isolated spot that afforded views west to Newport harbor and east to the sea. He commissioned Richard Upjohn—founder of the American Institute of Architects and an enthusiast of the Gothic Revival style—to design "a cottage containing eight chambers, besides two or three sleeping apartments for servants . . . [and] water closets [to] be in the house—also a bath." The house was completed in 1841. When the Civil War began, the Jones family and their Southern friends found the political climate in Newport unsympathetic, to put it mildly. In 1864 Kingscote was sold to William Henry Hunter King. A three-story addition was designed by McKim, Mead and White in 1881, and today the house still stands, gabled, dormered, painted gray with black and red trim. Though it is now actually in one of Newport's busiest commercial locations, large trees and fine shrubs seclude it from the avenue. The interior is indeed grand, but it has an intimacy and coziness missing in the "cottages" that came later.

Château-sur-Mer, built in 1852, was the residence of William Shepard Wetmore, who made his fortune in the China trade. The cottage represents a transition from the home-like qualities of Kingscote to the far gaudier and more ornate palaces that were to follow. A particularly interesting feature of the house is the painting on plaster of the "tree of life" under the staircase.

The stairs were designed by Richard Morris Hunt, who oversaw the extensive renovations in 1871. An impressive forty-five-foot balconied central hall with stained-glass landing windows is just one of the many impressive touches. Though the house is large, the rooms are still of a relatively modest size, appearing smaller perhaps because of an abundance of the heavy, dark furniture of the period. Some bright yellow and red fabric lightens things up considerably in the ballroom.

Marble House, William K. Vanderbilt's cottage built in 1892, has to be seen to be believed. Words such as sumptuous, lavish, and even vulgar and extravagant don't suffice when it comes time to describe this eleven-million-dollar edifice designed by Beaux Arts-trained Richard Morris Hunt. Vanderbilt wanted " the very best living accommodations that money could buy," and so Hunt, patterning the structure after Le Petit Trianon in Versailles, ordered quantities of Siena and Carrara marble and hired Italian stonecutters to ready it for construction. There was a keen sense of competition among Newport cottage owners, so Aubusson carpets, Venetian lace, Murano glass, and French walnut paneling were used with a vengeance. The Chinese Teahouse facing the sea on the grounds of Marble House was added in 1913 by Mrs. William Vanderbilt Belmont. A charming folly, it served as an extra pavilion for social teas and receptions.

Cornelius Vanderbilt II bought a wood and brick cottage called The Breakers in 1885 from Pierre Lorillard. In 1892 the house was destroyed by fire, and Vanderbilt engaged Richard Morris Hunt to design The Breakers as we know it today. Hunt's inspiration this time was "from palaces built for the merchant-princes of Genoa of the 16th century." Two thousand workmen took two years to complete construction. The Great Hall and sweeping staircase, the mosaic-decorated lower loggia that overlooks lawn and sea, and the billiard room—faced from floor to ceiling with matching slabs of blue-gray marble and yellow alabaster arches—are just some of the spectacular sights. On the grounds is the children's cottage—all that is left of the original Lorillard estate—where children's teas were served. It has a living room as well as a fully equipped kitchen that would be considered grand in a New York City apartment.

The Elms, designed by a relatively unknown thirty-two-year-old architect, Horace Trumbauer, for coal magnate Edward J. Berwind, was an almost exact copy of Château d'Asnières, the distinguished eighteenth-century French country house. Smaller than The Breakers, The Elms is splendidly proportioned with expansive views throughout, a house that flows gracefully. French ceiling paintings, beautiful parquet floors, and elaborate moldings are some of the outstanding touches. A bust of Marie Antoinette and a fireplace made of marble, onyx, and agate set an elegant tone in the dining room, as does a grand piano in gold leaf in the ballroom. The bedrooms are luxurious but livable, with some wall-coverings reproduced by Scalamandré. The toilet, in an adjoining bathroom, is disguised by a throne-like chair. In a bright conservatory downstairs it is said that sister Julia Berwind enjoyed bridge games, and when a fourth could not be found the butler filled in—but remained standing throughout the game.

Two bed and breakfasts are a mere hop, skip, and jump from the cottages. Ivy Lodge, at 12 Clay Street, has nine bedrooms in a cheerful, airy house. Only two of the guest rooms have private baths, so if you're fussy, inquire ahead. A full breakfast, served buffet style, features homemade seasonal specialties. The Wayside, at 406 Bellevue Avenue, once the home of an old Newport family, has ten large rooms and a heated pool.

The Newport Casino, at 194 Bellevue Avenue, was the brainchild of James Gordon Bennett, Jr., publisher of the *New York Herald* and the *Paris Herald.* Bennett was vexed at the Newport social establishment, which ran the exclusive men's club, The Reading Room, and so he decided to start his own meeting place for cottagers. In 1879 Bennett commissioned architect Charles McKim to draw up plans. The Casino, built in 1880, hosted the first National Lawn Tennis Championships the next year, and they were played there until they were moved to Forest Hills, New York, in 1915. The large shingled building with green trim and a handsome clock with Roman numerals exudes a charmingly old-world ambiance. When the Volvo and Virginia Slims tennis tournaments are played each year in July, red geraniums line courtside boxes, grass courts are lush and soft and green, and white awnings shade spectators. Colorful flags, representing the nationalities of all players participating in the tournament, blow in the summer breeze. Walking on well-tended gravel paths to the outer courts while sipping a Pimm's Cup or eating an Amaretto-almond ice-cream cone is a thoroughly pleasant activity. Croquet—serious croquet—is played here in August, when the grass courts are transformed into a perfect greensward. Players clad in white, thoughtfully considering their lies, give the scene an old-fashioned flavor. The United States Croquet National Open will be held at the Casino this September.

The International Tennis Hall of Fame, with memorabilia and photos of tennis since its earliest days, is also housed in the Casino, and a visit is a must for any tennis enthusiast. Here, too, is a court tennis facility, one of nine in the country. A game that evolved from thirteenth-century France's *jeu de paume*, court tennis almost defies description. Played on an indoor rectangular court, probably adapted from the monastery and castle courtyard, the game uses slant-headed rackets and heavy balls with a sagging net. Scoring is extraordinarily complex and beyond the comprehension of the average spectator. The pink and green porch of La Forge is an inviting place to lunch while watching croquet or tennis. Amid hanging plants and latticework, we enjoyed shrimp, lobster, and crab meat salad with a croissant and half an avocado filled with chicken salad; Dry Creek Chardonnay '86 was the perfect accompaniment. For a quicker bite, Cappuccinos, at 92 William Street, serves elegant sandwiches, pizzas and *frittate*, cappuccino and espresso, and delectable pastries.

The Redwood Library, a couple of blocks away at 50 Bellevue Avenue, is purported to be the oldest library in the country. It was designed in 1748 by Peter Harrison, architect of Touro Synagogue, and was added to in the nineteenth and twentieth centuries. The library has comfortable corners in which to read among the stacks, tables are laden with periodicals and newspapers, and walls showcase portraits by local artists. William and Henry James and Edith Wharton, we are told, read and studied here.

The wharves along Newport harbor boast all types of crafts, from dinghies to yachts. Shops featuring every conceivable souvenir—as well as much fancier items—can be found, and some of Newport's better eateries are located in this area. The Black Pearl, on Bannister's Wharf, offers three places to dine. The most casual is an outdoor café where we lunched on clam chowder, fragrant with dill, a unique Newport touch, and a tarragon chicken salad sandwich with bacon. On weekdays the café has a full menu for lunch and a limited dinner menu, but it is open on weekends as well for chili, chowder, and cocktails. Inside, The Tavern, an informal dining room, prepares lunch and dinner daily. One afternoon we opted for scallops amandine, which turned out to be a good choice, but a mussels marinara omelet sounded better than it tasted. Dinner only is served in the elegant Commodore's Room, which gives one the feeling of being on a fancy yacht, with its lacquered dark green walls with high-gloss black trim, romantically low lights, and candles and a lily on each table. One evening the starters included "black-and-blue" tuna, a sort of charred *sashimi*, with a red bell pepper sauce and a first-rate terrine of smoked salmon. Our main courses were a grilled striped bass and sweetbreads with Madeira, both accompanied by tiny pumpkins baked with brown sugar and butter. The wine list is impressive with some mighty costly bottles, but the house Chardonnay, a Sonoma-Cutrer, was in the lower price range and just fine. We ended our meal with an excellent *crème brûlée*.

Clarke Cooke, next door, has two dining rooms, a formal room upstairs and The Candy Store downstairs, the latter serving lighter meals both at lunch and in the evening. Downstairs we began with roast littlenecks—the clams in their shells with red peppers, corn, and cob-smoked bacon—and Locke-Ober's Caesar salad. (Clarke Cooke's owners acquired the venerable Boston eatery about six years ago.) Pumpkin pasta with scallops, *pancetta*, smoked ham, and chive *chévre* cream sauce and an order of stir-fried chicken with snow peas and ginger were exemplary. For dessert the house specialty is Snowball in Hell, "a slice of chocolate rouladine mousse cake, topped with vanilla ice cream, coated with hot homemade chocolate sauce and dusted with shredded coconut." The Locke-Ober Indian pudding was the best rendition I have had. Dinner upstairs features a variety of fish and game specialties in a dressier setting.

The Mooring, an informal spot on Sayer's Wharf, is lively, popular, and serves delicious simple fare. Old photos of the 1938 and 1954 hurricanes and of Fall River Line steamboats and a large model of the Governor Carr Ferry enhance the premises, which once housed The New York Yacht Club's station number six. On fine days an open deck overlooking the water serves as an extra dining area. Prizes have been awarded the restaurant for its clam chowder, but we thought a scallop chowder was even better. Seafood pie—a baked crock of shrimp, lobster, and scallops—and a seafood stew were well-prepared and served with state-of-the-art coleslaw. Key lime pie, made from authentic Key limes, was excellent. The menu is the same for lunch and dinner, and one has the option to enjoy a bite or a full meal. Admiral Fitzroy Inn, the third of the Admiral inns, is located at 398 Thames Street, in the heart of the harbor area. A shingled 1980s house with eighteen bedrooms, the Fitzroy has cable television and air conditioning, a must on humid summer nights.

Two tours, one on foot and one to be taken by car, might well appeal to visitors to this charming seaside resort. Cliff Walk, actually a three-mile path that winds along the rocky coast, affords views of the sea and cottages. However, because it is currently suffering from erosion, the walk is passable only from The Breakers to Newport Beach. Ocean Drive winds for ten pleasant miles past beach clubs, the semi-public Gooseberry Beach, and the more contemporary summer mansions inhabited today. Picnickers toting chairs perch on the rocks to take in the sights and sounds of the pounding surf and spray. The Inn at Castle Hill, at the midpoint of the drive, is the perfect place to pull in at sunset, sip a drink on the terrace, and savor the spectacular vista.

EXTRA TREATS

Key West

*K*EY WEST MAY BE part of Florida, but, a hundred miles from the mainland, it seems worlds away. The island is, in fact, the southernmost town in the continental United States. Blessed with a tropical climate and several economic booms, Key West has also been devastated by hurricanes and financial collapses.

Claimed by the Spanish around 1500 and dubbed Cayo Hueso (Bone Island), Key West remained sparsely inhabited until 1822, when it was sold to John Simonton, an American businessman, and the U.S. Navy set up a headquarters to guard against pirates. In the early 1800s, a lucrative business developed known as "the wrecking trade," the salvaging of sunken ships in the area. For a time later that century, Key West is said to have been the wealthiest town per capita in the country. Then sponging—the harvesting of those useful, absorbent marine creatures from nearby waters—flourished, and some of Key West's large Cuban population enjoyed success in cigar manufacturing (most production was moved to Tampa by 1930). Fishing always provided an economic base, but, as other sources of profit declined or moved away, the town became, by the 1930s, among the poorest in the nation.

Though Key West was broke and somewhat seedy when John Dos Passos came here around 1930, he recommended the island to Ernest Hemingway, calling it a place that "looked like something in a dream. " Hemingway settled here in 1931, and since then—no one is quite sure why—Key West has been home to many writers. In recent years, tourism has brought revival and restoration, and visitors of all kinds have discovered this exceptionally relaxed and welcoming island.

A good introduction to Key West is a ride on the Conch Tour Train, which leaves every day at frequent intervals from the Front Street Depot near Mallory Square. Although it may strike you as slightly absurd to be riding through town in an open train pulled by a motorized locomotive, with a conductor and a guide recounting Key West lore, the hour-and-a-half trip will give you a feel for the town's layout—and you're not likely to see anyone you know. The train passes Truman's Little White House, the Lighthouse Museum, the Wreckers' Museum, charming houses in Old Town—the quaint northwest section of the island—and dozens of T-shirt shops and bars on Duval Street, the busy main strip. The guide will explain that native Key Westers are Conchs and that the houses they live in are Conch houses: hence, "Conch Train."

Old Town is easily explored on foot, and the first stop for many sightseers is the Ernest Hemingway Home and Museum at 907 Whitehead Street. Built for Connecticut shipbuilder Asa Tift in 1851, it was bought by Hemingway and his second wife, Pauline, in 1931. They lived there until their divorce in 1940. The house has been open to the public for nearly thirty years. Guides conduct what are referred to in the brochures as "leisurely" tours (a half hour).

Visitors shuffle through Hemingway's former living quarters

and view his study atop a carriage house. The sixty-foot pool was built under Pauline's direction as a surprise while Hemingway was off on a trip. The docent pointed out that the real surprise was the price, $20,000, more than double the cost of the house and a tidy sum indeed in the 1930s. The grounds and house are overrun by polydactyl cats supposedly descended from one feline given to Hemingway by a sea captain. A recent census found forty-two here—no place for an ailurophobe. The food costs run about $700 a month. One cat is named Marilyn Monroe. Her father, Frank Sinatra, and her mother, Helen Hayes, have passed away, but her brother Charlie Chan was pointed out, taking his ease under a banyan tree. Hemingway was prolific in Key West. *A Farewell to Arms, To Have and Have Not, Death in the Afternoon,* and more were written here.

Tennessee Williams is on the long list of writers who have found Key West a congenial place to live and work. At the Tennessee Williams Fine Arts Center on nearby Stock Island, the Key West Literary Seminar has been held annually for ten years, during the second week of January. This event attracts both local and visiting members of the literary world. In 1992, "Literature & Film" was the seminar's topic, and Budd Schulberg, William Goldman, and Molly Haskell were among the speakers. Elizabeth Bishop, who was a Key West resident from 1938 to 1946, will be the focus of the 1993 gathering, and writers Octavio Paz, John Malcolm Brinnin, and James Merrill and publisher Robert Giroux—among others—are scheduled to take part.

The Literary Seminar also sponsors the Writer's Walk, which leaves from the Hemingway House on Sunday mornings (January through May) at 10:30. Novelist David A. Kaufelt frequently conducts the hour-long tour through Old Town. During our stroll, we learned about some typical Key West architecture. Eyebrow houses, so called because a roof overhangs second-storey windows, and shotgun houses, where a long hall from front door to back would enable a bullet to be fired straight through the house, are two common styles. Fretsaw or gingerbread carving is much in evidence along the quiet streets and lanes. Walking down William, Margaret, Elizabeth, and Eaton streets, we saw potted hibiscus, magenta bougainvillea, and huge ficus trees.

In her informative and colorful guide, *The Florida Keys*, Joy Williams, "believing that all living writers have enough problems, most of which are still with them . . . ," identifies only the houses of Key West's "fixed and illustrious dead," those of Elizabeth Bishop (624 White Street) and Tennessee Williams (1431 Duncan Street). But the Writer's Walk does not subscribe to this concept, so those taking the tour will also see the homes of writers of today, who might at that very moment be recording words for posterity—or maybe poaching an egg for breakfast.

Eight locals have won Pulitzer prizes, and a reliable source puts the present count of published authors at over a hundred.

Tickets for the walk are available at the Key West Island Bookstore, which has a good selection of all sorts of new, used, and rare books and specializes in works about Key West and by Key West authors. The shop sponsors frequent book signings and receptions for writers.

The literati are also honored at the East Martello Museum & Gallery—on South Roosevelt Boulevard near Smathers Beach—in a fort built by the Union during the Civil War. In the Authors' Room, photographs by Rollie McKenna of such local luminaries as James Merrill, John Hersey, Alison Lurie, Richard Wilbur, and Robert Frost share the space with copies of books by other Key

West residents—such as a first edition of *To Have and Have Not* and a copy of Tennessee Williams's *The Rose Tattoo* signed by the playwright as well as the cast of the 1955 film. Other exhibits display artifacts concerning Key West history, such as treasure chests from Caribbean pirates, model ships, and painted-wood folk art, and there are rooms from a wrecker's house and from a cigar factory.

Another destination of historical interest is the Audubon House and Gardens, in Old Town at the corner of Whitehead and Greene. John James Audubon never actually lived here—in fact, his connection with the house is somewhat tenuous—but it is nevertheless well worth a visit. The handsome structure was built by one Captain Geiger, a wealthy wrecker, in the first half of the nineteenth century. From the property Audubon acquired an orange-flowered branch from a native evergreen tree, known as the Geiger tree, which he used for his white-crowned pigeon engraving. Slated for demolition in the 1950s, the house was bought by Colonel Mitchell Wolfson and his wife, Frances, and has been restored and preserved by the Wolfson Family Foundation. It has been furnished with authentic pieces typical of nineteenth-century Key West. The collections of birds modeled by Dorothy Doughty at the Worcester porcelain factory in England and of original Audubon engravings were highlights of our tour. Two or three times a year, in a gallery on the second floor, special exhibitions about Audubon and the history of the house and Geiger family are mounted. I spent some time in the garden, amid Indian almond, tamarind, sea grape, and pygmy date and coconut palms.

House and garden tours are Key West events in which both locals and visitors participate. Four every year—during the winter season—are sponsored by the Old Island Restoration Foundation, each with stops at five houses and their grounds. There is always a variety: old and new, grand and simple, small and large.

A tour of a different sort makes its rounds at the Key West City Cemetery. Established in 1847 after a hurricane effaced the island's burial grounds, the 15-acre graveyard now has over 35,000 headstones. Our guide pointed out various symbols used by stone carvers: lilies of the valley on the graves of the very young, urns for the elderly, roses to indicate love, oak leaves and acorns for strength, and ivy signifying immortality. One well-known stone, of a B. P. Roberts, 1929-1979, reads, "I told you I was sick"—surely the hypochondriac's ultimate victory. Joseph Russell, "Sloppy Joe," whose famous namesake bar still thrives on Duval Street, is buried here. He died of heart failure while fishing with Hemingway on June 25, 1941. Guided tours—usually conducted by the very knowledgeable director of the Key West Art and Historical Society, Susan Olsen—start at 10 A.M. and 4 P.M., Saturdays and Sundays, at the cemetery's Margaret Street entrance.

Though there is plenty to occupy the sightseer, Key West is a place for relaxation. Luxury accommodations are available, and good food—especially seafood—is not hard to find. The PIER HOUSE RESORT, on the water at One Duval Street, is the grande dame of Key West hotels. It opened in 1963 with 55 rooms, and now 164 rooms make up the complex in a series of attractive low buildings, some overlooking the Gulf, some the pool area, all with terraces. The young staff is unfailingly obliging. They not only wish you a good day but want to know later if you had one. A recent addition to the hotel is the twenty-two-room Caribbean Spa, offering one- to eight-day packages of fitness and pampering. There is a tiny private beach where guests sun themselves and swim.

Another way to soak up the rays is to breakfast at the hotel's

HARBOUR VIEW CAFE, which sits at water's edge. The orange and grapefruit juices are always fresh, and the papaya is sweet and ripe. Here diners can enjoy a simple Continental breakfast, indulge in eggs Benedict or pancakes, or even choose from a spa menu. D.J.'S RAW BAR, also out of doors at the Pier House, serves a light seafood lunch in addition to sandwiches and salads. A creamy conch chowder is a delicious departure from the spicy Bahamian version of the soup generally served in Key West, and stone crab claws were among the best I have tasted. "Peel and eat" shrimp were savory, and house-smoked amberjack (a local fish) with a Key lime–mustard mayonnaise was attractively presented.

For a more formal experience try the PIER HOUSE RESTAURANT, inside but with views of the harbor. We dined on two intriguing starters: shrimp dumplings on warm salmon slaw (julienne strips of zucchini, yellow squash, red onion, and smoked salmon) and conch egg rolls with *wasabi* and pickled ginger. Grouper "Philippe," a main course, was all done up with almond chutney, spinach, plantains, and *pancetta* and served on a pool of roasted bell pepper sauce. A Simi Chardonnay went nicely with our selections.

Near the Pier House, the ROOFTOP CAFE is a pleasant spot for lunch or dinner. Dining rooms with ceiling fans and open terraces are good vantage points from which to view Key West's sometimes bizarre, always diverting, passing parade. On a cool day we lunched on warm Cuban sandwiches—sliced ham and pork, tomato, cheese, pickles, mustard, and mayonnaise on toasted Cuban bread. One hot afternoon, a spicy version of gazpacho was welcome, and the seafood special was dolphinfish served with coleslaw. The excellent Key lime pie was made with real Key lime juice, not always the case.

The charming fifteen-room MARQUESA HOTEL is at the corner of Fleming and Simonton. This former boarding house was reopened, after being meticulously restored and refurbished, in February 1988. The accommodations are deluxe, with tastefully furnished rooms, well-appointed baths, and breakfast served promptly in bedrooms or around the pretty, small pool.

In the hotel, but with a separate entrance, is the elegant CAFE MARQUESA. The pleasant dining room has stippled lemon-yellow walls, emerald-green chairs, purple banquettes, and a handsome Honduras mahogany bar. A trompe l'oeil of garlic and pepper ropes, hanging pots and pans, and other things for cooking decorates the kitchen serving window. Local artists' canvases are displayed. We began dinner one night with a sampling trio of soups: cold sun-dried tomato and goat cheese, duck consommé, and lobster bisque, all in black bowls and perfectly prepared. We also tried the duck liver mousse with a fig vinaigrette, which was smooth and rich. Grilled grouper with sun-dried tomato hollandaise was exemplary, as was a fragrant shrimp curry with garlic and coconut milk.

Cafe Marquesa has a well-chosen wine list, and a full-bodied Sonoma-Cutrer Chardonnay was just right with these flavorful dishes. Dessert portions are large enough to feed a small family, but the bread pudding with Jack Daniels hard sauce was so good that two of us had little trouble finishing it. Our companion's mango and coconut cake was terrific, too.

A walk of a couple of blocks will take Marquesa guests to ANTONIA'S, a northern Italian establishment on Duval. Polished wood, striped banquettes, ceiling fans, and votive candles create a pleasant ambiance. *Tre crostini* (toasted bread with olive paste, a pâté made of salami and other meats, and goat cheese with fresh herbs) was a sumptuous starter, as was the homemade mozzarella with roasted peppers and olive oil. Pasta, properly *al dente*, includes spaghetti sauced with shrimp and fresh tomatoes or with a spicy mixture of clams, tomato sauce, and garlic. Tender lamb coated with bread crumbs and herbs and served with *porcini* sauce was a special main course the evening we were there. Desserts were first-rate and unusual: peach spumoni and a Cabernet *sorbet*. A half bottle of the dessert wine Recioto di Soave made for a perfect ending to a fine dinner.

Nearby on Duval Street, YO SAKE, an outstanding Japanese restaurant, serves some of the best *sushi* I have tasted as well as an imaginative selection of other dishes.

A popular haunt for seafood is the HALF SHELL RAW BAR, by the harbor at the foot of Margaret Street. Wooden benches and tables are set in a large, beamed space decorated with old license plates. Clams and Gulf oysters, sparkling fresh, are served on the half shell, and fish selections vary according to the vagaries of the sea, with such choices as dolphinfish, grouper, and kingfish often available. But it was conch that tempted us: in chowder, spiced and fragrant, with a base of onions, garlic, peppers, and tomatoes; in fritters, which were dense but not heavy; and even smoked to a deep and assertive flavor. "Cracked conch" (conch steak sliced, breaded, fried, and served with tartar sauce) was delicious. The Half Shell Raw Bar is always busy, but service is efficient if without frills (plastic and paper tableware are part of the scene).

The Cuban influence is still palpable in Key West. There are Cuban restaurants as well as spots to stop into for *café con leche*. EL SIBONEY, on Catherine Street, serves a full repertoire of Cuban food in simple surroundings—oilcloth and the obligatory bottle of hot sauce on the table, pictures of Cuba on the walls. Roast pork with black beans and rice is the authentic stuff, as is the flavorful *picadillo* and *ropa vieja* (literally, "old clothes"; actually seasoned shredded beef). The menu features such side dishes as fried ripe plantains, the sweeter, softer variety; crisp, green plantain chips; and yuca, the potato-like tuber so dear to Latin hearts, served with garlic and lime. The soup of the day was red bean, thick with potatoes and pork sausage—the proverbial meal in itself. Venezuelan Polar beer is on hand, and also Presidente from the Dominican Republic. Iced tea is the alternative beverage of choice.

MARRIOTT'S CASA MARINA RESORT, on the beach on the south side of the island, offers a complete change of pace from Old Town and the rest of Key West. Built by Henry Flagler and completed in 1921, the hotel has added two modern wings, but the entrance and lobby retain twenties torchères, ceiling fans, potted plants, and wicker furniture. This is an ideal place for families with children, for it offers a private beach, pool, tennis courts, health club facilities, and water sports. The main restaurant, Flagler's, has a lovely shaded terrace, and less formal eating takes place on the beach at the Sun-Sun Pavillion.

LOUIE'S BACKYARD, a few blocks from the Casa Marina, is only about twenty years old but already has become a Key West institution. In an attractive captain's house with water views, this very good restaurant is a particularly pleasant place for lunch. One sunny day we sat under flowering hibiscus watching sailboats gliding along and colorful parasailors dropping into the balmy sea. Conch fritters with *wasabi* and pepper jelly were light but assertively seasoned, and a starter of beer-steamed shrimp with *rémoulade* sauce, coleslaw, and tomato-corn relish was a standout. The slaw consisted of red, green, and Napa cabbages; red, yellow, and green bell peppers; cucumbers; scallions; and a dressing spiked with cayenne, black pepper, and mustard. We went on to dolphinfish, the catch of the day, served with a Cuban twist of black beans, fried plantains, and lime. A signature dish of warm fried-chicken salad with honey mustard dressing presented strips of tender chicken on a bed of various greens. An Acacia Chardonnay rounded out our meal. Louie's lime tart with raspberry purée is a nice variation on the ubiquitous Key lime pie theme.

As for entertainment in Key West, almost every bar on Duval Street has music of one sort or another, some of it good, some of it not, most of it loud. But the best live "show" is at sunset. At least once, all visitors end up in Mallory Square to be part of what is surely the quintessential Key West happening. A juggler, an escape artist, a contortionist, and other talents show up to amuse residents and tourists, who might also have their fortune read in tarot cards. There are T-shirts and popcorn for sale, and brownies are peddled by a woman on a bicycle who announces her arrival with, "Here come the fudge." James Merrill in his poem "Clearing the Title" describes the event: "As the sun sets, 'Let's hear it for the sun!' cry voices. Laughter. Bells. Applause . . . ."

Baltimore

H. L. MENCKEN WAS not one of Baltimore's most distinguished citizens, he was one of that city's most enthusiastic epicures. "There is a saying in Baltimore," he commented, "that crabs may be prepared in fifty ways and that all of them are good." I may not have tried crab in fifty different guises, but after a number of visits to Baltimore restaurants I at least feel familiar with that extraordinary blue crustacean known as the beautiful swimmer. However, good as crab is, there is much more to Baltimore dining. The following three restaurants—two of which were going strong in Mencken' s day—offer a variety of culinary pleasures and distinctive ambiances for visitors to and residents of the city alike.

The Conservatory, which opened in 1985 atop the Peabody Court Hotel, at 612 Cathedral Street, is certainly where locals, decked out in their blue serge suits and pailletted gowns, go to celebrate. The restaurant provides elegant surroundings: marble floors, gas lamps, and expanses of glass revealing nighttime vistas of Mount Vernon Square, the Washington Monument (forerunner of the one in the District of Columbia), and the lights of Baltimore. Filigree, flowers, impeccable napery, and china with touches of burgundy and gold also help to set a tone of opulence. The menu changes seasonally but is always in keeping with the stylish setting.

One evening I started out with a warm lobster salad in a truffle vinaigrette. The generous pieces of Maine lobster, nicely teamed with a mix of greens and thin slivers of zucchini, were indeed redolent of truffles. A timbale of smoked Norwegian salmon garnished with herbed crème fraîche, another starter, was a perfect blend of textures and tastes. *Mille-feuilles* of wild mushrooms with a heady Chambertin sauce was a well-seasoned and appropriately light beginning. Little new potatoes stuffed with *escargots* were unique and delicious. Sauced with a pungent, garlicky hazelnut butter, the snails seemed to have found an ideal showcase. In fact, our only slight disappointment among the first courses was a rather routine quail and pistachio *pâté en croûte*, indifferently seasoned and served with a red currant *gelée*. Commencing on such a high level, we feared disappointments might follow, but such was not the case.

Medallions of beef tenderloin left one diner at our table purring with delight. After coaxing a morsel from him, I had to agree that this was possibly the best beef I had ever tasted, much enhanced by two irreproachable sauces, Choron and truffle. *Rouget* wrapped in thin slivers of crisp potatoes and napped with a Zinfandel-butter concoction was also something to smile about. Served with a carrot flan, the fish was perfectly fresh and contrasted splendidly with the crunch of the potato crust. Roast breast of wild pheasant stuffed with chanterelles, sauced with lentil purée, and accompanied by creamed cabbage was outstanding, as was roast veal, the tender slices served with their natural juices and a fragrant tarragon gravy.

Pouilly-Fuissé '86 and a Nuits-Saint-Georges seemed appropriate bottles to order with such elegant fare. The Conservatory's

wine list is extensive and equitably priced. There is also a generous choice of wines by the glass.

Last February The Conservatory reinforced its reputation
as a bastion of fine French dining by playing host to Jean-
Claude Vrinat and Claude Deligne, owner and executive chef of
Paris's legendary, three-star Taillevent. They presented dinner
for 140 at a charity event, the only meal Monsieur Deligne has
ever prepared in the United States. Michael Gettier, The Conservatory's young executive chef, had the thrill of assisting with
oysters, leeks, and shellfish with cream sauce; lobster enhanced
by Port and Cognac; and chicken breasts stuffed with *foie gras* in
a Sauternes sauce. All dishes were perfectly complemented by
Taillevent Champagnes.

Gettier has planned some delectable-sounding first courses
for his spring menu: a salmon *roulade* filled with spinach and
shallots and napped with a light curry sauce and *"délices marins
fumes"* (smoked tuna, sable, salmon, and sea scallops served with
mussel salad). For one of the main courses, Gettier will work his
magic on some of the halibut he finds impressively fresh.

When it comes time for sweets, there had better be a
bit of inclination left, for dessert here is something special. A
triple-chocolate—semisweet, milk, and white—mousse was the
answer to a chocolate lover's dream, smooth, dense, and rich. *Le
soufflé du Conservatoire*, which happened to be caramel when I had
it, was ethereally light and properly sweet. A savarin with raspberries and crème Chantilly was about as good as could be, as was
a raspberry tart. But it was an almond *succés* that truly showed
off the pastry chef's skills. With its luscious mocha buttercream
layered between delicate almond meringues—a combination that
almost anyone would find irresistible—the *succés* was as good as
that of the best French *pâtisserie*.

The Conservatory is open for breakfast and dinner only and is closed Sundays. Most first courses are between $7 and $10 ($16 for warm lobster salad), main courses range from $26 to $32, and desserts run about $8. Reservations are advised and may be made by calling (301) 727-7101.

Maison Marconi, at 106 West Saratoga Street, is known as simply Marconi's and has been a cherished Baltimore institution since it opened, in 1920. The black and white awning, marble stairs, and neatly trimmed bushes outside and the linoleum floors and slightly faded murals inside probably have not changed in the restaurant's seventy years. Even some of the tuxedo-clad waiters seem as though they have been accommodating happy diners for nearly that long. Regulars are seated in their favorite waiter's section and sip drinks mixed by him from a bottle-laden tray right at the table. Even Pink Ladies and Manhattans are still on the cocktail list.

Manager Ahmad Rozegar is proficient and diplomatic and makes everyone feel at home. On our first visit, we—four enthusiastic diners, two old enough to feel instantly comforted by Marconi's nostalgic ambiance—perused the impressively extensive printed menu and the smaller, typed enclosure with twenty-one specials. The menu endures, untouched by the heyday of *nouvelle cuisine.* Sole Marguéry, chicken à la king, and six kinds of potatoes—including "hash, creamed" (cubed potatoes with cream sauce), julienne, lyonnaise, and au gratin—will transport anyone back to blissful memories of Grandmother's home cooking.

A spectacular-looking antipasto consisted of chunks of lobster, a couple of perfectly cooked large shrimp, salami, hard-boiled egg, anchovies, and crunchy coleslaw. Minestrone had a fine stock base, and chicken consommé with rice was vintage comfort fare. Lobster Cardinal, a house specialty, was very much like the lobster

Thermidor of yore—diced lobster bathed in a rich cream sauce, returned to its shell, and glazed under the broiler. A small decanter of Sherry is brought with the dish so that diners can spike it to their hearts' content. Curried shrimp on rice was classic, the shrimp fresh and plump and the curry sauce assertively spicy. These dishes are on the regular menu, therefore always available.

From the daily specials we chose a lobster and crabmeat sauté and broiled sweetbreads with mushrooms. The sauté, a simple dish in which ingredients are all, was flawlessly prepared. Both the lobster and carefully picked lump crab meat were abundant, sparklingly fresh, and cooked to the proper degree. The sweetbreads, also perfectly cooked (to a slight crispness), were served on toast, which soaked up the buttery juices, and garnished with broiled mushroom caps. Marconi's doesn't just garnish plates with a dwarf carrot or two; vegetables are a serious matter here. The creamed spinach, sheer bliss, would be difficult to surpass, and the potato really comes into its own on West Saratoga Street. The julienne potatoes were crisp and addictive, and the lyonnaise (sautéed with onion) were satisfying and nicely seasoned. Being inordinately fond of fried oysters, we could not resist sharing an order. They were quite simply superb accompanied by fabulous tartar sauce.

Another visit to Marconi's was just as pleasing an occasion. This time we had crabmeat and lobster cocktails, both with a fiery cocktail sauce and the latter served with its roe, and went on to sample four main courses from the daily specials. Red snapper with peas was very fresh and straightforwardly presented, and the soft-shelled crabs, happily in season, were sautéed *meunière* to a turn. And Marconi's is to be reckoned with when it comes to crab cakes. Here they are nearly quintessential specimens. Bay scallops, delectable little ones, were in season, too, and served with slices of crisp bacon. Of course we had the creamed spinach, and this time the restaurant's house salad, very finely chopped greens in a creamy, flavorful dressing.

Chef Antonio Sartori has been at Marconi's for thirty-three years, starting work here when he was eighteen. He is a wonder, managing to produce a vast number of consistently fine dishes day after day and year after year. Marconi's' wine list, brief but adequate, includes a 1987 Pouilly-Fuissé ($24), a fine foil for local shellfish. The hot fudge sundae, always one of the city's best desserts according to *Baltimore Magazine*'s readers' poll, is in a class with the legendary Schrafft's version. And *meringue glacée*, with the same slightly bitter chocolate sauce, rates nearly as well.

Maison Marconi is open Tuesday through Saturday, noon to 3:30 for lunch and 5 to 8 for dinner. First courses range from $1.20 for soup to $9.50 for the lobster cocktail; main courses are from $4 for an omelet to $17.25 for the lobster Cardinal, with many choices under $10; and desserts are around $2. The telephone number is (301) 727-9522, but the restaurant does not accept reservations.

Obrycki's, one of Baltimore's older and better-known crab houses, could be called crab heaven. The restaurant, actually two restaurants across the street from each other, in the Fell's Point historic district, specializes in serving the beautiful swimmers in many different ways. Rose and Richard Cernak bought the smaller restaurant, at 1729 East Pratt Street, from the Obrycki family in 1976. The building, a tavern site from 1865 until the Obryckis expanded by serving food, became known as Ed Obrycki's Olde Crab House by the late 1940s. The Cernaks built a larger eatery across Register Street at number 1727 in 1986 and now operate both establishments with the help of their children and in-laws.

The newer place accommodates 250 mallet-swinging, crab-picking diners, and the original spot handles 100. Veteran customers know what to expect here, and the patrons who will wait more than an hour for seats at brown-paper-covered tables tell all. The smaller restaurant's nineteenth-century building is divided into small, cozy rooms, whereas the larger restaurant is more spacious and spare, with brick floors, turn-of-the-century touches, and a large oak bar at the entrance. The no-nonsense atmosphere is in keeping with the untidy ritual of crab eating.

If you have not visited a crab house before, it will be quite an experience. Your waitress will cover the table with sheets of stiff brown paper; provide lots of extra napkins, a crab knife, and a wooden mallet; and then unceremoniously dump a steaming heap of the famous blue crabs on the paper. (In case you fear you have been served the wrong crustacean, be advised that the beautiful blue of the shell changes to a mottled red with cooking.)

The crabs have been coated with a piquant pepper and salt mixture, Obrycki's' own top-secret blend, and then cooked in large steamers. Picking out the delectable white meat takes a bit of knowledge of the crab's anatomy, practice, and at least a modicum of dexterity. The staff at Obrycki's is not too busy to be helpful and will instruct the neophyte, but the best strategy is to invite a veteran crab eater along to provide hands-on instruction. The crabs are available in small, medium, large, and jumbo sizes and are sold by the dozen. Your waitress will advise the appropriate quantity for your table. Order draft beer, put on your bib, and roll up your sleeves—forget table manners and enjoy.

In addition to steamed crabs, Obrycki's has a varied and copious seafood menu. For starters, savory crab soup, a tomato and crab broth with vegetables and bits of crab meat, has a real kick to it; cream of crab soup is less spicy, richer, and also delicious; and crabmeat cocktail, accompanied by a zesty sauce, must be one of the most generous and carefully picked that I have sampled. Backfin crab cakes are considered a house specialty and with good reason: Almost all crab meat, held together perhaps with the slightest hint of egg and bread crumbs, they are deftly seasoned and deep-fried (or broiled, on request). Deep-fried deviled crab cakes are more assertively spiced and crisper. Both styles of crab cake seem complete when accompanied by the perfect tartar sauce and creamy coleslaw. Soft-shelled crabs, sautéed in butter, are expertly cooked, and for a rich, elegent dish try broiled backfin crab-meat imperial, a combination of lump crab meat and velouté sauce, redolent of Sherry and cheese.

The well-chosen, reasonably priced wine list includes a selection of California Chardonnays, reds, and "blush" wines. Obrycki's also offers several wines by the glass. It is difficult to imagine wanting dessert after this crab feast, but if there's room try the special called éclair supreme: two éclairs, ice cream, coconut, walnuts, whipped cream, fudge sauce, and a cherry.

Obrycki's' larger restaurant is open daily during crab season (roughly early April to the middle of December), from 11:30 A.M. to 11 P.M. weekdays, 4 to 11 Saturdays, and 4 to 9:30 Sundays. The original and smaller eatery is open only Friday and Saturday evenings, from 5 to 11, from the Preakness (May 19 this year) through Labor Day. Starters range from $3 for chowder to $8.25 for spicy steamed shrimp. Steamed hard-shelled crabs are priced according to the market, and because catching them is inextricably bound to climatic caprices it is wise to call the restaurant at (301) 732-6399 for information on availability. Other main courses run from $10.50 for a one-crabcake dinner to $18.25 for crabmeat and shrimp imperial. The éclair supreme will set you back $4.95. Obrycki's does not take reservations, but good things will come to those who wait.

Garden Week in Charlottesville

*T*HE SMOOTH BLACKTOP roads of Albemarle County, Virginia, wind through some of the prettiest country extant: White plank fences enclose lush green fields where Herefords and Holsteins graze, red-clay earth abounds, and everywhere flowering Juda, dogwood, and azaleas exist in profusion. The third week of April is, and has been for the past fifty-four years, Historic Garden Week in Virginia. Throughout the state special events are held at museums and historic buildings, and private houses and gardens are open to the public.

All the arrangements and plans are the work, and work it is, of The Garden Club of Virginia's forty-five member clubs. Three of these clubs, Rivanna, Albemarle, and Charlottesville, sponsor the festivities in Charlottesville. Hostesses from the member clubs sell tickets, answer questions, and generally enlighten horticultural enthusiasts. They do this with the graciousness that one would expect in .the land of Southern hospitality, offering glasses of punch or iced tea and homemade cookies to revive flagging spirits. Proceeds from Garden Week admissions are used by The Garden Club of Virginia for the restoration and preservation of historic gardens throughout the commonwealth. A visit to Charlottesville during Garden Week is not just a happy springtime fix but an experience that both instructs and delights.

Sunday and Monday kick off the week with a tour of a half dozen or so small, "friendly" city gardens, maintained by their owners with little outside help, gardens to which the average gardener can relate. The tour is arranged so that the sites chosen are in the same general area and are well marked by signs bearing the Garden Week slogan, "Follow the green arrow." (A program of the week's activities is a must for visitors and is available at all of the houses on the tour and at most hotels and guesthouses.)

The gardens are all spring gardens, intended to be at their best during the third week of April. Different gardens are open every year, and though they are varied and reflect the personalities of the owners the range of spring blooms remains the same. A few late daffodils and lilies of the valley sit under elm trees. A wild-flower walk boasts Virginia bluebells, may-apples, wild pink azaleas, and wild pale blue phlox. Slate walks winding through hosta and columbine, deep blue hyacinth, primrose, and a variety of pale peach pansies lead to a formal garden, where Carolina jasmine almost covers a brick wall, and neat rectangular beds lined with low boxwood hedges are planted with pink tulips and deep red pansies. Peonies in pale and dark pinks stand next to a tiered bed of yellow and blue irises. Azaleas in shades of pink, purple, magenta, and white are everywhere, and snowball trees mix with dogwoods.

The Boar's Head Inn is a fine place to establish headquarters during Garden Week. Located just outside Charlottesville, the inn has grown from a small country guesthouse to a 175-room resort complex. If possible reserve a room in the old part, where comfortable, beamed ceilinged rooms look out onto a pond with geese, ducks, and swans. The grounds are attractively landscaped, and two tennis courts are available for the use of guests. Beyond the new wing of the hotel is The Boar's Head Sports Club, which has three indoor and fourteen outdoor tennis courts, squash and racquet ball courts, two paddle ball courts, an outdoor pool, and a health club with a fully equipped gym—all at guests' disposal for a nominal fee. Two gift shops enhance the inn complex: The Boar's Head Inn Store has cookbooks and garden books, antiques, and a gourmet department featuring the famous Virginia peanuts and hams; and next door The Very Thing! sells charming painted baskets, trays, pillows, potpourri, and clothing.

Entering the inn, one is greeted in the small lobby by a large urn filled with carnations, snapdragons, and lilies, and sporting prints and replicas of boars' heads grace the walls. The main dining room is actually an old mill that was dismantled, moved, and painstakingly reconstructed. Morning here gets off to a good start with a sumptuous breakfast buffet. Fruit and juices are kept iced, and dishes of creamed chipped beef, country ham, sausages, scrambled eggs, fried potatoes, and grits would tempt even a non-breakfast-eater. Baskets of warm biscuits and corn bread are also on hand. Lunch is served in the dining room, where one can have sandwiches, salads, or something more substantial. Downstairs is the Tavern with an adjoining patio; here less elaborate fare is offered, and a special buffet is always available during Garden Week.

Dinner in the dining room is an atmospheric affair: The staff is in Colonial dress, and tables are set with pewter porringer candle holders, white and blue napery, and lovely flowers. Melon with country ham is a good starter, and fresh Chesapeake Bay seafood is usually on the menu. The distinctive, salty country ham is also served as a main course with a raisin and apricot sauce. Another regional treat is spoon bread made with yellow cornmeal. For dessert don't miss the pecan pie. A good accompaniment to all of this is one of the local wines. In just a decade Virginia has developed over two thousand acres of wine grapes. Oakencroft wines—from a Charlottesville vineyard in the Monticello viticultural area—are available at Boar's Head, and I especially enjoyed the Seyval Blanc. During Garden Week the Oakencroft Vineyard and Winery offers tours and tastings by appointment.

The next event in the Garden Week program is a tour of the University of Virginia's Pavilion Gardens, Lawn Rooms, and Carr's Hill, the home of the president of the university. The Pavilions are faculty residences, and neither they nor Carr's Hill is open to the public at any other time. The president's house is a handsome brick structure designed by Stanford White and first occupied in 1909. White said that he sought in this house to give the university an example of "a lighter, more airy type of classic form" than Jefferson's noble and dignified buildings. The interior boasts fine antiques and elegant chintzes, and the whole exudes architectural good manners. Most of the ten Pavilions that line the colonnade are open. Once, when the university was young, they were used as schoolrooms in addition to providing faculty housing; most are now furnished with appropriate period pieces and enhanced by colorful flower arrangements provided by the Garden Club.

The varied and charming Pavilion Gardens—maintained by the Garden Club—are open to the public year round. Pale brick serpentine walls with cascading wisteria separate one from the other, and tulips, lilacs, and dogwoods proliferate. Several student Lawn Rooms—neat enough to satisfy even the most demanding mother—are also open for inspection.

Visitors to Charlottesville should make it a point to have a guided tour of the university. These tours are given daily by campus guides when school is in session. It is considered an honor for students to be chosen as guides, and they are indeed well informed and articulate escorts.

The Galerie, nine miles west of Charlottesville on Route 250, is worth the drive for the imaginative French food that is served in this country setting. The restaurant has two dining rooms, one a wine cellar with bins of bottles and the other a pleasant, white room filled with hanging plants and artwork by local artists. Several first-rate starters included quenelle of scallops, an unusual dish of avocado stuffed with frogs' legs, and *salade Galerie*, which combines Belgian endive, Boston lettuce, watercress, Brie, kiwi, and almonds. For main courses duckling Shallottesville, pun clearly intended, was a rich presentation of duck in an intense shallot and Port sauce, and lamb with tarragon came off very well. Among our favorite desserts were a showy hazelnut soufflé with a hazelnut sauce and a *vacherin glacé* (meringue with vanilla ice cream, whipped cream, and chestnut sauce). The wine list—as befits a cellar—is amply endowed with French, California, and Virginia vintages.

Wednesday and Thursday of Garden Week are set aside for visits to country houses and gardens. Located in the more rural areas surrounding Charlottesville, those places on view might include anything from an energy-efficient solar-heated house with indoor pool and terrariums to a working horse farm or a formal slate-roofed Georgian house with extensive gardens and barns. Again, the houses chosen change each year except for Morven, the five-hundred-acre estate of Mrs. Whitney Stone, which is always on the tour. Morven is a Scottish name that means "ridge of hills." The terraces of the main brick house, which was built from plans drawn by Thomas Jefferson and completed in 1820, command a view of rolling countryside with Monticello in the distance. The garden was redesigned in 1930, using brick walls and boxwood to retain the original flavor. Deutzia, a willowy shrub with delicate white blooms, mixes with coralbells, yellow irises, and columbines in lush beds. The early kitchen house is now filled with memorabilia of the family's involvement in the breeding and racing of Thoroughbred horses. Down the road is the carriage house, where a remarkable collection of carriages, including a pony coach, an old mail coach, and a wicker phaeton, are stored in pristine condition and are well worth viewing.

The C & O Restaurant, across from the old C & O railroad station in downtown Charlottesville, is a unique little gem. The run-down, turn-of-the-century brick building with a blinking neon Pepsi Cola sign resembles an eerie Edward Hopper painting and gives the distinct impression that one has arrived at the wrong address. But persevere and walk through a dark bar and up a flight of stairs to the tiny dining room (only ten tables). The stark décor, with white floors, walls, and napery, creates a kind of elegance, and the small menu changes daily. An order of *terrine de campagne*, a well seasoned blend of veal, pork, lamb, and pistachios served with *cornichons* is hearty yet elegant; and fettuccine with morels was napped with a particularly rich and delicious Marsala cream sauce. Main courses of veal with marrow and of sweetbreads and pears in a brioche were an unexpected and enjoyable departure from the more standard offerings of small, French-accented enterprises. The pears had been soaked in an *eau-de-vie de poire*, giving them intense flavor. Vegetables served from a trolley featured asparagus with hollandaise sauce and new potatoes mashed with leeks, sour cream, butter, and garlic, flecked with bits of their red skin. An excellent salad of Boston lettuce and a fine selection of cheeses made a delicious transition to dessert, coffee parfait and white cake with buttercream, strawberries, and walnuts.

It is virtually impossible not to become deeply interested in Thomas Jefferson and Monticello on a visit to Charlottesville. His presence everywhere is palpable, and he is spoken of as one would speak of a beloved and revered friend or neighbor. In addition to his many and extraordinarily diversified other talents, Jefferson was a gardener *par excellence.* While serving as Minister to France he visited dozens of gardens and concluded that gardens as an art form in England surpassed those of all the rest of Europe. From these visits he adopted the concept of *ferme ornée,* or "ornate farm," which Monticello ("little mountain") was to become. The connection between this Garden Club sponsored week and Jefferson's notions of humanized horticulture is inescapable. He exchanged seeds and plants with neighbors, and he even organized contests every spring to celebrate the season's first crop of peas. For over fifty years Jefferson also kept a detailed garden diary with records of the weather, plant yields, and his botanical successes and failures. The Garden Club of Virginia began the extensive restoration of the Monticello gardens in 1939.

A slide show and lecture is given twice during the week at the Thomas Jefferson Visitor's Center by Peter Hatch, superintendent of Monticello's gardens. Afterward small groups of visitors are led on a special tour of the grounds by one of the members of the young staff. At this time of year the twenty large oval flower beds are dominated by tulips, columbine, wallflowers, and Crown Imperial lilies to add variety and color contrasts. Near the house are linden trees, tulip poplar trees, and lilacs. A special effort has been made, for the sake of authenticity, to use species plants that were available during the late eighteenth century rather than today's extensive variety of hybrids.

The vegetable, or kitchen, garden, placed on the sunny southern slope of the mountain for maximum shelter and to extend its growing season, is a thousand feet long. Vast rows of asparagus, cabbage; cauliflower, broccoli, garlic, lettuce, tomatoes, spinach, artichokes, and peas flourish in the dense red earth. Mounds of tarragon, thyme, and rosemary give the warm air a heady perfume, and with all of this bounty the birds naturally proliferate. The cardinal is Virginia's state bird, and here at Monticello its distinctive song can be heard from the highest branches of aspens and catalpas. Tours of the house are given year round, and those who have not visited Monticello may be surprised to find that the house is not, in fact, overly grand or elaborate but rather a manageable, workable, and cheerful spot, surely one of our national treasures.

Historic Michie Tavern, on Route 53, just down the mountain from Monticello, is a pleasant stop for lunch. One of the oldest homesteads (1784) of Virginia, the tavern was operated as an inn seventeen miles northwest of its present site. In 1927 the building was dismantled, moved, and reconstructed. Lunch in "The Ordinary" is buffet style and can be enjoyed indoors or out. The menu never changes: fried chicken, black-eyed peas, beets, coleslaw, green bean salad, potato salad, stewed tomatoes, biscuits, corn bread, and apple cobbler. Cider, wine, and beer are available, and refills are passed by waitresses in Colonial attire. Visitors take great pleasure in sampling this hearty, authentic Southern fare. A fine old grist mill houses a general store, and upstairs a museum traces the history of Virginia's wine production from Jefferson's time to the present.

Ash Lawn-Highland, the home of James Monroe from 1799 to 1826, is located on Route 6 just two-and-a-half miles from Monticello. Jefferson, a close friend of Monroe's, selected the site in the hope of creating "a society to our taste" near Monticello. The 550-acre working plantation was bequeathed in 1974 to the

College of William and Mary and opened to the public in 1975. The members of the Rivanna Garden Club have for the past five years made potpourri from the cuttings of their own gardens to sell at the Ash Lawn Gift Shop. Proceeds finance the maintenance of perennial borders planted by the club, which also cares for the charming herb garden around the well house.

The cream-colored wooden farmhouse is furnished with period pieces—many of which belonged to the Monroe family—and the gardens are laid out with brick walls, box hedges, and foundation plantings. Peacocks wander about, and on our visit one, particularly bold, spread his tail like a giant rainbow, strutting his stuff. Box lunches are for sale at Ash Lawn, as they are at several other locations on the tour, and when the weather is good myriad picnic spots in the vicinity may be enjoyed. A champagne and candlelight tour of Ash Lawn is conducted one evening during Garden Week, when the house and gardens glow with two thousand lights.

Opened in time for the 1986 Garden Week, 200 South Street is a bed and breakfast that has twenty rooms, all with private bath, in two nineteenth-century houses on a quiet street a block from the historic downtown mall. The houses have been refurbished by four Charlottesville businessmen, according to the specifications of the Virginia Landmarks Commission. The rooms and suites, some with fireplaces, are furnished with fine seventeenth-, eighteenth-, and nineteenth-century antiques, and in the halls is a collection of sepia photos of old Charlottesville. Flowered chintz, Oriental rugs, and handsome Belgian armoires give Old World comfort to the bedrooms. But the baths, where modern comfort is a must, are totally up-to-date—some even have whirlpool tubs. Complimentary breakfast is served in either the guest rooms, the pleasant library, or on the veranda. And a delightful breakfast it is, served on handsome black lacquer trays set with Ginori china and a vase of primrose. We enjoyed fresh kiwi and strawberries, apple and cheese tarts, banana nut bread, brioches, jam, and coffee and tea. Tea and Virginia wine are also served in the afternoon. Cynthia and Steve Deupree are the hospitable innkeepers.

Only breakfast is served at 200 South Street, but this is not a problem, for there are two good restaurants nearby. Memory and Company—named for its owner, Ann Memory—is a first-rate establishment, just across the street on the first floor of an old town house. Quality is clearly a top priority here, and only twenty-five to thirty can be seated in a front dining room, in the ample kitchen, and on a small garden deck. A *prix fixe* lunch is served each day, and among the specialties are pasta with seafood and peas, Chinese chicken salad, London broil, pork roast, and chicken with balsamic vinegar. The delicious pork roast was accompanied by asparagus vinaigrette and new potatoes. Desserts are an event in themselves with a choice of "my cousin's chocolate cake," old-fashioned biscuit strawberry shortcake, gingerbread with lemon curd, and a world-class orange chiffon cake.

South Street, at number 106, is a casual and busy restaurant with a heavy emphasis on seafood. Brick walls, exposed wooden rafters, and butcher-block tables in two spacious rooms create the open and informal feeling, and a delightful collection of marine paintings reinforces the nautical setting. Chincoteague oysters, Chesapeake Bay soft-shelled clams, shad roe, Eastern Shore back fin crab cakes, and special Sea Island shrimp are fresh, well cooked, and well presented. Cajun blackened redfish and a Chesapeake platter consisting of delicately battered oysters, clams, scallops, and shrimp are both exemplary. Moist and light corn muffins are an ideal accompaniment. Portions are large, and the service is remarkably efficient.

Charlottesville welcomed 13,239 visitors to its 1986 Garden Week and collected over $20,000, which is earmarked for historic garden restoration projects. Not only is the cause a worthy one, but a visit to Virginia's springtime gardens provides a lift to the senses as well as the spirit after long winter months.

John Gardiner's Tennis Ranch and Carmel Country

*J*OHN GARDINER'S TENNIS RANCH in the Carmel Valley of California was conceived to teach tennis in an atmosphere of beauty and comfort. It succeeds admirably. One's first impression upon negotiating the sharp right turn off Route G16 from Carmel is of an enchanted garden. The grounds consist of twenty-five acres, with masses of flowering shrubs, perennials, and annuals everywhere—in gazebos, flower beds, and hanging baskets. The plantings are watered, clipped, pinched back—in other words, lovingly tended—throughout the year. The public rooms and fourteen cottages for guests are housed in rough-cut redwood buildings, landscaped so cleverly that they are scarcely visible. In addition to an office and tennis shop, the complex includes two swimming pools, a Jacuzzi, and, lest the purpose of one's visit be forgotten, fourteen tennis courts and two training courts. The atmosphere exudes luxury.

John Gardiner started the ranch twenty-six years ago. It was an innovative idea in those days to provide adults with twenty-five hours of tennis instruction over a five-day period. The average tennis player in the 1950s took an hour lesson a week, perhaps two if he was a real enthusiast. No one thought of going off to a tennis clinic for a week or of sending children to a tennis camp for three weeks, and no one had yet provided the facility. John Gardiner, an Easterner who ended up as the sports director of the Pebble Beach Club after serving in World War II, decided that here was an idea whose time had come. In golf-oriented Pebble Beach he had his problems acquiring a loan to finance the dream, but he finally succeeded and chose the beautiful Carmel Valley for his first venture. Now Gardiner operates clinics in Scottsdale, Arizona; Sun Valley, Idaho; Sugarbush, Vermont; and West Palm Beach, Florida. He subscribes to the theory that there are three requirements for running a successful tennis hotel: first, good tennis; second, great food; and third, deluxe accommodations.

Guests check into the ranch on Sunday afternoon and stay until after lunch on Friday. A typical day begins with a flower, a glass of fresh-squeezed orange juice, and *The Wall Street Journal* and the *San Francisco Chronicle* delivered in a golf cart by a cheerful young staff member at precisely seven-thirty. The pool steams like a sulfur spring in the crisp air as guests walk to breakfast, served on cooler mornings in front of a cheery fire in the glass-roofed breakfast room. And what a breakfast! One helps oneself to fresh raspberries, strawberries, and melon from a serving table, and then orders are taken for eggs Benedict, any sort of pancake or omelet, ham, Canadian bacon, sausage, croissants, and toasted sourdough bread—all accompanied by the freshest butter and jams made from local fruits.

The clinic starts at nine-fifteen with fifteen minutes of warm-up exercises. Court assignments are given, and the twenty-eight participants fan out, four to each instructor, to spend the morning perfecting forehands, backhands, volleys, and serves. A quick break at ten-forty-five for fruit and juice and a little conversation, and then back to the courts until noon. From noon to one the swimming pools and Jacuzzi are the places to be, after which a buffet lunch is served on the terrace outside the dining room. Tennis instruction and some play start again at two-thirty and last until five, when it is time to put one's pleasantly aching bones into the Jacuzzi or a hot tub.

At seven o'clock, refreshed and all dressed up, clinic members, along with a few local guests, gather for cocktails in the clubhouse. (John Gardiner's is also run as a club in the Carmel Valley, with some seventy-two members who may come for meals and use the facilities when they are not occupied by clinics.) The clubhouse is simply but comfortably furnished with an antique Welsh dresser, a copper-hooded fireplace, roughhewn beams, and tennis memorabilia. Adorning the walls are old wooden rackets, a far cry from today's sleek graphite, and action photos of such tennis greats as Don Budge, Bill Tilden, and Alice Marble. There is a large clock that has elected to abandon timekeeping and always reads six-ten and a miniature piano. Around a fire—welcome as temperatures drop abruptly in the evening—guests are served steak tartare, tiny pizzas, smoked salmon, and bacon-wrapped water chestnuts along with their drinks. Schuman, the bartender, remembers everyone's order from the first day, many from the first visit to the clinic.

Though for a tennis buff the pleasures implicit in a well run clinic tend to revolve around overheads, backhand volleys, and half volleys, the food at John Gardiner's is so good that it becomes a major part of the enjoyment. As a matter of fact it would be difficult to imagine any resort that consistently serves better, fresher, or more varied fare. A great advantage of the tennis ranch is that it is located in a part of the world known for its produce. This area of California supplies much of the country's fruit and vegetable bounty, and the lucky guests reap the benefits of such abundance.

Lunch, served on a terrace banked with impatiens and fuchsia, is an embarrassment of riches. There is invariably a soup: pungent and intriguing oatmeal soup, velvety smooth cold avocado and lime, or spicy gazpacho. There is usually a soufflé, perhaps sole with shrimp sauce or one based on artichokes from nearby Castroville, which calls itself the artichoke capital of the world. Then a mousse of ham with mustard sauce or salmon with dill. The hot dish might be lamb curry with condiments, beef bones diablo, or chicken crêpes with mushrooms. There are always salads of avocado, tomato, hearts of palm, and artichokes in all sorts of marinades, and desserts include peach cobbler with brandied ice cream sauce and a perfect cold strawberry soufflé with raspberry sauce. Vernon Griffith is the talented chef, and Mr. Gardiner's first wife, the late Barbara Gardiner, set up and planned the menus. Her interest in and knowledge of food have been passed down to her son Tom, who has much to do with the excellence of the cuisine.

Dinner is always a major cause for celebration. It is served in the dining room, where guests sit at tables of six or eight. Butterflied leg of lamb grilled over charcoal is a specialty of the kitchen, and there is fresh seafood at all times. Some of the possibilities are red snapper or petrale sole, the king of Pacific soles, with lemon and caper sauce, tender *calamari* (squid) with marinara sauce, or salmon with béarnaise. Again there are soufflés. of mushrooms or sweet Carmel Valley corn and for dessert perhaps a chocolate or lemon or almond soufflé. As Tom Gardiner says, "the egg man loves us." Tom is a knowledgeable oenophile and matches California wines with these wonderful dishes. A Mondavi Chardonnay from Napa, a Durney Cabernet Sauvignon from the Carmel Valley, and a Chateau Montelena Zinfandel were among the choices we sampled from the comprehensive list. It was indeed a pleasure to be treated to first-rate American food accompanied by fine American wines.

Accommodations at the ranch are, in Mr. Gardiner's words, "deluxe." Each center court cottage houses one couple in a comfortable bedroom with spacious bath and well planted private terrace, and the larger cottages—Pool Lanai, Forest Hills, Grand Slam, and Wimbledon House—have space for two couples totally separate from one another. These larger cottages have living rooms with wood stoves, refrigerators, and percolators for early morning coffee, and there are Jacuzzis in the patios of Grand Slam and Forest Hills. Wimbledon has had three presidents as inhabitants: Nixon, Ford, and Reagan. Beds are turned down at night and curtains drawn. The staff is first-rate, unobtrusive but efficient, and unfailingly affable.

The magnificent gardens and general landscaping of the tennis ranch are a testament to the talents of Janos Toldi, the charming Hungarian head gardener. Sycamores and eucalypti, magnolias and live oaks shade the lawn, and English ivy, clematis, wisteria, countless varieties of fuchsia, mock orange, violets, calendulas, and primroses cohabit in colorful confusion. In his greenhouses Mr. Toldi starts chrysanthemums and carnations from seed to put out when they are hardy enough to stand the chilly nights. Whole banks of blooms are removed when they begin to show the slightest sign of wilting and are instantly replaced with fresh reserves.

All in all John Gardiner's Tennis Ranch is a special spot. The staff of young instructors is exemplary; their patience is inexhaustible and their tact is such that even the most inept are made to feel that somewhere, deep within them, is buried another Chris Evert Lloyd or John McEnroe just waiting to emerge. Mr. Gardiner, a legend in the tennis world, has achieved and maintained his goals: excellence in tennis instruction, food, and accommodations. Like all hostelries that are really successful, this one is run without a hitch and without the guests being aware of how much effort is involved. The ranch is in operation from the end of March through November. Most clinics are for mixed doubles play, but there are three or four weeks during the season that are set aside for the ladies. Further information may be obtained from John Gardiner's Tennis Ranch, Box 228, Carmel Valley, California 93924. Telephone: (408) 659-2207.

The town of Carmel has a make-believe quality; the streets are immaculate and the sidewalks planted with flowers of every hue. Ocean Avenue is the main street through the town, and on it and the streets that intersect it are shops galore. The most compulsive of buyers will certainly be satisfied and perhaps even satiated here. The Carmel Bay Company, at Ocean Avenue and Lincoln, is filled with unique items for the house. Pierre Deux, in a little courtyard at Ocean Avenue and Derling Lane, has charming French country antiques and fabric as does La Fille du Roi Antiques, on San Carlos between Seventh and Eighth. There is Dansk II (Ocean Avenue and San Carlos), an outlet for the well-known Scandinavian housewares, and the Mediterranean Market, Inc. (Ocean Avenue and Mission), a specialty foods and wine shop where a variety of picnic and party supplies is available.

Carmel also seems to have an inordinate number of bakeries, some where one can have coffee with a pastry or a croissant and others that just sell cakes and cookies. The Tuck Box, a tearoom and gift shop on Dolores Street, is a Carmel institution, and breakfast there is a local tradition. Hungry patrons queue up early to savor homemade scones and olallieberry jam, the luscious concoction made from a berry indigenous to this part of California. Lunch and afternoon tea are also served. The Secret

Garden, off Dolores Street between Fifth and Sixth in a pictur-esque alley, has animals cast in bronze to fit on garden hose bibs, ivy balls, and a huge selection of plants; and William Ober, on Dolores between Fifth and Sixth, is another shop with an unusu-al selection of housewares.

Carmel is also an active art and gallery center. First Im-pressions, on Dolores Street at Sixth, and Poster Graphics, in the Carmel Plaza, have a wide assortment of posters. Some of the most decorative are done by Big Sur painter and designer Kipp Stewart, and many other California artists are represented. The Saar-Jarvis Gallery, at Dolores and Fifth, has charming flower paintings by Dorothy Saar and landscapes by her husband. This is one of the few artist owned and operated galleries in town, and the artists' work is now sold only in Carmel.

The Carmel Art Association Galleries, a little farther along Dolores Street, presents new shows each month. The associa-tion was started in 1920, incorporated in 1927, and exhibits only member artists who live within thirty-five miles of Carmel. The Fireside Gallery, off Dolores between Fifth and Sixth, features paintings and sculpture. The two Zantman Art Galleries, both on Sixth Avenue, one near Mission and the other near San Carlos, are among Carmel's oldest and largest galleries. Kipp Stewart's paintings are exhibited here. Ansel Adams is a longtime resident of this area, and photography is pursued with great enthusiasm. The Weston Gallery features many twentieth-century photog-raphers including Adams, Edward Weston, Yousuf Karsh, Eugene Atget, and Man Ray and some rare nineteenth-century work. The Friends of Photography on San Carlos also has a va-riety of shows.

The PINE INN on Ocean Avenue is a pleasant place to stay. In this white stucco building guests are greeted by a flamboyant Victorian lobby with walls covered in red fabric, a bright red carpet, a gas fire, and brass chandeliers. One double bedroom on the top floor boasts brass bedsteads, a marble-topped bureau and nightstand, and a glimpse of the sea over the pine trees. If the wind is right, the pounding of the surf is audible. The Gazeboé is a glass-domed dining room in the hotel, "very Carmel" we were informed. There is a jolly bar and prompt room service. Breakfast is served in the bedrooms, not generally the case in the town's other inns, and it is an amenity that we consider virtually essential.

At the foot of Ocean Avenue is Carmel's crowning glory: one of the world's most beautiful beaches. The white, powdery sand is as fine as one could imagine, and the views south to Point Lobos and north to Pebble Beach are breathtaking. The beauty of the scene, however, belies the danger that exists in the severe rip-tides and undertows. On a glistening autumn day only wet-suited youths with surfboards braved the fifty-degree water, though we were told of a hardy group of Carmel's older women, raised in the spartan days of yesteryear, who apparently ignore the temperature and tides and swim in the early morning.

The Carmel Mission, consisting of two museums, the church, and the gardens, is a picturesque reminder of California's colonial past. Junípero Serra, a Franciscan priest originally from Majorca, came to Mexico in 1749 and in 1769 established a mission at San Diego. From there he made his way by sea to Monterey and in 1770 started a religious enclave in Carmel where the mission stands today. Thousands of Indians were baptized and ministered to at the mission, and Padre Serra remained there until his death in 1784. He is buried in the sanctuary. In the early days the mission buildings were made of wood, but Padre Lausen, who succeeded Padre Serra, set about to fulfill a dream of his predecessor and in 1793 took over the building of the present stone church. The Indian population gradually dwindled, and by 1836 the mission was secularized and the padre settled in Monterey, taking with him the ornaments of the church for safekeeping. The mission fell into decay and not until the late 1800s was the task of saving this landmark undertaken. The restoration has preserved a historic monument and created a delightful haven. The old mission, now with the status of Minor Basilica, is surrounded by gardens, a veritable bower of dahlias, fuchsias, and hydrangeas. Purple-blossomed Mexican sage serves as a watering spot for hummingbirds, and a perennial impatiens that blooms continuously and grows to a height of over eight feet is massed around the chapel. Huge cactus and bougainvillea complete the joyous scene.

Tor House, residence of the late poet Robinson Jeffers on Carmel Point, is a highlight of any trip to this part of California. The house was named by Jeffers for the craggy knoll on which it was built in 1918-19. Deliberately simple and small, it was designed by the poet as a dwelling place for himself, his wife, Una, and their twin sons. Hawk Tower, the stone tower in the garden, was built by Jeffers as a hideaway for Una, and it is an extraordinary construction feat. Using wooden planks and other manual methods to move three-hundred-pound stones, he completed it in four years. The poet lived and worked at Tor House for over forty years and died there in 1962. His books and mementos have been preserved with such care that one has the feeling that the family departed minutes ago on some short errand and will be returning soon. Jeffers' chair is made from timbers cut at the Carmel Mission, and Una has a keepsake in her tower of a few dried leaves that were collected at the graves of Shelley and Trelawny in Rome's Protestant cemetery. The garden is quintessentially English. Roses, a perennial border, and Una's herb garden coexist happily with fragrant geraniums. The sea is of great importance at Tor House: Jeffers said that he sited the house on a point that juts into the ocean like the "prow and plunging cutwater" of a ship. The last seven lines of his poem "Tor House" aptly express the atmosphere of the place:

> Come in the morning you will see white gulls
> Weaving a dance over blue water, the wave of the moon
> Their dance-companion, a ghost walking
> By daylight, but wider and whiter than any bird in the world.
> My ghost you needn't look for; it is probably
> Here, but a dark one, deep in the granite, not dancing on
>   wind
> With the mad wings and the day moon.

Docent-led tours of the house are conducted on Fridays and Saturdays only from ten to four. The tours are limited to six people an hour, so advance appointments *must* be made. The Tor House Foundation, Box 1887, Carmel, California 93921. Telephone: (408) 624-1813.

Carmel offers many restaurant choices to the visitor. L'ESCARGOT, on Mission Street and Fourth Avenue, is a French restaurant of the sort that one found in New York City a decade or so ago. There are banquettes, menus from such French greats as the Restaurant de la Pyramide in Vienne, and old maps and prints. Dinner one night started with house-smoked Pacific salmon and a hearty country pâté, followed by an honest tomato soup and commendable main courses of *poulet à la crème* and sweetbreads with mushrooms. The meal ended with a tart of Carmel strawberries and excellent brewed decaffeinated Colombian coffee. L'Escargot has a comprehensive wine list of both

French and California wines and, like many California restaurants, does not serve cocktails.

FLAHERTY'S SEAFOOD GRILL AND OYSTER BAR, centrally located (Sixth Avenue between Dolores and San Carlos) in the heart of the galleries and shops, is a smart establishment specializing in—what else?—seafood. The Oyster Bar has blue-and-white-tiled counters, caned barstools, and the day's specials on blackboards. They serve chowders, oysters, and seafood entrées. The Grill, next door, has a more extensive menu, and lunch one day of *cioppino* (Italian-style fish stew), a helping from the salad bar, and a good chilled Soave was thoroughly satisfying.

CASANOVA restaurant, in a small house on Fifth between San Carlos and Mission, has three comfortably appointed rooms usually filled with enthusiastic diners. In the back is a large walled garden strung with lights, where one can also dine alfresco during most of the year in this temperate climate. There was the reassuring smell of garlic, and a young woman walked among the umbrella-topped tables with a basket of pink roses the night we dined. Dinner began with an antipasto for two of avocados, tomatoes, and delicately grilled mushrooms followed by excellent homemade ravioli. Our entrées were a rack of lamb with Zinfandel sauce and chicken breasts Chandon, and for dessert we chose from tempting chiffon pies and fruit tarts. A Frog's Leap Sauvignon Blanc '81 from the Napa Valley accompanied dinner. Casanova always seems to be crowded and does not take reservations, but in some magical way they accommodate all corners.

RAFFAELLO, on Mission Street between Ocean and Seventh, is a first-class northern Italian restaurant. A handsome etched-glass mural of the Duomo and Campanile of Florence and two red Florentine tapestries set the scene, and a blazing fire, white napery, and flowers on each table put one on notice that dinner will be an event. Remo d'Agliano, the owner and host, describes the day's specialties with care and quietly sees that all goes smoothly from then on. The prosciutto and mushrooms of the antipasto were exemplary, and cauliflower soup was velvety and well seasoned. Carefully prepared cannelloni and veal *piccata* came next and then a simple but classic green salad. Italian Pinot Bianco was an apt wine selection.

Californians are known to be partial to motoring, and it is easy to see why; in the vicinity of Carmel there are some not-to-be-missed jaunts that can only be made by car. The Seventeen Mile Drive, which we embarked upon at the Carmel Gate, is a must with its spectacular views of the seacoast and the lush and justly famous local golf courses. From the Cypress Point Lookout on clear days one can see Point Sur and the Point Sur Lighthouse twenty miles to the south and be regaled by dozens of sea lions sunbathing and generally disporting themselves on the offshore rocks. The Lone Cypress, clinging precariously to bare rock, and Pescadero Point are two familiar landmarks. The drive takes an hour or two, and a good stopping place is The Lodge at Pebble Beach. There one can explore a handful of boutiques and lunch at the lodge's CLUB XIX. The view from tables set on the terrace is dazzling, and the food and service match it. Pacific salmon with lemony hollandaise, perfect fresh spinach, and excellent pilaf with a bottle of Lambert Bridge Sonoma Chardonnay made an ideal lunch.

The coastal scene changes with the weather. Sometimes the Pacific is shrouded in eerie fog and the wild surf makes the ocean's name a curious irony, and other times the sea is clear and glistening. Whatever the day, it is almost impossible to tire of the spectacle.

GOURMET | SEPTEMBER 1991

In Praise of
Boarding School Fare

T SEEMS DIFFICULT to believe that one could actually remember meals eaten half a century ago, but in my case it is indeed a fact. In the autumn of 1940, I left a New York City brownstone for Miss Porter's School in Farmington, Connecticut. Perhaps unusual for a teenage girl, I was far more interested in food than in clothes and jewelry, and thus my recall of my boarding school fare is almost total.

The school consisted of a dozen or so grand village houses on either side of Farmington's Main Street. These houses contained classrooms; three dining rooms; and bedrooms that two, three, and sometimes four girls shared with double the number of stuffed animals. In the largest dining room, which was situated in Main, the school's principal building, a hundred girls ate at tables of ten or twelve with a teacher at each. Here, too, Mr. and Mrs. Keep, the headmaster and headmistress, took their meals. Three times a day girls filed in, nodding to and making eye contact with whoever was at the head of the primary table. New Place and Humphrey, smaller dormitories across the street, housed two other dining rooms, each accommodating fifty. Seating assignments were changed twice a semester so that everyone had her turn with a beloved (or despised) teacher. Mademoiselle

Nédèlec presided over the French table, where only that language was spoken, severely limiting mealtime pleasantries for all but a fortunate few. Mademoiselle loved salad and referred to herself as Pierre Lapin Nédèlec. Such was the level of boarding-school wit. But my most vivid recollection concerns the toast: In New Place toast was buttered while still warm, which made it far superior to the cold version, served with butter on the side, that was the rule in Main and Humphrey.

Breakfast, precisely at 7:25 in all the dining halls, started with fruit juice and a choice of dry or hot cereal. Then came a most extraordinary egg ritual. Each girl was asked how long she wanted her egg boiled—two, three, or five minutes—and the said egg arrived cooked exactly to the moment. I would invariably select a five-minute egg, which I especially savored mashed with a good dollop of sweet butter and a dash of salt and pepper. No egg since has ever tasted as good to me. Small wonder those eggs were so delicious, for the school had not only its own dairy herd but also its own chickens. Toast, either buttered warm or buttered cold, and crocks of delectable homemade raspberry jam rounded out our first meal of the day.

Annie O'Shay, a large, white-uniformed lady, ran the main dining room with all the discipline of a Marine Corps drill sergeant. In those days maids, attired in black uniforms and white aprons, waited on tables and made the beds. One, known as Diet Mary, was thin to the point of emaciation. Our teachers liked to threaten us with the warning that we would one day look like Diet Mary if we did not eat everything that was put before us.

Lunch, served at 1:10, frequently featured such typical boarding-school fare as meat loaf, shepherd's pie, or New England boiled dinner, but I remember best an open-faced grilled-cheese sandwich. The chef concocted a mixture of grated Cheddar, mustard, and Worcestershire sauce, which he would generously slather on thick pieces of white toast, cover with bacon and a slice of tomato, and broil. Divine.

On Saturdays, when there were no afternoon classes, we had a celebratory meal of hamburgers and, as a special treat for dessert, thin butter crackers with jam and either peanut butter or cream cheese. Sunday lunch, or actually dinner, starred roast or broiled chicken. Hans, our resident baker, turned out voluminous quantities of bread, rolls, biscuits, and cakes. We also enjoyed homemade jams, tomato juice, and chili sauce. What very lucky girls we were!

But, as it was fashionable to complain about boarding-school food, we had our pet nicknames for certain dishes: An often-served casserole of lima beans and tomatoes bore the sobriquet "train wreck," hash became "refrigerator" (that is, clean out the fridge), and croquettes were known as "floor sweepings."

Dinner, at 6:30, always started with soup and toast fingers or cranberry juice. Wednesday night featured chicken in such guises as potpie, shortcake made with baking powder biscuits, or fricassee. Friday's menu centered around fish. Depending on the chef's whim, we were served either "good" fish, which was fried and accompanied by tartar sauce, or "bad" fish, which was baked in butter. In the springtime we relished Connecticut River shad, boned in the kitchen and served with its roe.

When World War II started, "Golden Rule" meals entered our lives. Partly to comply with rationing restrictions and partly as a gesture of economy, we had two meals a week that were meatless and cheap. Pancakes, macaroni and cheese, and baked beans and brown bread made frequent appearances. Along with these dishes we nibbled on a most bizarre "salad." It consisted of bananas, halved lengthwise, rolled in pulverized peanuts, laid to rest on a leaf of lettuce, and covered with a creamy dressing. We loved it!

But war or no war, the menu for special occasions remained inviolate. Study Hall Tea, an eagerly anticipated buffet served before Saturday night entertainments two or three times a semester, was savored on one's lap in the front parlors of the main house. The buffet usually included link sausages, Waldorf salad, chicken salad, potato chips, and fragrant Parker House rolls. And for dessert Hans prepared a lavish assortment of layer cakes, among them chocolate, maple walnut, and mocha. Another special event we always enjoyed was the "Ice-Cream Concert," which took place once a semester. José Iturbi presided over the piano, and bass Mark Harrell sang. We students wore our best dresses. Following the concert we feasted on ice cream and beautiful petits fours with our invited guests.

On holidays, of course, we looked forward to more festive fare. We always celebrated Thanksgiving with our Farmington schoolmates, when we would dine on a half grapefruit to start and then roast turkey, bread stuffing, jellied cranberry sauce, candied sweet potatoes, and acorn squash. Decorating our holiday tables were starched white cloths and napkins, flowers, crystal dishes with celery hearts and olives, and baskets of candy and nuts. Pumpkin and mincemeat pies and ice cream ended this all-out gorge.

On Thanksgiving night we watched a movie in the gym, and afterward we opened packages from home. This was the only day of the year that we were allowed to receive food, a custom that brought out the competitive instincts of some parents. Elaborate hampers from fancy caterers like Day Dean in New York City often arrived as part of the bounty, and some girls suddenly became popular.

The last night before Christmas holidays the whole school

gathered at the Keeps' residence to sing carols, drink hot chocolate, and devour Toll House cookies and candy from Hilliards,
West Hartford's premier candymaker.

On Valentine's Day, Hans baked heart-shaped cookies with
pink icing and on Washington's Birthday, an evocative cherry-tree
log cake complete with chocolate hatchet. On Field Day in May,
the Minks, the Possums, and the Squirrels, our school teams, dis-
ported themselves enthusiastically playing intramural games.
Following the games we picnicked on such typical teenage re-
freshments as hot dogs, potato salad, chocolate éclairs, and Cokes.

On Saturday afternoons, girls were allowed "callers," boys
from neighboring boarding schools—or even the occasional Yale
"men." Tea was served at the Keeps' grand house, "Next Door,"
and the delicious spread made it well worth putting up with a
dull caller for an hour's walk beforehand. Hot biscuits with marmalade, jam, and cream cheese; perfect watercress and cucumber
sandwiches; and Banbury cakes (flaky pastry filled with mincemeat) accompanied tea.

In a course called Domestic Science, some of us tried our own
hands at cooking. We met once a week in the "domestic" kitchen,
and at the end of the semester the class cooked a meal for the
Keeps—always the same meal, term after term. The prescribed
menu comprised fish chowder, rolls, Russian salad, and peach
upsidedown cake. The poor Keeps must surely have considered
themselves the definitive authorities on fish chowder.

Although we enjoyed our share of good food at boarding
school, we still needed a place to go for snacks, and so we often
headed for the Gundy. A half-mile walk up Mountain Road, the
Gundy was a charming little white house with a sign nailed
outside that read, "Benjamin Judd, 1697." The proprietors, two
gentlewomen of a certain age, were known simply as Lady and

Lady's Sister. We retreated here, and only here, after classes and on weekends to eat cookies and toasted English muffins with peanut butter and strawberry jam and to drink Coca-Cola. In the spring, we sat outdoors under the blossoms of an old apple tree and guzzled the world's best iced tea. For birthdays, roommates would arrange, with money extracted from parents, to have Lady bake a cake for a surprise party in one of the Gundy's inner rooms. Lady's superlative chocolate and marshmallow cake or her yellow cake with caramel icing made for a gala celebration.

Singing in the garden preceded closing exercises. Dressed in white, we sang to the tune of Cole Porter's "An Old-Fashioned Garden" our own lyrics:

It was a quaint, shaded garden,
where we first came as new girls,
and we listened to songs
that forever so long
have been sung at Farmington.

After graduation, teary but still hungry girls and their guests dined alfresco on creamed sweetbreads in pastry shells, baked hams, rice and cheese croquettes, and ice cream and cake. Pitchers of iced tea replaced our usual milk.

Unquestionably the highlight of my memories of Miss Porter's School food can be described in one word: Icebox. Icebox was a dessert with which we were surprised once a semester, always on a Friday night and usually after "bad" fish. It combined a lusciously rich chocolate mousse with layered ladyfingers and whipped cream. Rumors would start to fly during the first month of the term: Someone had smelled chocolate, someone else had seen Annie whispering to a teacher. Would it be tonight? When the great moment arrived, the maids—holding large crystal bowls in what I remember as a triumphal, reverential manner— marched single file into the dining room to cheers and applause. For me this was certainly the high point of the semester. Otherwise reasonable and properly brought up girls were known to hold back their hair and lick their dessert plates.

Here is the recipe that prompted our delight: 2 squares of bitter chocolate; 3 eggs, separated; 1 cup confectioners' sugar; ladyfingers; 1/2 pint whipping cream; 1/2 teaspoon vanilla. In the top of a double boiler melt the chocolate, gradually add beaten yolks and sugar. Cook over whispering water till well blended and slightly thickened. Cool. Beat the whites till stiff peaks form and then carefully fold into the chocolate mixture. Line a glass bowl with split ladyfingers, pour in some of the chocolate mixture and layer with more ladyfingers. End with ladyfinger layer. Chill at least overnight and cover with unsweetened whipped cream mixed with the vanilla.

POSTSCRIPT

VOGUE | FEBRUARY 1980

Back to School . . .
After Twenty-Seven Years

*I*N FEBRUARY OF 1973, I became a matriculated student at Barnard College, after having "dropped out" for a period of twenty-seven years. During those years, I married a Columbia Law student (my reason for leaving Barnard after my sophomore year), had three children, and spent my days as a suburban "superwoman." But when the youngest child went to college and life had changed from the demanding daily routine of running a household, I started to think seriously of going back to school. I think that I had really always had it in the back of my mind and had a feeling of something unfinished. In retrospect, I see that I took the step with remarkably little foreboding.

After having received staggering numbers of forms, applications, questionnaires, etc., I was ready to register for the spring semester in November. The young students of today (and perhaps I did the same in the '40s) seem to handle the intricacies of registration serenely. Not so the middle-aged dropout. I was overwhelmed by instructions, numbers, and the ritual of getting registered. The initiated student knows that one must have a "packet" which contains everything germane to a successful registration: a blue card with housing clearance, a pink card from the bursar, a green card from the registrar, a yellow card from the office of student activities, a pale-mauve card from public relations, two grey cards from the Barnard and Columbia libraries, and a solemn white card from the chaplain's office. Without this packet there is no hope and, even with it, one must follow instructions with great precision, as the whole process is as complex as anything the Internal Revenue Service could devise. In any case, after several near-disasters, I was registered and ready to start classes.

There was only one problem. Under the extreme pressure of all of this heavy paperwork, I had misread the calendar in the catalogue and showed up for my first class, fresh, alert, with three new felt-tip pens, two days early. I sat alone in a dark and empty room in Barnard Hall, awaiting the forty other students and the professor of a modern theater course, which was to cover theater from Ibsen and Strindberg through Beckett and the theater of the absurd. Indeed, it was absurd when I realized the class started at 2:10 on Thursday, *not* Tuesday. So much for my first day of college.

I did get into the academic swing after that and found rewards and challenges along with terrible moments of stark panic and fear of failure. The students, my friends, were one of the great pleasures. I really gave little thought to the fact that my peers were half my age and younger than my youngest child.

The only exception to my feeling of agelessness was when I took a course in the Humanities entitled "The Concept of Death." As the title would indicate, it was a study of attitudes toward death: suicide, euthanasia, afterlife, etc. The texts were Kübler-Ross' *On Death and Dying*, Tolstoy's *Death of Ivan Ilych*, Thomas Mann's *Death in Venice*, and other appropriate readings.

As I sat and listened to eighty young women—and a few men—talk about death and—dying I felt every one of my fifty years. Few of the students had experienced more than the death of a grandparent, and I found their attitudes excessively rigid and overly simplistic. When I expressed this later to the professor, she said that from her point of view having an older student in the class had given the course a new dimension!

The younger students and I soon had the same problems and interests: classes, papers, mid-terms, finals, marks, and holidays. It had little to do with how many years one had happened to live. Perhaps owing partly to my lack of self-consciousness about age, I think that my fellow students did not dwell on it too much. As a matter of fact, one of my friends in an Italian course strongly recommended that I take more courses at Columbia because, as she put it, "you'll get to meet more boys." The ones who did mention age did so in a most affirmative and supportive way, saying that they wished their mothers would, or could, do the same thing. They often kept me going with their encouragement and help, the reverse of what one would have expected. I did notice, however, that I was always the one who was asked for a Kleenex. Perhaps, after all, I represented the mother figure, matriculated or not.

I enjoyed my days at Barnard; the classes, my work on papers, and reading in the library. The part that was by far the most difficult was studying to be done at home on weekends or vacations. It was an impossible problem to be home for the Thanksgiving weekend with papers due, finals coming up, and a family who were used to my attention and didn't see why anything was different now. I think this is a problem that the younger student (except, of course, the one who has a part-time job) does not face. Since I never took more than three courses in one semester, I managed, for the most part, to work in the library during the day and rarely took more than reading home.

As an English major and one who is totally unmathematical

and unscientific, the most challenging—nay, terrifying—course that I had to take was physics. I had not fulfilled my science requirements when I was first at Barnard and though I tried desperately, even petitioning the committee on academic requirements, to be excused from fulfilling the requirement, it was to no avail. I was to be a well-rounded Barnard graduate. So I embarked on a History of Physics, known to the students as "physics for poets" and a course that was designed to be science for the unscientific. I think that, until I came along, it was impossible to know how unscientific an unscientific person could be.

I took my "science" the fall semester of what was to be my graduating year; and by then I had good friends with whom I had shared the toils and tribulations of such courses as Developmental Psychology, Dante's World, and Arts and the Vernacular. They were all more prepared for what was to come than I, having been exposed to such things as the New Math, calculus, and the like. I managed to get through the course, but on the advice of my fellow students took my first pass/fail, a decision I never regretted. When my term paper on "The Starry Messenger" was written, my final exam over, and a beautiful, wonderful "P" displayed on my record, I knew then the feeling that nothing was beyond my capabilities. This must have been what the Committee on Academic Requirements had in mind.

There were many experiences peculiar to me, or I imagine to any student of my age. I found that I was conscientious to a fault. I never handed in a paper late, took an incomplete or, for that matter, cut a class. I did my assignments to the last page and generally all the suggested outside reading. I am certain that anyone who decides to go back to college at middle age has a great awareness of how precious are the time and opportunities that present themselves. I was frequently mistaken for a teacher or staff member by the students and even by other staff members, and I had a bothersome recurrent dream that I was cleaning Milbank Hall and never got it done. Once I developed excruciating back spasms before a particularly demanding French exam and almost missed the final altogether.

My diploma is handsomely framed now and hanging in my bedroom, and it is easy to laugh at some of the memories of student life. When spring of my senior year came, I had my picture taken for the yearbook, attended both the baccalaureate ceremonies and commencement so that I could wear my cap and gown twice. It was a rare May day, all of my children came to see me get my diploma, and my husband was either so moved or so relieved to see me in my academic robes that he cried unashamedly.

Acknowledgments

THANK YOU TO:

Jane Montant, way back when the editor-in-chief of *Gourmet* magazine (1980-1991), who either approved or assigned these travel adventures. She's the one who gave me all the work.

Melody Lawrence, whose always encouraging and patient guidance took these articles from the attic closet to the light of day. And to Michael Putnam.

Elaine Richard, gifted editor, who was there at *Gourmet* and has helped me ever since.

Gail W. Berry.

Margie Weeks, who brought the images to the words.

Chris Weeks, for astute proofreading.

Mindy Brandt (manager), Patricia Harrison, and the staff at Brightwood, who put everything together—especially Chris Rutherford.

Ann Weeks. Louis Weeks.

About the Author

TERRY WEEKS went back to Barnard at fifty, after raising three children, and got a degree in English literature and creative writing, then went to the New School to learn how to send out articles and get them published. *Gourmet* bought the first article she sent them, in 1980, and she eventually became a contributing editor to the magazine. Over the next two decades, appearing regularly in *Gourmet*, she also wrote for Andy Birsh's *Restaurant Reporter* in New York for six years, and reviewed restaurants in Key West for Frank Taylor and David Ethridge's *Solares Hill*. A longtime resident of Stonington, Connecticut, Weeks currently lives in Baltimore near her son and daughter-in-law.